FROM GAY TO Z

FROM GAY TO Z

By **JUSTIN ELIZABETH SAYRE**

Illustrations by **FREDY RALDA**

CHRONICLE BOOKS
SAN FRANCISCO

Text copyright © 2022 by JUSTIN SAYRE.
Illustrations copyright © 2022 by FREDY RALDA.
All rights reserved. No part of this book may be reproduced in
any form without written permission from the publisher.
Library of Congress Cataloging-in-Publication Data

Names: Sayre, Justin, author.
Title: From gay to Z / by Justin Elizabeth Sayre ; illustrations by Fredy
   Ralda.
Description: San Francisco : Chronicle Books, [2022] | Includes index.
Identifiers: LCCN 2021045719 | ISBN 9781452178028 (hardcover)
Subjects: LCSH: Gays. | Gay culture. | Gays in popular culture.
Classification: LCC HQ76.25 .S397 2022 | DDC 306.76/6--dc23
LC record available at https://lccn.loc.gov/2021045719

ISBN: 978-1-4521-7802-8

Manufactured in India

Design by MICHAEL MORRIS
Illustrations by FREDY RALDA

10 9 8 7 6 5 4 3 2 1

Chronicle books and gifts are available at special quantity discounts to cor-
porations, professional associations, literacy programs, and other organizations. For details and discount information, please contact our premiums
department at corporatesales@chroniclebooks.com or at 1-800-759-0190.

Chronicle Books LLC
680 Second Street
San Francisco, California 94107
www.chroniclebooks.com

Dear friends,

Before we begin this journey together, I would like to get a few things clear:

The task of boiling down the entirety of queer culture into one book is impossible. It would take up several volumes, and while the lovely folks at Chronicle Books seem to like me, I don't know how many volumes they or I have signed up for. Also, because queer culture is continually evolving, as our awareness and our presence grows in the world, so too does our history. As we begin to learn about ourselves, we hope to hand that knowledge over to the next generation of queer people to do with as they will. This book is an attempt to pass along as much as I can.

It's also a book to make you laugh. The opinions in these pages are mine and mine alone. I am a humorist rather than a historian or a social scientist. I believe that a culture is made up of people, so in some ways this is a who's who of the LGBTQ+. I have concentrated on artists and activists who are gay, or have a gay following, to illuminate the compendium of art created by and for gay people, and because I think in many ways they tell the stories of the LGBTQ+ community. In these pages, I hope to celebrate all that we are and all that we can be, but in a very queer way—to throw a little shade and to make a little joy. To me, the core of queer culture is how a group of people maligned and mistreated come together and try to make the world more beautiful, more fair, and perhaps more loving.

It is with these two objectives that I begin this book and we begin our journey together.

I wish you lots of laughs, lots of insight, and lots of hope to go out and make more of the same. Queer culture isn't just what we have been but what we still can be.

Much love,
Justin Elizabeth

A is for . . .

A Fantastic Woman

The visually brilliant 2017 film by Sebastián Lelio tells the story of a young transgender woman living in Chile. This groundbreaker took the world by storm, nominated for the prestigious Golden Bear at the Berlin International Film Festival and the Oscar for Best Foreign Language Film in 2018. With a title right out of the golden era of Hollywood and a stellar performance by transgender actress Daniela Vega as Marina, this film became a modern classic in the LGBTQ+ cannon.

A Single Man

Written by Christopher Isherwood, this novel that was one of the first to openly deal with homosexuality and love. It sounds strange, but most novels until then dealt with homosexuality in terms of tragedy, even those by gay authors. Isherwood's novel broke the mold by having George, a bookish professor, deal with the loss of his partner not as some sort of redemption but as a genuine loss born from a deep love. It was adapted for film in 2009 by fashion designer Tom Ford, starring Colin Firth and Julianne Moore. While this adaptation made some changes, it brought style, grace, and some of the best smoking in modern cinema, making this classic even more classy.

ABBA

This Swedish supergroup of the 1970s, famous for songs like "Waterloo" and "Dancing Queen," have become gay music you and your mom both like. ABBA's songbook later became the source material for the musical *Mamma Mia*, and you know how we love a musical. The film adaptations starring Meryl Streep (and in the sequel, Cher) have become gay hallmarks, or as I like to call them, "movies you can see with your parents when visiting for the holidays and can be enjoyed by all for very different reasons."

Kathy Acker (1947–1997)

Acker wrote books, plays, and poetry, sometimes using the works of other writers to create a new vision of the world as she saw it. She searched for new forms and was unafraid to talk about identity and politics, which, in some ways, were intermingled for her. Her 1984 novel *Blood and Guts in High School* remains her most popular work, but in recent years all her novels and life have been reexamined as she finds a host of new fans and accolites to this day. Acker used a myriad of forms in her works, adapting other stories, illustration, playwriting, and prose, all to make a new form of storytelling. Who knows what she could have done had she only had more time. Acker died of cancer in 1997 at the age of fifty.

ACT UP

ACT UP stands as an example of how disenfranchised people can educate, organize, and mobilize themselves while fighting for their lives. Many in the organization were suffering with AIDS and knew they would not live to see the outcome of the movement, but fought nonetheless. Formed in 1987, this direct-action group took the AIDS crisis to the streets and showed America and the world that we were not going out without a fight. The group was founded by writer and activist Larry Kramer after he was asked to leave the GMHC for his "cantankerous" views about taking on the system. People were angry, and they were dying, and nothing was getting done. Out of this despair and righteous anger, ACT UP was born. Members created powerful images calling out the delinquency of the Reagan administration. They held protests on Wall Street demanding drug companies push for better research and development of new AIDS treatment drugs. They shut down the post office in New York. They debuted the slogan and image that would forever be associated with the organization: Silence = Death. They reappropriated the use of the Pink Triangle, now used to signify solidarity. They shut down the FDA, demanding that the organization approve medications for a dying population. They marched on Saint Patrick's Cathedral in New York and shut down that hate-monger, Cardinal Spellman. These were angry queer people fighting for the life of a community. And they won.

Calpernia Addams

Calpernia Addams (1971–)

Addams is a groundbreaking trans actress and personality who brings wisdom and charm to everything she touches. She has been lighting up the screen for decades and encouraging the work of other trans actors. She coached Felicity Huffman for her role in *Transamerica*. She performed in the *Vagina Monologues*. She was even the subject of her own reality dating show called *Transamerican Love Story*, which debuted in 2008 on Logo TV.

Jane Addams (1860–1935)

Jane Addams is considered a pioneer in the world of social work for founding Hull-House in Chicago in 1889.

It's frequently overlooked that she co-founded this landmark with her lover Ellen Starr. Hull-House was a settlement house that helped immigrants get acclimated to their new country, but eventually offered health and humanitarian services to the Chicago community at large. Addams started a movement with Hull-House, and throughout her life stayed true to her advocacy for the rights of women and all oppressed peoples. She cofounded the ACLU in 1920, and in 1931, she became the first woman to win the Nobel Peace Prize.

Adele (1988–) ICON

The queen of the "breakup album," this British pop diva reminds us what it feels like to get the chills when we hear a great voice singing the truth. Adele first came onto the scene with her 2008 album, *19*, but it wasn't until 2011, with *21*, that she captured our hearts. Songs like "Rolling in the Deep" and "Someone Like You" captivated the world and made us hungry for more. Her 2015 follow-up *25* was no exception with her mega hit "Hello." So far, Adele has named her albums after her age at the time she created them, and a league of eager fans can't wait for *31, 40, 50, 75*. Let's just hope she doesn't have to suffer a breakup every time she records a new album.

The Advocate

If the *New York Times* is called the "Gray Lady," then perhaps *The Advocate* should be called "The Pink Lady." Founded in 1967—two years before the Stonewall Riots—*The Advocate* is one of the oldest LGBTQ+ publications in this country. Concentrating on news, politics, and cultural commentary, *The Advocate* remains one of the best LGBTQ+ publications around. Not too bad for the old girl, is it? Thanks, Pink Lady.

After Dark

From the late '60s to the early '80s, there was a famous gay (not gay according to the publisher) magazine called *After Dark*. It was fabulous, a mélange of high and low gay culture. With cover girls like Chita Rivera, Angela Lansbury, and Bette Midler, the magazine reported on everything in entertainment, from dance to disco, and always with a fair amount of male nudity. There were ads for bathhouses and Spanish fly next to interviews with Patti LaBelle. Unfortunately, the magazine folded in the early 1980s, but if you ever get your hands on an old copy, leaf through it and just ride the gay wave. It's marvelous.

Christina Aguilera (1980–) ICON

The diva with THE VOICE, this pop princess continues to show the world how to SANG. With her amazing vocals and a string of hits like "Genie in a Bottle," "Come on Over Baby," and "Ain't No Other Man," Aguilera became a staple of the 1990s and early 2000s club scene. A favorite for drag queens to lip-sync, she has given us so many songs where girls are allowed to live their proverbial lives. She continues to produce impressive music and starred as a host of NBC's *The Voice* from 2011 to 2016 and in the film *Burlesque* opposite Cher.

AIDS/LifeCycle

This endurance bicycle ride from San Francisco to Los Angeles raises millions of dollars for AIDS charities. The route is 545 miles, and every year hundreds of people participate in this life-changing experience to raise money for AIDS and AIDS research. The marathon race takes place over the course of a week, with celebrations and festivities all along the California coastline. So bring your joy, your endurance, and your baby powder (chaffing is an issue), and join this amazing journey toward an AIDS-free tomorrow, or at least Los Angeles.

AIDS Walk

This annual walkathon raises money for all sorts of charities assisting people living with AIDS. A great community event, it keeps the spirit of advocacy and awareness for the disease alive. The first AIDS Walk was held in Los Angeles in 1985 and has since spread to cities around the globe.

Alvin Ailey (1931–1989)

Ailey changed the world of American dance by widening the vocabulary and breadth of dancers of color on the stage. Born to a teenage mother in Texas in 1931, Alvin Ailey found his way to New York City where he danced on Broadway in shows like *House of Flowers* with Pearl Bailey and *Jamaica* with Lena Horne. He founded the Alvin Ailey American Dance Theatre in 1958 and began creating works for dancers of color. Ailey's choreography celebrated and glorified the African American experience with dignity and glorious technique. His most treasured work, *Revelations*, still shocks and awes audiences around the world and has become a hallmark of American dance. Though Ailey died of AIDS in 1989, his company continues to thrive to this day.

Edward Albee (1928–2016)

One of the most important playwrights of the twentieth century, Albee brought absurdist grit and poetry to the American stage for more than fifty years with works like *Seascape*, *The Goat*, and *Three Tall Women*. For his work in playwrighting, Albee was awarded three Pulitzer Prizes. His most famous play, *Who's Afraid of Virginia Woolf?* (1962), is often revived, and with its stunning film adaptation starring Richard Burton and Elizabeth Taylor, it has become a quotable masterpiece. Rumor has it there's a clause in the contract that, to acquire rights to perform the play, the parts of George and Martha can never be performed by two people of the same gender. I'm guessing Albee knew gay couples would be acting it out all on their own.

Alkyl Nitrate, a.k.a. Poppers

An inhalant that has been keeping the gay sex party going for nearly five decades. When inhaled, poppers are said to cause a rush that helps with "relaxation" and provides a brief flush of blood to the head. Countries throughout the world have tried to ban these happy little whippets, but to no avail. A recent study in France linked excessive use of poppers to blindness, but when legislation was proposed to ban the products, there simply wasn't enough support. Folks still love their poppers.

Edward Albee and Poppers

Peter Allen (1944–1992)

This Australian singer-songwriter hit the United States in the 1970s with a flamboyant style that shocked and awed audiences—and even impressed some gay royalty. Allen was taken under the tutelage of famous lesbian cabaret singer Frances Faye and met his idol Judy Garland—he even married her daughter, Liza Minnelli. Allen was bisexual and wrote a thinly veiled song about his identity titled "Bi-Coastal." With numerous hits, like "I Go to Rio" and "Don't Cry Out Loud," Allen became a highly sought-after singer and songwriter. His biggest hit, Oscar-winning "Arthur's Theme (Best That You Can Do)," came out in 1981. Allen died of AIDS in 1992 and his life story was turned into the 2003 musical *The Boy from Oz* starring Hugh Jackman.

Pedro Almodóvar (1949–)

One of the world's most respected and acclaimed auteurs, Almodóvar has widened the world's cinematic vocabulary with his wild and often humorous takes on contemporary life through a very queer lens. His films vary in tone from the visually delicious *Volver* in 2006 to the campier *Women on the Verge of a Nervous Breakdown* in 1988. He challenges his audience with startling visuals, stellar performances from the likes of Antonio Banderas and Penélope Cruz, and a stunning musicality that draws on Spanish romanticism. Almodóvar shows no sign of slowing down despite the long list of classics in his rear view, like *All About My Mother* (1999) and *Talk to Her* (2002); in 2019 he released the critically acclaimed *Pain and Glory* starring Antonio Banderas and *The Human Voice* with Tilda Swinton in 2021.

Marc Almond (1957–)

Marc Almond first came on the scene with the 1980s' synth pop duo Soft

Cell and their hit cover of Gloria Jones's "Tainted Love." Though Soft Cell split up in 1984, Almond continues to make music and push the boundaries of pop with literate and poetic lyrics that speak to his own queerness and that of his audience.

Hilton Als (1960–)

Social criticism and insight are a time-honored tradition in the LGBTQ+ community, and we're not just talking about your best friend's shady comments at brunch. In a lineage that traces back to Oscar Wilde, Als emerged in the twentieth century as a writer of keen insight and cutting social critique. He has been a mainstay at the *New Yorker*, writing on a myriad of subjects with subtlety and a signature wit that earned him a Pulitzer Prize in 2016. His 2013 collection of essays, *White Girls*, was shortlisted for the National Book Award. The collection has become a must-read for those interested in contemporary culture and its deeper meanings.

Hilton Als's
White Girls

Brian Jordan Alvarez (1987–)

A writer, actor, and filmmaker with hilarious deadpan and stellar delivery, Alvarez is a comedy star on the rise. He initially found success in a series of shorts and web series that he wrote and produced himself. His humor was evident, and soon enough he started making films like *Grandmother's Gold* (2018) and *Web Series: The Movie* (2019), both released on Amazon. He also appears in Netflix's *Special* and had a recurring role as Estefan, Jack's husband on the *Will & Grace* reboot.

Tori Amos (1963–) `ICON`

In every generation, and to every genre, a diva is born. If you were a moody teen in the 1990s, your diva was Tori Amos. This Canadian multi-instrumentalist singer-songwriter first came to national prominence with her 1990 album, *Little Earthquakes*. She was and remains an artist willing to go there. Writing songs about everything from sexual abuse to political awareness, Tori brought angst and anger to a fevered pitch that leaves queers feeling like someone was writing just for them. Her unique take on the world and love has earned her a huge LGBTQ+ following, whom she loves very deeply in return.

And the Band Played On

Published in 1987, it is often considered the greatest book ever written on the AIDS crisis. Written by Randy Shilts, a journalist on the frontlines of the epidemic in San Francisco, this harrowing masterpiece chronicles a community dealing with a horrendous disease and finding the will to fight back. The book was adapted for HBO in 1993 in a movie of the same name starring Matthew Modine and Ian McKellen. Shilts died of AIDS in 1994.

Angels in America: A Gay Fantasia on National Themes

This modern classic debuted on Broadway in 1993. From playwright Tony Kushner, the two-part play explores America during the AIDS crisis, taking on everything from race and conservative politics to environmental breakdown and the American character. The two plays that make up the work, *Part 1: Millennium Approaches* and *Part 2: Perestroika*, are revered for their poetic brilliance. The original repertory production on Broadway starred actors like Stephen Spinella, who won a Tony for his role as Prior; Marcia Gay Harden; Ron Leibman, who won a Tony for playing Roy Cohn; Joe Mantello; Kathleen Chalfant; and Jeffrey Wright; and was directed by George C. Wolfe. It won the Pulitzer in 1993 and has been in almost constant revival since its opening. A major Broadway revival in 2018 starring Andrew Garfield and Nathan Lane saw both win Tony Awards for their roles. A 2003 HBO miniseries version of the play from director Mike Nichols starred Meryl Streep, Al Pacino, and Mary-Louise Parker.

Angels in America

Anohni (1971–)

There are voices like Anohni's once in a lifetime, and how lucky we are to be around for hers. She is a performance and visual artist, singer and musician who thrills audiences with her unique sound and take on melancholy. Anohni first came to prominence with the band Antony and the Johnsons. She won the Mercury Music Prize for her album with the Johnsons, 2005's *I Am a Bird Now*. Anohni then went out on her own, changing her name and releasing *Hopelessness* in 2016, which aided her commitment to the environment and work toward world peace with songs like "Drone Bomb Me." Anohni is a visionary artist and the second transgender person to be nominated for an Oscar for her song "Manta Ray" from the film *Racing Extinction*.

Gregg Araki (1959–)

Araki is the director of 2010's *Kaboom*, which won the first Queer Palm award at the Cannes Film Festival. His movie *Mysterious Skin*, starring Joseph Gordon-Levitt as a hustler, added new voices to gay cinema. Araki has also directed for television, where his short stint on the CW's *Riverdale* gave us Archie in a wrestling onesie. Thanks, Gregg.

Penny Arcade, a.k.a. Susana Ventura (1950–)

A chronicler of culture and its decline, she creates performance art and plays that push the boundaries of storytelling and identities. Arcade consistently confronts the homogenization of American culture that gnaws away brilliance and freedom. In the 1960s she performed with friends Jackie Curtis and Jayne County and took a small role in a Warhol film. In the 1980s, she started exploring more solo work, debuting pieces at the Poetry Project and working with friend Quentin Crisp. In 1990, Arcade developed her most popular work, *Bitch! Dyke! Faghag! Whore!*, which toured around the world to universal acclaim. In the decades since, Arcade has continued to make daring and impressive work, like interviewing artists about that hotbed of artistic life in Manhattan for the Lower East Side Biography Project, and recently writing and performing the radio play *Longing Lasts Longer* with collaborator Steve Zehentner.

Reinaldo Arenas (1943–1990)

Arenas was a Cuban novelist and poet who wrote insightfully about the Cuban Revolution and criticized Fidel Castro's treatment of LGBTQ+ Cubans. His most famous work in English, *Before Night Falls*, was adapted into a movie directed by Julian Schnabel in 2000, starring Javier Bardem as Arenas. Arenas came to the United States as part of the Mariel boatlift, a mass emigration of Cubans between April and October 1980, where many LGBTQ+ Cubans escaped the Castro regime. He lived and continued to write in New

York, where he died by suicide after battling AIDS.

Joey Arias (1949–)

A true original and master performance artist, drag queen, singer, and raconteur, Joey Arias has been pushing the limits of drag since the beginning of his long and storied career. Whether he's singing with friend and collaborator Klaus Nomi (including backup for David Bowie on *Saturday Night Live* in 1979) or channeling the spirit and voice of Billie Holiday at New York's legendary Bar'Do, Arias has created a world of his own. He continues to wow audiences in collaborations with puppeteer Basil Twist in his famous play *Arias with a Twist*. His drag performances defy, dare, and demand attention; luckily he gets a lot of it.

Alexis Arquette (1969–2016)

Though part of the acting dynasty that is the Arquette family, Alexis was always a bit of the outsider. An actor, cabaret performer, and activist, Arquette took a path not tread by many and that made her life all the more interesting. She took on eclectic roles, debuting at nineteen in *Last Exit to Brooklyn*, with other memorable roles in movies like *The Wedding Singer, Pulp Fiction*, and *Bride of Chucky*. Arquette was open about her transition and made a documentary about the process called *Alexis Arquette: She's My Brother* in 2007. Arquette died of complications from AIDS in 2016.

Dorothy Arzner (1897–1979)

One of few female film directors in the golden age of Hollywood and a pioneer in the field, Arzner was the sole female director in the industry for many years. She began working in silent pictures, proving herself to be a capable editor and writer. She found success as a director with 1929's *The Wild Party*, starring Clara Bow in her first talking role. The film was a major hit, allowing Arzner to continue as a singular female director in a male-dominated field. Arzner went on to direct Katharine Hepburn in 1933's *Christopher Strong*, Rosalind Russell in 1936's *Craig's Wife*, and Joan Crawford in 1937's *The Bride Wore Red*. Arzner retired from filmmaking in 1943 but continued to teach until the 1970s.

Dorothy Arzner and Joey Arias

John Ashbery (1927–2017)

Influential artist and writer John Ashbery's work both exemplified and defied the deeply personal work of the New York school of poetry that emerged in the 1950s and '60s. He was one of the most awarded poets in American literature, winning the Pulitzer Prize in 1976 for his collection *Self-Portrait in a Convex Mirror.* He rarely wrote about his sexuality, and while that fact has often been a bone of contention with his queer readership, his poems are laced with a queer sensibility and richness that tell a deeper story.

April Ashley (1935–)

A great trans-cestor who garnered a bit of fame from her role in the 1962 Bob Hope and Bing Crosby vehicle *The Road to Hong Kong* when she was outed as a trans woman. She was dropped from the film but went on to be an outspoken advocate for trans people. In 2012, she was rewarded as a Member of the Most Excellent Order of the British Empire (MBE) for her services to the transgender community. To this day, Ashley continues to be a shining example of elegance and grace.

Howard Ashman (1950–1991)

Many critics have made the case that Ashman has influenced a whole generation of lyricists in American musical theater, and with good reason. He collaborated with Alan Menken on musicals like *Little Shop of Horrors* (1986), but then got picked up by Disney to write the songs for *The Little Mermaid* and *Beauty and The Beast.* During the writing of *Beauty and The Beast*, Ashman was suffering from AIDS, and some of his own pain can be felt in the story and the hope for love in the movie. He died in 1991 before fully completing the songs for *Aladdin.* A documentary about Ashman's life and work called *Howard* was released by Disney in 2018.

Athletes

We're LGBTQ+, we do everything— even sports! Putting my inherent sassiness aside for a minute, it's a great day to see LGBTQ+ players in almost every major US sport. Not just the heroes of the past, like basketball's Jason Collins and tennis pros Martina Navratilova and Billie Jean King, but to see current superstars like figure skater Adam Rippon, skier Gus Kenworthy, and everyone's hero, soccer megastar Megan Rapinoe. LGBTQ+ people continue to prove that we are capable of doing amazing things in many fields.

W. H. Auden (1907–1973)

One of the most celebrated poets of the twentieth century, Wystan Hugh Auden achieved a brilliance with lyrical poetry that spoke to the modern age. He took on everything from the cruelties of war to the brilliance of love in first flowering. Auden traveled with his friend Christopher Isherwood to Germany, where both found sexual freedom in Weimar Berlin. Auden eventually emigrated to the United States, and became a citizen in 1946, where he lived for the rest of his life. Auden continued to write and teach, and was also a prolific essayist. For those of you who don't read much poetry, Auden wrote "Funeral Blues," which is read in *Four Weddings and a Funeral.*

Auntie Mame

The quintessential queer childhood fantasy of being whisked away to live with a fabulous drag queen who loves you and teaches you about the world, *Auntie Mame* is a novel written by Patrick Dennis in 1955. It became a stage play starring Rosalind Russell, and was then adapted to film in 1958. In 1966 it was also adapted into a musical by Jerry Herman starring Angela Lansbury. The musical was made into a not-so-great film in 1974 starring Lucille Ball. That's a whole lot of Mame. *Mame* has it all: love, loss, and lots of costume and apartment changes. It's hard for me to write about it now without gushing. When a young boy goes to live with his wild and eccentric Auntie Mame after the death of his father, she tries to open up the world for little Patrick, for as she says, "Life is a banquet, and most poor suckers are starving to death!" Aside from being one of the most dazzling examples of Technicolor, with the brilliant Russell glowing from scene to scene,

the film has in some ways become a philosophy for me. Mame charges into the future looking for further evidence of just how brilliant the world can be. She's open and accepting and kind and tries to impart that kindness to everyone she meets. Never losing sight of expression and expansion, Mame is the dream of constant evolution. She never looks back at the way things were, but always forward at the way they can be if we're all just a little freer and know how to accessorize. If we escape the life of small-mindedness and the trappings of respectability, we can be something greater than whatever we dreamed. It's not just a movie, it's a creed. To move, to try, to fail, but to always push

Auntie Mame

forward and most importantly to live! Live! LIVE!

Kevin Aviance (1968–)

Words like *fierce* were invented for performers like Kevin Aviance. This drag performer and musician pushes the bounds of drag with an energy and stage presence matched by very few. Aviance moved to New York in 1993, where he joined the House of Aviance, a legendary house in the New York ball scene. Once in New York, he began getting a lot of attention for his performance and musical abilities. He's appeared in multiple films and has had number one hits on the Billboard dance charts like "Give It Up," "Strut," and "Rhythm Is My Bitch." In 2006, Aviance was attacked walking home from a gig in the East Village. He insisted on continuing his career, so despite his injuries he appeared at the Gay Pride Parade a few weeks after his attack. Aviance continues to create work today that maintains his powerful and unbelievable standard of excellence.

B

is for...

Cardi B (1992–) ICON

Our lady of the tongue pop and those nails, Okkkuurrrr? Cardi B is here to tell you a thing or two, and her fans can't wait for more. She is the second female rapper of all time to top the charts with a solo effort. She first broke out as a cast member of *Love & Hip Hop: New York*, but her musical talents couldn't be denied. Her first major hit, "Bodak Yellow," was released in 2017 and spent three weeks at the top of the charts, shooting her into the public spotlight. Which is exactly where she belongs. With her unapologetic Bronxisms and her bold sense of self, Cardi B solidified her gay appeal with the controversial 2020 hit "WAP" (Wet-Ass Pussy) with Megan Thee Stallion. We'll never think of a bucket and mop in the same way again.

The B-52s

Everybody knows "Love Shack," but that's just the tip of the massive rainbow iceberg. The B-52s are a New Wave band originally formed in 1976 by Cindy Wilson, Kate Pierson, Keith Strickland, Fred Schneider, and Ricky Wilson who played guitar with the band until his death of complications from AIDS in 1985. The band always had a kitsch aesthetic, with live shows resembling performance art more than standard rock and roll. They became an indie darling of the New Wave scene in the 1980s with songs like "Rock Lobster" and "Planet Claire," until 1989 when they took that playful kitsch to the mainstream with "Love Shack." After a hiatus in the late 1990s, the band got back together in 2008 to release the album *Funplex* and continue a busy schedule of touring to this day.

Francis Bacon (1909–1992)

A painter of violence and energy whose work both excites and entrances viewers around the globe to this day, Bacon came to painting relatively late, trying his hand at interior designing and gambling before he settled on art. He was a key figure in Soho's gay artist community and painted many of his friends and fellow artists. He created his first major work, a triptych titled *Three Studies for Figures at the Base of a Crucifixion*, in 1944. He would return to the triptych form throughout his career. He was an artist obsessed with the seedy underbelly of London and the darker, more painful sides of love.

Jim Bailey (1938–2015)

If you were a child of the 1970s, Jim Bailey was your singular vision of female impersonation and all the glamour that came along with it. Why lip-sync with your favorite Judy Garland record when you could sing it live? He did just that. Bailey started his career in Las Vegas in the early 1960s, impersonating legends like Judy Garland, Barbra Streisand, and Peggy Lee. He made the leap to television in the 1970s and became a hallmark of comedy variety shows of the time. Bailey was a sensation, playing solo concerts at Carnegie Hall in New York and the Palladium in London. He toured the world until his death in 2015, raising money for many AIDS charities and singing just like the divas who inspired him.

Josephine Baker (1906–1975)

Singer, dancer, icon of the Jazz Age, and spy, Josephine Baker did it all, and for that and so much more she is often seen as the first African American international star. Baker grew up poor in St. Louis, Missouri, and began her career as a comedian and dancer in vaudeville. In 1925, at age nineteen, she appeared in the famous banana skirt in La Revue Negre in Paris and all of Paris went *insane* for la Josephine. Throughout the 1920s and '30s, she made films and appeared on stages across Europe, collecting accolades and lovers of both sexes. When the Second World War broke out in the late '30s, Baker became a spy for the French Resistance and was later awarded the Legion of Honor by Charles De Gaulle. She was an outspoken critic of race relations in the United States and a staunch supporter of civil rights. She adopted twelve children of different races from around the world, and referred to them as her "Rainbow Tribe." She died in 1975, after opening a huge show celebrating her life and work at the Bobino in Paris.

James Baldwin (1924–1987)

When asked in an interview what he thought about the disadvantages of growing up poor, black, and gay, Baldwin laughingly replied, "I thought I'd hit the jackpot." There are voices of such rarity and precision that they block out of the rest of the noise around them to achieve something solitary and rare. James Baldwin was such a voice. Brilliant, brave, and brazen,

Josephine Baker and James Baldwin

Baldwin asked tough questions about power and its uses from his first book, *Go Tell It on the Mountain*, until the end of his career. His collections of essays, like *The Fire Next Time* and *Notes of a Native Son*, have become classics of political thought and social-justice writing. After all these years, Baldwin's brilliant work continues to strike readers at the heart of where they live. From his novels like *If Beale Street Could Talk* and *Giovanni's Room*, his gay novel published in 1956, to plays like *Blues for Mister Charlie*, each and every work affirms Baldwin's place as an icon of American Literature.

Ball and Ball Culture

Yes, a ball, dawling! Why you gagging? She brings it to you every ball! Events for gay communities to show off and show up for each other, gay balls go back to the early years of the twentieth century. Operating under the guise of "fancy dress," queer communities were able to circumvent cross-dressing laws and show off for one another. Balls were hugely popular in Harlem among African American communities. They continued throughout the century and were brought to the attention of the mainstream public with the classic 1990 documentary *Paris Is Burning* by Jennie Livingston. The documentary provided rich context about the details that made ball culture thrive—houses, strutting, and voguing. Balls survive into the modern day as detailed in the 2016 documentary *Kiki*, and as the major backdrop for the FX show *Pose*. In 2020, HBO Max debuted *Legendary*, a competition show celebrating the moves and the attitudes of all things ballroom!

Les Ballets Trockadero de Monte Carlo

Drag queens can truly do anything, including dance on pointe. The Trocks, as this drag troupe of highly trained ballet dancers are affectionately known, was co-founded by Peter Anastos, Natch Taylor, and Anthony Bassae in 1974. An offshoot of the 1972 Trockadero Gloxinia Ballet Company, they initially produced small, late-night shows in off-off-Broadway spaces to poke fun at the world of ballet and perform the roles denied to men. After the troupe's first show in a second-story loft on Fourteenth Street in the Meatpacking District, they received a favorable review in the *New Yorker*. The Trocks eventually toured the world, and in 2017 they were profiled in the documentary film *Rebels on Pointe*.

Tallulah Bankhead (1902–1968)

A legend is often talked about but rarely understood. Such is the case for this larger-than-life personality Tallulah Bankhead. Tallulah came to New York in the 1920s with her sister to be famous by hook or by crook, and she did a little of both. She was a hanger-on at the Algonquin Round Table and a frenemy of Zelda Sayre

Fitzgerald, but from the very beginning Bankhead was building her own legend. She'd cartwheel at parties. She'd drink all manner of booze and take all manner of drugs. As she said, "My father warned me about men and liquor, but he never mentioned a word about women and cocaine." Her biggest hit came in 1934 with Lillian Hellman's play *The Little Foxes*, later played on film by her rival, Bette Davis. Bankhead did few films, preferring the life and freedom of the theatre, but we luckily have the camp-tastic *Die! Die! My Darling!* from 1965.

Tallulah Bankhead and Barbette

Azealia Banks (1991–)
This Harlem-born rapper first hit the scene in 2012 with a self-released mixtape. Her lyrics were frenetic and powerful, and her beats were solid. When her song "212" started to make its way to clubs that year, she easily started to build a strong following among gays looking for a new female rapper to celebrate. When she later came out as bisexual, the community thought they had found a new hero. But there's been trouble for Banks along the way—she's been at the center of online feuds with people like Perez Hilton and Zayn Malik. Her use of homophobic slurs have caused many to take a second look at this performer with a lot to say but not always the best delivery.

Samuel Barber (1910–1981)
One of the most revered American composers of the twentieth century, Samuel Barber made his first splash on the classical-music scene with his *Adagio for Strings* in 1936. Throughout his career Barber wrote amazing works and was awarded the Pulitzer Prize twice for his efforts: once for his opera *Vanessa* in 1956, and again for his *Concerto for Piano and Orchestra* in 1962. Barber's most controversial work was his opera *Antony and Cleopatra* written for Leontyne Price to open the new Metropolitan Opera House at Lincoln Center. It was heavily criticized and caused Barber to withdraw, though he continued to write music until he was seventy years old. He had a lifelong relationship with fellow composer Gian Carlo Menotti.

Barbette (1898–1973)
This darling of the flying trapeze was a man. Barbette was born Vander Clyde

Broadway in Round Rock, Texas, and began performing in the circus at the age of fourteen with an act called the Alfaretta Sisters. After the sisters split up, Barbette went solo, performing on the high wire and trapeze in full drag and revealing his male identity at the end of the act. The performance became so popular in America that in 1923 he took it to Europe and became an international star. Jean Cocteau compared Barbette to ballet star Nijinsky and championed the performer throughout Europe, commissioning Man Ray to photograph the gender-bending star. After retiring, Barbette became the artistic director for Ringling Brothers and a consultant for the film industry. Tony Curtis and Jack Lemmon hired Barbette to coach them on getting their drag just right for the film *Some Like It Hot.*

Clive Barker (1952–)

Feeling ghoulish, are we? Well happily, or miserably as the case may be, we have the work of novelist, visual artist, and filmmaker Clive Barker. There is little Barker can't do when it comes to terrifying an audience. Early in his career, Stephen King wrote of Barker, "I have seen the future of horror and his name is Clive Barker." Barker's work hit the big screen with *Hellraiser* in 1987, which was based on his novella *The Hellbound Heart.* Barker continued with the franchise with two more movies, which besides being

bloodcurdlingly frightening also had a strangely fashionable feel. He also began the *Candyman* franchise. He continues to create horrifying works across genres and be an advocate for LGBTQ+ rights and causes.

Djuna Barnes (1892–1982)

Mysterious, alluring, and aloof, she is most remembered today for her novel *Nightwood*. Barnes got her start in journalism, writing for ladies' magazines in the 1920s. In 1921, she was assigned to Paris, where she started associating with the Natalie Barney circle, an enclave of lesbian artists and socialites. It was there that she first met artist Thelma Wood. Wood and Barnes carried on a relationship that would be the basis for *Nightwood*. Her work was highly experimental, finding a compatriot in the writings of James Joyce. After Barnes and Wood separated in 1928, Barnes traveled between New York, London, and North Africa. She eventually settled in New York at 41 Patchen Place where she became a famous recluse. Her neighbor, e. e. cummings, would often check in on her by yelling across the street, "Are you still alive, Djuna?" She stopped answering in 1982 at age ninety. *Nightwood* has since become a classic in the queer literary cannon.

Natalie Clifford Barney (1876–1972)

If you were a lesbian in the 1920s in Paris (and I hope you were because it had to be a good time), you would want an invitation from socialite, writer, and artist Natalie Barney. Inheriting a large fortune from her father, Barney moved to France determined to live her life as an openly queer person. Barney wrote of her sexuality, "My queerness is not a vice, is not deliberate and harms no one." She wrote openly to female lovers in her novels and poetry, and used her talents to promote the work of other female writers. When the French Academy would not accept female writers, she started her own by founding the Académie des Femmes, offering readings of some of her writer friends like Colette, Gertrude Stein, and Djuna Barnes. Barney continued her salon into the 1960s when she finally began to retreat due to ill health. She died in 1972 at the age of ninety-five.

Susanne Bartsch (1962–) `ICON`

There's one queen of the party, and that's the legendary Susanne Bartsch. She started as a party girl in London in the late 1970s but found her home and calling in New York in the 1980s. As a small-boutique owner in New York's Soho area, Bartsch showcased the work of fashion-forward British designers like Vivienne Westwood. But it was the club kids that started to give Bartsch her biggest inspiration. As the 1980s continued, Bartsch began throwing parties. It was a chance to see and be seen, and from the beginning she had an eye for what could make a night in New York special. She fostered young talent from among the club kids, giving RuPaul one his first big breaks, and put a philanthropic spin on partying with her first Love Ball in 1989. This event raised $400,000 for the fight against AIDS. And the party continues: Bartsch still throws major events in New York, and a documentary about her life and work, *Susanne Bartsch: On Top*, was released in 2017.

Shirley Bassey (1937–) `ICON`

Shirley Bassey

After a rough day, I always play a Shirley Bassey song and let her get out all the drama for me. With booming vocals, a sparkling and over-the-top stage presence, Dame Shirley has been a favorite of the gay scene for more than fifty years. This marabou-covered diva is mostly known to the larger public for her songs for the James Bond series of films, including *Goldfinger* in 1964, *Diamonds Are Forever* in 1971, and *Moonraker* in 1979. But it's her highly performative song styling that has endeared her to a legion of LGBTQ+ fans. One need only look at televised performances of her hits, like *I, Who Have Nothing*; *The Greatest Performance of My Life*; and *I Am What I Am*, to see that Dame Shirley brings the vocals and the drama to everything she sings.

BDSM

Bondage and sado masochism are sexual practices that play out power dynamics and the enjoyment of a pain/pleasure principle. BDSM has been a part of queer sexuality since long before *Fifty Shades of Grey* came along to get everybody turned on. The early days of the AIDS crisis saw a rise in the prevalence of BDSM among gay men, as it concentrates on many different kinds of activity and not solely on penetrative sex. The push and pull and power exchange in sex have always been in play in queer sexuality, and BDSM is one of the ongoing conversations the community has when it comes to gender and subverting roles in sexual spaces. (Did I get it right, Daddy?)

Beach Blanket Babylon

There are some gay events that are hard to describe, and *Beach Blanket Babylon* is one of them—part musical, part costume showcase, part drag show, part comedy, all camp. *Beach Blanket Babylon* was the brainchild of Steve Silver who started the show in 1974 at the Savoy Tivoli in San Francisco. The show follows Snow White on her trip around the world to find a Prince Charming, and guess where she finds him? San Francisco! The show was an immediate hit with its over-the-top performances and costumes.

In the grand tradition of the *Ziegfeld Follies*, performers came out in huge headdresses and costumes showcasing landmarks of San Francisco and the United States. The show ran for over forty years before finally closing in 2019.

Bears

A genre of gay people that tend to be bigger and furrier than the stereotypical gay. The bear movement started in earnest during the AIDS crisis, in an effort to show that gay men were not all wasting away—some of them were bulking up. A quick guide:

BEAR: A hairy gay man, usually bulkier and probably over forty.

CUB: A younger hairy gay man, bulkier and probably under forty.

EWOK: A small hairy gay man.

OTTER: A hairy gay man, on the skinnier side of bear-dom.

WOLF: A hairy gay man, on the skinnier side, with whitish hair.

POLAR BEAR: A hairy gay man on the bulkier side, with whitish hair.

And my own addition . . .

MINK: A hairy-ish femme-ish gay-ish person, who much like the animal they are named after is useless and looks best when draped over a dowager's shoulder.

(But that's just me.)

Jackie Beat (1963–)

Few drag performers can make you laugh as long and as hard, but don't

Jackie Beat and Bears

say "long" or "hard" in her presence, because she'll go right in for the joke. It's what she does; Jackie Beat is the queen of the song parody. Entertaining audiences for decades, Beat performs in cabaret with her solo shows like *Jackie Beat Is a Whole Lotta Love*, and releases videos for her wild song parodies like "Baby Got Front" and "Filthy Whore." She's also worked behind the scenes as a writer for comedians like Rosie O'Donnell, Joan Rivers, Roseanne Barr, and Margaret Cho. She continues to tour the country with her one-woman shows and her adaptations of the Golden Girlz Live, where she plays Dorothy Zbornak.

Cecil Beaton (1904–1980)

Photographer, painter, interior designer, and costume designer, Beaton was an aesthete on the level of Oscar Wilde, and his wit and insight were not far off either. He started taking photos for *Vogue* in 1931, and his beautiful work quickly caught the attention of the rich and famous. He was the official royal family photographer for many years, and a particular favorite of Queen Elizabeth II's mother. He designed the costumes for the original Broadway production of *My Fair Lady*, and then the film, for which he won an Oscar. Besides his visual work, Beaton was also a dedicated and gossipy diarist. Published in six volumes, his diaries are the funniest and bitchiest ride through a who's who of the twentieth century. He had an opinion about everyone, and luckily for us, he wasn't afraid to dish.

Alison Bechdel and Cecil Beaton

Alison Bechdel (1960–)

This graphic artist, writer, and originator of the famous Bechdel test has been making work that is proudly personal and political for more than forty years. Bechdel's first major strip, *Dykes to Watch Out For*, began in 1983 and ran for twenty-five years in gay and lesbian publications across the country and in a series of compilations from Firebrand Books. She debuted her now-famous Bechdel test in *DTWOF* in 1985. For those unfamiliar, it's a litmus test for assessing female characters in media. The test is simple: to pass, there must be at least two women who talk to each other about something besides a man. It seems simple enough, but it's shockingly sad to see how few films pass the test. Bechdel has also pushed the limits of the graphic novel format with two visual memoirs, *Fun Home* and *Are You My Mother? Fun Home* became a Tony Award–winning musical in 2013.

Alan Bennett (1934–)

This beloved performer and playwright created plays and monologues for television, bringing the music of the North of England to almost all his works. Bennett was part of the legendary Beyond the Fringe group with Dudley Moore, Peter Cook, and Jonathan Miller in the 1960s. Following that success, Bennett continued to write plays and television. His *Talking Heads* series for the BBC, where stories are told directly to the camera by a single character, featured actresses like Maggie Smith, Eileen Atkins, and Patricia Routledge. Bennett had one of his greatest successes in 1991 with *The Madness of King George.* The play was turned into a film with Nigel Hawthorne, who originated the role on stage. Bennett's next huge hit was 2004's *The History Boys*, which became an international hit and launched the careers of Russell Tovey, Dominic Cooper, Samuel Barnett, and James Corden.

Michael Bennett (1943–1987)

The man who gave us *Dreamgirls* and *A Chorus Line* left the world before we could experience the full effect he might have had on the face of the American musical theatre. Bennett was a director and choreographer whose work continues to resonate almost forty years after his early death from AIDS. He began as a dancer on Broadway and television in the early 1960s. On the set of the pop music TV show *Hullabaloo*, Bennett met his friend and muse, Donna McKechnie. Bennett started choreographing in 1966 but had his first breakthrough in 1968 with the musical *Promises, Promises*, his "Turkey Lurkey Time" number, featuring McKechnie, is a classic from that year's Tony Awards telecast. He followed up with two Sondheim musicals, co-directing and choreographing the original productions of *Company* and *Follies*. Bennett continued this streak of hits with *A Chorus Line* in 1975, which won nine Tony Awards and the Pulitzer Prize. Bennett was also the visionary behind the original production of *Dreamgirls* on Broadway, for which he won the Tony Award for Best Choreography.

Bent

This play by Martin Sherman exposed the treatment of homosexuals by Nazis during the Holocaust. It debuted in 1979 with Ian McKellen and Tom Bell in the lead roles and was an instant smash. A brutal look at life for gay men inside the concentration camps, it is also a powerful piece about the survival of the spirit under the most difficult of experiences. A 1997 film adaptation starred Clive Owen, Lothaire Bluteau, Mick Jagger, and Ian McKellen, this time playing a smaller role.

Gladys Bentley (1907–1960)

Always dapper in her white tuxedo, Bentley was a star entertainer and queer symbol of the Harlem Renaissance. She set herself apart during the 1920s by always appearing in male drag and singing her own risqué compositions about the love between ladies. She often flirted with female audience

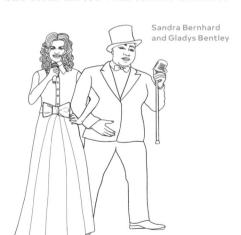

Sandra Bernhard and Gladys Bentley

members and was out and open about her sexuality in her work. By the mid-1930s, her career started to stall, and she faced trouble with the law for performing in male drag. After the Second World War, Bentley abandoned her lesbianism and married a man, saying she had been cured by hormone therapy, which sounds crazy in LGBTQ+ circles today, but people bought it in the '50s.

Greg Berlanti (1972–)

If you're into teen dramas with smart, witty dialogue and love scenes that make you believe in a sweet, surrendering love that will last forever or at least until the end of the season, look no further. Writer, director, and producer Berlanti has been the voice behind shows like *Dawson's Creek*, *Everwood*, and most recently driving the kids wild with *Riverdale* and *Chilling Adventures of Sabrina*. While Berlanti has stepped out of the teen drama with hits like *Brothers and Sisters* and the Netflix hit *You*, he's even taking on the DC universe by producing shows like *Arrow* and *Supergirl*. Throughout his career, Berlanti has pushed for LGBTQ+ representation in his shows, like introducing Jack, an out gay teenager, to his first major series, *Dawson's Creek*.

Peter Berlin (1942–)

The man and the look of the '70s. He was all sex, when sex was becoming the vogue. If Instagram was a thing back then, Berlin would have been its first thirst trap. He curated his look from the start—the famously low-resting, tight-enough-to-tell-exactly-what-he-was-packing jeans, and the open shirt—acting as his own photographer, model, and designer. Berlin starred in early gay sex films like *Nights in Black Leather* in 1973 and *That Boy* in 1974. These films made Berlin an international star and put him in contact with successful artists of the period. He posed for Warhol, Mapplethorpe, and even Tom of Finland. A documentary about his life as a sex symbol, *That Man: Peter Berlin*, was released in 2005.

Sandra Bernhard (1955–)

Cabaret star, actress, and voice of righteous indignation and ribald commentary of stardom and status who has been making us laugh and think for almost forty years, Bernhard started doing stand-up in Los Angeles, where she set herself apart by combining her offbeat observations and musical numbers. Her performance as Masha, the crazy stalker in Martin Scorsese's *The King of Comedy* in 1982, won her the National Society of Film Critics Award for Best Supporting Actress. She launched her career as a solo cabaret performer in 1985 with her first one-woman show, *I'm Your Woman*. In the 1980s, she became a staple guest on *Late Night with David Lettermen* and the best gal pal of Madonna during her *Truth or Dare* period. Since then, Bernhard has continued to do solo shows and tour internationally, acting on television shows like *Roseanne* and *Pose*, and even hosting her own talk show on Sirius XM, *Sandyland.*

Leonard Bernstein (1918–1990)

Likely who you picture when you think of an orchestra conductor, Bernstein, with his big and excited gestures, jumping off the stand in time with the music, represented the best of American classical music for most the twentieth century. Bernstein wrote symphonies, ballets with Jerome Robbins, and crossed into the world of popular music with musicals like *On the Town* and *Wonderful Town*, written with friends Betty Comden and Adolph Green. His greatest commercial success came in 1957 with *West Side Story*. He conducted with the New York Philharmonic for more than a decade before eventually becoming the first American conductor of the Vienna Philharmonic. He continued to write musicals like *Candide* and *1600 Pennsylvania Avenue*, operas and operatic works like *Mass* and *A Quiet Place*, and educated American children on the glories of music in his Young People's Concerts.

Beyoncé (1981–) `ICON`

It's hard to compare her, and with good reason. In a world that throws around the term *icon* willy-nilly, there are few who have the same gravitas

Beyoncé and
Leonard Bernstein

in the creative world as Beyoncé does. She's beloved. She's revered. She's close to worshipped in some circles (I know a guy who has an altar). Beyoncé Knowles is the icon of the twenty-first century. Everything she touches turns to gold—just look at Solange. Her life is already a story of legend. Born in Texas in 1981, she started singing in malls and climbing her way to the top—first with the super-group Destiny's Child and then, in a Diana-Rossian twist of fate, as a solo artist, eclipsing the group and taking over the world. Since going out on her own, Beyoncé has only continued to slay with albums like 4 and *Lemonade,* visual albums to accompany the music, and unbelievable stage performances. She promotes the talents and the visibility of women of color and creates something akin to a revival in live performance. You don't have to believe in a lot in this world, but you can surely believe in Beyoncé.

Tom Bianchi (1945–)

Bianchi, the king of the gay Polaroid, is a writer and photographer whose Polaroids capture gay life and sex since the 1970s. You just want to land in a Tom Bianchi picture. Or maybe land on one of the men in his pictures. Within Bianchi's photographs, there's the hint of nostalgia—the skies are bluer, the waters are clearer, the bulges are bigger. Perhaps it's that he chronicled a world that would be forever changed by AIDS, but it may also be the medium. His exploration of gay desire through the male nude elevates Bianchi beyond a casual chronicler to a true artist.

James Bidgood (1933–)

Bidgood was a glittery and gay artist way ahead of his time whose genius lay open for all to see but was uncredited for decades. He was a costume designer and window dresser in New York in the 1950s and '60s, but his secret passion was photography. He would create wonderlands of frisky fantasy right in his own little apartment and then pay hustlers to come and pose in them. This work eventually became a movie, *Pink Narcissus,* that was released anonymously in 1971. The film became an underground cult classic and had a rare appearance by downtown New York theatre legend Charles Ludlam. The lushness of the sets and the suppleness of the boys became a huge influence for later artists like David LaChapelle and Pierre et Gilles. And all in his apartment. Can you imagine? Makes you feel bad about not yet fixing that light in the bathroom, doesn't it?

Big Dipper (1985–)

Rapper and comedian all about the body-ody-ody, Big Dipper has been putting it all out there to make us laugh and to help us shake that ass, no matter the size. The Chicago-born artist raps about being a plus-size beauty and his outlook on the gay world. His music video "LaCroix Boi," celebrating his love of the seltzer-y drink, reached hundreds of thousands of views on YouTube. He tours the world with his dance beats and his powerful and playful message of body positivity and loving yourself.

Big Freedia (1978–)

Nobody makes it pop like Big Freedia, the undisputed queen of bounce. Born and raised in Louisiana, she has taken this local music, with its fast-paced lyrics and chronic beats, and celebrated it across the country. If you love to twerk, you need to write Freedia a thank-you note, because she brought that booty bounce to a nation in need. Freedia released her first single in 1999 and her first studio album, *Queen Diva*, in 2003. But things really started taking off for her with the release of *Big Freedia Hitz Vol. 1* in 2010. She's since starred in her own reality TV show, collaborated with everyone from Drake to RuPaul, and so famously said on Beyoncé's "Formation," "I did not come to play with you hoes. I came to slay, bitch." Long may this queen slay.

Bikini Kill

A much-revered band in the Riot Grrrl movement of the 1990s, thought by many to have even started it. Founded by Kathleen Hanna, Billy Karren, Kathi Wilcox, and Tobi Vail in 1990, Bikini Kill was set apart from the rest of the music scene at the time by their unique combination of beach guitar, punk, and feminist strains. They were a band for thinking and fighting girls who wanted to rock. The band released their first album *Revolution Girl Style Now* in 1991 as an independent cassette, and started to build a major following. Avast! Recording signed them and in 1993 they recorded the now-classic *Pussy Whipped*. The album includes the song "Rebel Girl," which *Rolling Stone* listed as one of the "Most Excellent Songs of Every Year Since 1967." They released their final album, *Reject All American*, in 1996 and broke up in 1997. Its reputation has only grown and, in 2019, the band did a reunion tour.

Alexandra Billings (1962–)

Trans actress, singer and, pioneer, Billings has been making art since the 1980s. After starting out in the drag clubs of Chicago, she took her talents to the pageant circuit. She began working with theatre companies in Chicago and eventually joined the Steppenwolf Theatre Company. Billings continues to work in the theatre, as well as on television with a major role in *Transparent*, and most recently on *The Conners*. She's a true triple threat and continues to be a source of strength for the community at large. She supports trans and HIV rights and has always been an outspoken proponent for love. If you have the chance to see her do her thing, run to her.

Bingo

A game played in gay bars around the country—I will never understand why. Is it the balls?

Dustin Lance Black (1974–)

A screenwriter, director, and activist, Black has been telling gay stories since his first short film, *Something Close to Heaven* in 2000. Following his Oscar-winning screenplay for the movie *Milk*, Black became an outspoken gay activist for marriage equality, fighting hard against the passage of California's Proposition 8. He wrote a play about the *Hollingsworth v. Perry* case that ended up overturning Prop 8 in California, bringing marriage equality to the United States. Black continues to work writing films like *J. Edgar* about the former head of FBI, J. Edgar Hoover, and the ABC miniseries *When We Rise*, about the life and activism of Cleve Jones. Black is married to Olympic diver Tom Daley, with whom he had a child in 2018.

Black Cat Riots

It's New Year's Eve, and you're out on Sunset Boulevard in Los Angeles looking to ring in 1967 with a bang. Pun intended. The lights get low, everyone around you is counting down, and you snuggle up close to the nearest man and lean in for a kiss when . . . cops bust up the joint. They used the holiday as a sting to arrest gay men and it worked like a charm—until word got out. Not just a case for gay rights, but also a strong case for entrapment, Personal Rights in Defense and Education (PRIDE) headed up peaceful protests called the Black Cat Riots. PRIDE's newsletter later became *The Advocate*. Two years before Stonewall.

Black Cat Riots

Black Girls

The originators of gay culture. Next time you hear two Black girls talking on the subway:
(1) Take notes, because that's what your friends'll sound like in five years;
(2) Thank those girls.

Black Party

The Black Party was a debaucherous circuit party that ran for almost forty years in New York City. A night of leather, latex, and getting laid, this notorious bacchanal harkened back to a different time in gay culture. It also brought out all kinds of people with all kinds of ideas about how to celebrate. For years, the party where anything and everything goes was held in the Roseland Ballroom in Hell's Kitchen. But after the Ballroom's closure in 2014, the Black Party moved around a bit, and at the time of writing, its future is uncertain.

Mykki Blanco (1986–)

There are artists who change the rules of the game and then there are others who blow it up. When you're looking for someone to blow it up, look no further than Mykki Blanco. Rapper, performance artist, and activist, Blanco first hit the scene in 2010 with performance pieces on YouTube. They released their first mixtape, *Cosmic Angel: The Illuminati Prince/ess*, in 2012. Since then, Mykki has been a groundbreaker for LGBTQ+ hip-hop and gender identity. Blanco has been

Mykki Blanco

open about their search for the best expression of their identity, questioning whether to undergo reassignment surgery and the limitations of pronouns. He has been open about their HIV-positive status, trying to break the stigma in both gay and hip-hop communities. Blanco released their first studio album, *Mykki*, in 2016 to excellent reviews.

Panti Bliss (1968–)

An Irish Icon of drag, Panti Bliss had been delighting audiences for decades in her home of Dublin, Ireland, with her hilarious takes on politics and the world at large. In 2014, Panti got to do just that on a larger scale. While on RTÉ's *The Saturday Night Show*, Panti took the Irish press to task for being homophobic. At first there was outcry for Panti to apologize, but the drag queen stood her ground. Panti took to the stage of Dublin's famous Abbey Theatre, and talked openly and honestly about the real effects of homophobia in her day-to-day life. The speech went viral, making Panti an international sensation. Panti continues to speak out for the rights of LBGTQ people and tours the world with her newfound fame.

Marc Blitzstein (1905–1962)

An American composer largely forgotten today, but whose mark on American opera and theatre can still be very deeply felt, Blitzstein first came to prominence in 1937 with his pro-union musical, *The Cradle Will Rock*. The show was produced by the Works Progress Administration (WPA) and directed by Orson Welles. Complaints about the play's "communist undertones" forced the WPA to pull its funding and the show was shut down by dramatically locking Blitzstein and the company out of the theatre. Undeterred, Blitzstein, Welles, and the cast of actors found another venue, and on June 16, 1937, with Blitzstein acting as narrator and accompanist, *The Cradle Will Rock* made its unofficial debut. It's since become a night of theatrical legend. A film about the legendary performance of *The Cradle Will Rock* was produced and directed by Tim Robbins in 1999, in which Blitzstein is played by Hank Azaria. There's a 1985 recording of the musical in its entirety by the Acting Company and featuring a very young Patti LuPone.

Blue Is the Warmest Color

This French graphic novel by Jul Maroh, which was adapted into a film in 2013 under the French title, *La Vie d'Adèle–Chapitres 1 & 2*, tells the lesbian coming-of-age story of Adèle, a young French teenager, and her first crush on a young painter named Emma. The film charts the beginnings of their relationship in early high school to early adulthood, providing an honest and graphic portrayal of two young women in love. (It's *very* hot and I'm *very* gay.) Co-written and directed by Abdellatif Kechiche, the film won big at the Cannes Film Festival with a unanimous vote for the Palme d'Or and was nominated for Best Foreign Language Film at the Golden Globes in 2014.

Mickey Boardman (1971–)

The editor and advice columnist at *Paper* magazine, Boardman is a favorite in the fashion world with a keen eye and a sense of kitsch that is both smart and playful. His advice column, Ask Mr. Mickey, has appeared in the magazine since 1993. Boardman is a huge part of New York art and fashion scene, doling out his particular brand of style to all he encounters. He is always at fashion shows, and *New York* magazine named him one of the most photographed faces in town. Boardman is also a philanthropist—his Mr. Mickey's Celebrity Sidewalk Sale raises money for many notable causes.

Dirk Bogarde (1921–1999)

A matinee idol who refused to live a lie and paid the price for it, Bogarde was an actor with charm and good-enough looks to launch him to the top. He fought bravely in the Second World War and then starting acting in the late 1940s and '50s. Bogarde played homosexual characters with humanity and panache. In 1961's *Victim*, he played a man being blackmailed for his homosexuality, and in 1971's *Death in Venice*, he played the aging Gustav von Aschenbach obsessed with the untouchable Tadzio. Though he never came out publicly, his sexuality was seen as a liability simply because he took on gay roles. A favorite of many directors and actors, he never achieved the matinee idolhood of which he was truly capable.

Justin Vivian Bond (1963–)

A cabaret artist, actress, performer, and perfumer who has been the epitome of downtown New York cool for almost thirty years, Justin Vivian Bond got their start working in the plays of trans-artist Kate Bornstein. The breakthrough for Bond came when they met Kenny Mellman and formed the legendary duo of Kiki and Herb. Bond played the gritty chanteuse Kiki DuRane, singing songs from all over the musical landscape in a style that gave fresh energy to the rage and ferociousness of the gay community in the waning days of the AIDS crisis. As Kiki and Herb, Bond and Mellman played Carnegie Hall, Broadway, and concert halls around the world. Bond retired Kiki in 2008 to concentrate on their solo work and their transition. They have since released three LPs and one memoir, *Tango*, and continue to be stalwart talent of downtown cabaret and a legend the world over.

Chaz Bono (1969–)

When your mom is Cher, what can you do? Well, a lot it seems. Chaz Bono was first introduced to the nation on his parents' television show, *The Sonny and Cher Comedy Hour.* Then Chastity, she came out at eighteen and lived as a lesbian for many years. In 2008, Chaz began transitioning from female to male. He shared his story of transition in the OWN network documentary *Becoming Chaz.* He has since appeared on *Dancing with the Stars* and *American Horror Story* and has been a vocal advocate for the trans community. Mama should be proud.

Justin Vivian Bond
and Rae Bourbon

Born This Way Blog

Before the infamous Lady Gaga song, there was this online blog created by Paul Vitagliano (a.k.a. DJ Paul V). Participants submitted stories and pictures of their younger selves, showing everyone that queerness shows up early in the lives of LGBTQ+ people. The results were often touching and mostly hilarious, but overall it broke down the myth of choice when it comes to LGBTQ+ identity. The blog became so popular that a companion book was published in 2012.

Kate Bornstein (1948–)

Activist, playwright, author, and gender theorist who has always been out front and out proud, questioning the role of gender in our lives and in our happiness, Kate Bornstein has done it all. She was a Scientologist and a performance artist. She's written about her transition and her sex life, all the while pushing our understanding of what gender is and can be. Bornstein is the author of *Gender Outlaw*, a revelatory memoir of her trans experience. Here's one of my favorite quotes of Kate's: "I have this idea that every time we discover that the names we're being called are somehow keeping us less than free, we need to come up with new names for ourselves, and that the names we give ourselves must no longer reflect a fear of being labeled outsiders, must no longer bind us to a system that would rather see us dead."

Boston Marriage

A term used for a formalized "romantic friendship between two women," starting in the late nineteenth century, a Boston marriage was seen as something respectable and common and was apparently so common at Wellesley College at the time that it was also called a Wellesley marriage. These marriages were usually formed between educated upper-class women, and seen by the public as a pairing of spinsters who just needed to split the rent while they taught school. But what do you think was going on? One famous Boston marriage was between Katharine Lee Bates, who wrote the lyrics for "America the Beautiful," and Katharine Ellis Coman, who wrote the first industrial history of the United States. An excellent book on this topic is Lillian Faderman's *Surpassing the Love of Men*.

Ivy Bottini (1926–2021)

A comedian and activist who started her career as an advocate for women in the 1960s, Bottini helped found the New York chapter of the National Organization for Women (NOW) in 1966. While fighting for rights of women, Bottini staged huge actions, like a protest at the base of the Statue of Liberty. She opened up the conversation about lesbianism in the women's movement and was pushed out of the organization by Betty Friedan in 1970. When she relocated to Los Angeles in

1971, Bottini founded AIDS Network LA, the first AIDS organization in Los Angeles. A natural wit, she wrote and started performing the one-woman show *The Many Faces of Woman* around the country in 1972. In 1981, she was appointed by Governor Jerry Brown as the first LGBTQ+ person on the state Commission on Aging.

Rae Bourbon (?–1971)

To this day, we still don't know exactly when this female impersonator and comedian was born. Bourbon was so successful as a female impersonator in the 1930s that by the late '40s Mae West asked him to star on Broadway in her production of *Catherine Was Great.* He performed across the country and put out wildly successful little party records of his routines. In 1956, Ray—now Rae—claimed that they'd gone to Mexico for a sex change. The claim was never proven, but it made a great topic for one of their party records, *Let Me Tell You About My Operation.* Rae had a hard life and when, in the late '50s, their act was seen as too dirty for a regular audience, they went into semi-retirement. That's where things got weird. Rae liked to travel with dogs, but as the gigs dried up, so did the money for puppy chow. So Rae dumped the dogs with a friend, promising to pay for their upkeep. When Rae didn't pay up, the friend sold the dogs for medical experiments. Rae was so mad they hired two guys to beat the friend up and they accidently killed him. They all went to jail and Rae died in prison in 1971. Now that may sound dark, but to me it sounds like the gayest season of *Fargo* yet.

Bette Bourne (1939–)

Peter Bourne wanted to be an actor, so he studied at the Central School of Speech and Drama in London and made his way to the stages of the West End and the soundstages of the BBC. But in the early '70s, as the Gay Liberation Front started making strides for LGBTQ+ equality, he felt called to change his life and the lives of others. So young Peter Bourne, a successful West End actor, changed his name to Bette and started performing in drag. In 1976, Bourne joined the gay cabaret group Hot Peaches and toured with them around Europe. He went on to form his own group, Bloolips, working with playwright John Taylor on shows like *Lust in Space* and *The Ugly Duckling.* Bourne continued to work in the theatre, writing shows about his life and playing his friend Quentin Crisp in the play *Resident Alien.* Playwright Mark Ravenhill made a documentary about Bourne's extraordinary career and life in 2014 called *It Goes with the Shoes.*

Matthew Bourne (1960–)

Bourne started dancing late—at a whopping twenty-two. But he brought something new and exciting to the world of ballet. As a choreographer, he has changed the face of contemporary ballet and theatre forever. He formed his first company, Adventures in Motion Pictures, in 1987 and ran it until 2002. Bourne became an international sensation with his 1995 reimagining of *Swan Lake* featuring all-male swans. The first time I saw it, I never thought I could be attracted to a bird, but there I was. The work was thrilling and edgy, introducing a new physical language to the world of contemporary ballet. Bourne continues to make other new ballets: *The Car Man*, based on the music of Bizet's opera, *Carmen*; *Edward Scissorhands*, based on the Tim Burton film; *Dorian Gray*, based on the novel by Oscar Wilde; and *The Red Shoes*, based on the 1948 film. He also works in the theatre, choreographing and directing musicals in London. Bourne was knighted in 2016 for his contribution to the theatre and dance.

Leigh Bowery (1961–1994)
Drag queen, club kid, and provocateur Leigh Bowery took London by storm in the 1980s. His imaginative and envelope-pushing costumes brought him immediate attention, but there is also a great mind behind the mask. Leigh was born in 1961 in Australia and moved to London in 1980, where the underground punk scene was morphing into something more gay and experimental. How lucky that Leigh was there. He was a club promoter who created the club Taboo, which

Leigh Bowery

inspired a short-lived musical by friend Boy George and Charles Busch. A zaftig character, Leigh became a muse of painter Lucian Freud. He also formed a punk band called Minty and at performances was known to fill his ass with an enema and then share that bounty with the audience. Yup. What you do in the shower before drinks and a light dinner, Leigh Bowery made people pay to see. That's pretty punk. Bowery died at the height of his career from complications with AIDS.

David Bowie (1947–2016)
Some have called him the greatest rock star that ever lived. Some say he brought gender-bending and glam rock to the mainstream. Some see him as musical visionary, whose constant evolution set the standard for the twentieth century. Whatever you find yourself saying about David Bowie, there's so much more still unsaid. He was a

cultural icon whose music and style set up a whole generation to dream outside the realms of the real. Bowie revealed his alter ego Ziggy Stardust in 1972, putting the "glam" in glam rock by starting a trend in music that made the whole presentation more theatrical and gay. Bowie also came out as bisexual in 1972 and carried on a relationship with Iggy Pop in the '70s. Bowie moved away from his Ziggy persona in the '80s but continued to inspire queer artists looking to push the envelope when it comes to performance and persona.

Paul Bowles (1910–1999) and Jane Bowles (1917–1973)

If you follow the story of American literature of the twentieth century, there are certain figures who pop up everywhere. Paul and Jane Bowles are two such figures. Paul started out writing music and studying with the famous Nadia Boulanger in Paris. When he visited Tangier with friend and composer Aaron Copland in 1931, he fell in love with the city. He married Jane Auer in 1938. Both were gay and open about it but liked each other's company and thought, why not? Jane's first novel, *Two Serious Ladies*, published in 1943, became a favorite of writers Tennessee Williams and Truman Capote. Jane and Paul moved to Tangiers in 1947, where Paul wrote his novel *The Sheltering Sky* in 1949. It has been listed many times as one of the best American novels of the twentieth century. The

Bowleses played hosts to a sea of literati traveling through north Africa—from Gore Vidal to Allen Ginsberg and William S. Burroughs. Jane had a stroke in 1957 at the age of forty and spent the rest of her life in ill health. She died in Málaga, Spain, in 1973. Paul continued to write music and books until his death in 1999.

Boy Erased

Garrard Conley's 2016 memoir is a national bestseller that told of Conley's experience with Christian conversion therapy. It was heralded for its honesty and stunning detail about the reality of this hated practice. It was adapted into a play and then a movie starring Nicole Kidman, Russell Crowe, and Lucas Hedges. The film was nominated for multiple awards and brought this brilliant and harrowing story to life for a wider audience.

Boy George (1961–)

If Bowie gave us a taste of androgyny, Boy George gave us a sissy twist that made the '80s a lot more bearable. George came out of the London club scene, heavily influenced by folks like Leigh Bowery, and hitting the music scene with his band Culture Club. The band had a number of hits like "Karma Chameleon" and "Do You Really Want to Hurt Me," highlighting George's smooth and soulful vocals. But it was often his outfits that made the sensation. George' makeup and gender-bending persona quickly became a symbol of the sexual androgyny that club kids were exploring at the time. Boy George played coy about being gay early on but has since become a loud and outspoken advocate for the community. After Culture Club broke up in 1986, George went out on his own, then formed a new band, Jesus Loves You, in 1989. George has worn many hats since the 1980s (they've even become a staple of his get-up): whether DJing, singing with Culture Club again, or even writing a musical— Taboo debuted on Broadway in 2004— about his early days. Boy George keeps breaking bounds with a whole lot of style while he's doing it.

Boys Don't Cry

This 1999 biopic tells the story of hate crime victim Brandon Teena. Teena was a trans man living in Nebraska when he was raped and murdered in 1993. The movie, written and directed by Kimberly Peirce with Andy Bienen, starred Hillary Swank as the young Teena. *Boys Don't Cry* was universally acclaimed for showing a more sympathetic view of Teena, whose reputation was often tarnished in the media. The movie also relied heavily on a documentary about the case, *The Brandon Teena Story*, released in 1998. For her role as Brandon Teena, Swank won the Academy Award for Best Actress, and her co-star, Chloë Sevigny, was nominated for an Oscar for her role as Lana, Teena's girlfriend.

The Boys in the Band

A play about a gay party that ends in tears and heartbreak: Sound familiar? *The Boys in the Band* by Mart Crowley was the first runaway hit written by a homosexual that deals with the real turmoil in our lives rather than the perceived troubles from the straight world around us. It takes place at the home of Michael, who is throwing a party for Harold, his self-described "ugly" friend. The evening spins out of control, when Michael's former "friend" from college, Alan, shows up. Michael goes around drinking too much and forcing everyone to confront their demons in a party that goes off the damn rails. The play was a huge but controversial hit when it opened in New York in 1968 and ran for over a thousand performances. It was made into a now-classic movie in 1970 with most of the original cast. The play was most recently revived on Broadway in 2018 with Jim Parsons, Zachary Quinto, Matt Bomer, and Andrew Rannells.

Boys in the Sand

Wakefield Poole hoped gay people could look at this film and say, "I don't mind being gay—it's beautiful to see those people do what they're doing." Shot on Fire Island in 1971, this X-rated film has no dialogue, though the story spreads over three acts. Act One: Bayside. Lonely, dark-haired Peter Fisk sits on the beach wishing to find something substantial. From the water, the beautiful blond Casey Donovan appears. They do it. Act Two: Poolside. Casey responds to a personal ad and days later gets a reply in the mail. It's a pill that he throws into the pool. It turns into a guy. They do it. Act Three: Inside. Casey's alone in the house, showering, because he's been a lot of places by this point. He checks out the hot telephone operator up on the pole. Casey goes back to his room to carry out his fantasy where he and the operator do it. After the fun, the real operator arrives and we're left to imagine they do it for real. It was a huge hit because—at least from my theory—it gives credence to the fact that sex is often better in your head than in your bed.

Boystown

This section of Lakeview Chicago holds the record for being the first officially recognized "gay village" in America. From Irving Park Road in the north all the way to Wellington Avenue in the south, Boystown continues to be the center of gay life in Chicago. It's still a hell of a good time, and nobody knows how to party likes gays in the middle.

Joe Brainard (1942–1994)

Brainard was a writer and visual artist who lived and worked in the creative haze of the 1960s, '70s, and '80s in New York. A draftsman and cartoonist, Brainard collaborated with many of the great writers of his time, including poets like Ted Berrigan, Anne Waldman, and John Ashbery. Deeply influenced by the pop art movement, Brainard's Nancy drawings, based on the comic strip *Nancy*, have become iconic. Brainard is most recognized for his *I Remember* series of writings. The book is a series of non sequitur memories that vary from the banal to the deeply personal, work that creates a full and often quite funny picture of Brainard's life.

Guy Branum (1975–)

Guy Branum is one of those comedians who makes you feel smarter for laughing at his jokes. With cool erudition and a sharp eye, he is in a league all his own on the LGBTQ+ comedy circuit. He got a big break writing for *Chelsea Lately* in 2007 and was eventually put on camera to offer his own hilarious commentary on the events of the day. From there he moved on to *Totally Biased with W. Kamau Bell* and *The Mindy Project* with Mindy Kaling. Branum's own show, *Talk Show the Game Show*, ran for two seasons on truTV. He also released a hilarious memoir, *My Life as a Goddess: A Memoir through (Un)popular Culture*, in 2018.

Benjamin Britten (1913–1976)

One of the most celebrated English composers in the twentieth century, he is most remembered today for his stunning opus *War Requiem* and the opera *Peter Grimes*. His works are moody and yet eerily tuneful, expressing both the anxiety and the cruel beauty of the twentieth century. Britten wrote a lot of vocal music for children and loved the cacophony of sounds that comes from young or amateur musicians. His music is still very popular today and performed all over the world, but in England in particular his works are a source of pride.

Brokeback Mountain

The 2005 film that has us all weeping, reconsidering spit as a lubricant, and promising that we "just couldn't quit" whoever was listening, was based on a short story by writer Annie Proulx. Heath Ledger and Jake Gyllenhaal portray two lonesome cowboys who fall in love over the course of a single summer and spend the rest of their lives trying to reconnect with the love they found on the titular mountain. Directed by Ang Lee, the film was a critical and box office hit, and was one of the first films with an LGBTQ+ story line nominated for Best Picture at the Oscars.

Romaine Brooks (1874–1970)

Any good salon needs a good painter, and luckily for Natalie Barney's circle in Paris of the 1920s, they had Romaine Brooks. At the age of nineteen, Brooks moved to Paris to study art, followed her studies to Rome, and eventually married her gay friend John Ellingham Brooks. The marriage didn't work out, so Brooks returned

to Paris in 1908. Her first solo show in 1910 caused a sensation when she included two nudes—unheard of for a female artist at the time. Brooks met Barney in 1916 and the two carried on an open relationship, at times as a contented thruple, for almost fifty years. As the twentieth century moved on to the abstract, Brooks's work was often dismissed as too figurative, but later scholars looked at her work with a keener and more expressive eye. She died in 1970, at the age of ninety-six.

Jericho Brown and Romaine Brooks

James Broughton (1913–1999)

People called him Big Joy, for his exuberance and commitment to playfulness in his art and life. A poet and filmmaker, Broughton was the elfish queen of the avant-garde film scene and poetry circles for the latter part of the twentieth century. His film *The Pleasure Garden* was heralded at the Cannes Film Festival in 1953. *The Bed* in 1968 became a staple of the experimental and midnight movie scene of the late '60s, as it highlighted several differently gendered couples hopping into and being intimate in bed. He wrote openly about his homosexuality, though he lived for many years in a heterosexual relationship. He eventually left his marriage for a much younger partner, Joel Singer, in the late 1970s. Broughton was very involved with the Radical Faerie movement of the late '70s with activist Harry Hay, who had been a lover of his.

Jericho Brown (1976–)

Jericho Brown is a major American poet of tremendous emotional depth, whose work has been almost universally praised since his first published collection, *Please* in 2008. Brown takes on America's deeply held racism, with a stunning clarity that is as human as it is harrowing. As he writes, "Nobody in this nation feels safe, and I'm still a reason Why." Brown uses his experiences as a Black gay man to illustrate a common humanity, thus continuing a legacy put forth by other LGBTQ+ Black poets like Essex Hemphill. Brown has been award the MacArthur Genius Grant and Guggenheim Fellowship, and his 2019 collection, *The Tradition*, was awarded the Pulitzer Prize for Poetry.

Brunch

A gay sacrament, brunch typically involves day drinking and gossip. People will tell you that it should be sometime before noon, but those people aren't doing it right. A proper gay brunch should take place after noon, to give all those concerned the chance to wake up and get their lives together. You can still have eggs at 2 p.m., so relax.

Buck Angel (1962–)

A trans-male porn star and activist who has created a market for himself and made way for other trans performers while pushing the conversation about trans sexuality forward. After Angel's transition at the age of twenty-eight, he began bodybuilding and eventually moved into pornography under his own imprint, Buck Angel Entertainment. Calling himself "The Man with a Pussy," Angel made waves and turned heads as he put himself out there. Since his breakout, he has worked with other companies like Titan Media and won many awards for his work in film, but it's been his role as an advocate for trans people that has truly made Angel a legend. He has continued to push for positive trans portrayal in pornography and help his fellow trans men, first by opening his own dating site and then working with Perfect Fit to design sex toys specifically for trans men.

Lady Bunny (1962–)

What can you say about Lady Bunny that hasn't been said? Rude, crude, lewd? You betcha. But she's also a multitalented legend in the drag world and one of the sharpest minds in the biz. Bunny got her start in Atlanta with her good friend RuPaul and both moved to New York in 1984. It was in New York in 1985 that she organized the first Wigstock, the groundbreaking celebration of drag and performance that would go on for the next twenty years. Lady Bunny does it all: writing her own song parodies and jokes, acting in shows with Ethyl Eichelberger, and DJing to keep the party moving. In recent years, she's become more political in her comedy, taking on the religious right and anyone on the public scene who's not making sense. Though her profile has grown with the advent of *RuPaul's Drag Race* and the short-lived *RuPaul's Drag U*, for many Lady Bunny is and always will be the queen of New York drag.

Lady Bunny

Tituss Burgess (1979–)

In world full of gay drones on their merry way to normalhood, a gay flamboyant savior emerged to make us laugh and shriek with delight. Actor Tituss Burgess as Titus Andromedon in *Unbreakable Kimmy Schmidt* is outlandish, outspoken, and out every other way you can imagine. Burgess brings heart and endless quips to a performance that is recognizable but endlessly new. He started working with Tina Fey on *30 Rock* as D'Fwan, then made the leap with her into this new project in 2015. Prior to his success on television, Burgess starred on Broadway in the musical *The Little Mermaid* in the role of Sebastian the Crab and in *Guys and Dolls* as Nicely-Nicely Johnson. Burgess is a true gay star of the twenty-first century. In the words of Titus Andromedon, "I envy you. I've never been able to meet me."

Charles Busch (1954–)

If camp had a mother, well that would be Joan Crawford, but if it had an aunt, a playful, fun, and glamourous aunt, she would be this playwright, actress, and icon Charles Busch. Busch continued the legacy of the gay-camp leading lady laid out by Charles Ludlam and Jackie Curtis, but with a sparkle and a glamour all his own. With his unique take on Hollywood glamour, Busch began his theatrical legend with *Vampire Lesbians of Sodom*, a major hit off-off-off-off-off-Broadway. More plays followed, with bigger theatres and audiences and hits like *Times Square Angel* and *Psycho Beach Party*. Busch writes and performs his own works and luckily some of his greatest stage roles have made their way to film with *Psycho Beach Party* and *Die, Mommie, Die!* Busch has also written plays in which he has not starred, like *The Tale of the Allergist's Wife*, which appeared on Broadway in 2000. A documentary about Busch's life and career, *The Lady in Question Is Charles Busch*, was released in 2005.

Bushwig

Founded in 2012 by Brooklyn drag royalty Horrorchata and Babes Trust, this offbeat drag fest started as a celebration of the wild and burgeoning drag scene that was happening in Brooklyn. The festival filled a hole that was left by the loss of Lady Bunny's Wigstock in the East Village and continued with much of its renegade spirit. It has continued to grow year after year, attracting acts and attention from all over the world and extending from one to two days of fun and fabulousness with over two hundred performers.

But I'm a Cheerleader

In 1999, Natasha Lyonne and Clea DuVall fell in love at True Directions, a camp for "troubled gay people" run by Cathy Moriarty and RuPaul. Or at least they did in this now-classic film. The colorful send-up of reparative therapy was directed by Jamie Babbit

and has since become a laugh-out-loud hilarious classic of LGBTQ+ film. Lyonne plays a sweet and wholesome cheerleader who's feeling through certain downstairs rumblings we all know and love, so off she goes to True Directions. Dressed in pink for days alongside a cast of other gays who aren't buying it either, Lyonne finds herself and a little love in the beautifully butch DuVall.

But I'm a Cheerleader

Butch

They've been called everything from "mannish" to "masculine" to "bulldaggers," but butch lesbians are a personal favorite. Short-haired, handy, usually clad in something utilitarian and simple, these women have been a visible staple of LGBTQ+ life. Some poke fun at the typical uniform of the Butch—Birkenstocks, a flannel, the ring of keys—but when I see a butch lesbian walk by, I see a woman who doesn't have time for your crap; she's got things to do. And I salute that. And her.

Rhea Butcher (1982–)

With a wit this dry, it's almost absorbent, Rhea Butcher is a comedian on the rise. Butcher began their career in

Chicago with Second City and quickly began performing stand-up around the country. They made their television debut on *Conan* in 2016. They performed with their then partner and fellow comedian Cameron Esposito for BuzzFeed in "Ask a Lesbian," *She Said* for the Amy Poehler's Smart Girls Network, and finally in the Seeso series *Take My Wife*. The couple have since gone their separate ways, but both Butcher and Espesito continue to gay up comedy stages around the country.

Judith Butler (1956–)

A feminist and gender philosopher who has written seminal texts on queer and gender politics starting in the late twentieth century, Butler blew open the conversation about gender in her 1990 work, *Gender Trouble*. In it, she put forth that gender as we see it—or rather as it exists in the world—is mostly performative. You act like a man or a woman, but who knows what you are. To Butler, it's a list of characteristics rather than a predetermined state, making extraordinary room for gender variance. This major theme in her work has changed the way scholars and educators think about gender. In some ways, Butler has brought to the fore deep conversations about who we are and how we as queer people exist in the world.

BUTT

The thinking gay's guide to art, attitude, and ass. Founded in 2001 by Gert Jonkers and Jop van Bennekom, this deliciously dirty magazine was the height of porny art, all printed on gorgeous pink paper. *BUTT* broke a mold of gay content by mixing high and low culture in one forum without shying away from sexuality. In any given issue, you could see a collection of nudes as well as an interview with author Edmund White or John Waters. In 2014, Taschen released a special edition anthology of the magazine called *Forever Butt*.

C

is for . . .

Paul Cadmus (1904–1999)

With his incredible sense of fun, Paul Cadmus presented a gay world that was bubbling under the surface in the 1930s and '40s. Growing up on the Upper West Side of New York, Cadmus from an early age was witness to the burgeoning queer life in the city that he would later detail in his work. In 1934, while working for the Public Works of Art Project for the WPA—a program set up by the federal government to help artists find work during the Great Depression—Cadmus painted *The Fleet's In!* A group of sailors, often a ready trick for gays out on the prowl, start their shore leave with a bunch of freewheeling ladies of the evening. In a stunning turn, Cadmus included a single and fae looking gentleman wearing a red tie—an early flagging signal that homosexuals used in New York in the 1930s. The painting was deemed unsavory by Navy officials and eventually withdrawn. Cadmus went on to create work that celebrated gay visibility almost until the very end, dying just five days short of his ninety-fifth birthday.

Caffe Cino

Caffe Cino was the birthplace of the off-off-Broadway movement that boasted the early plays of writers like Robert Patrick, Lanford Wilson, Tom Eyen, and Doric Wilson. It was founded in the late 1950s by Joe Cino who invited gay friends and writers to create plays that dealt openly with queer themes. While many gay playwrights were first seen on the Cino's stage, it also launched the careers of performers like Bernadette Peters, who got her start as the lead in the musical *Dames at Sea*. Joe Cino committed suicide in 1967, and while the Caffe tried to stay open without him, it eventually closed its doors in 1968.

John Cage (1912–1992)

John Cage is the bright-eyed trickster of twentieth-century avant-garde music, whose most famous piece, *4'33"*, is a work where no notes are played—the experience with the audience *is* the music. Written in 1952, it was seen as part of Cage's aleatoric, or chance-controlled, music. He wanted to broaden the understanding of what music was, using sounds from the modern world as instruments. Cage believed that music was a series of sounds, and while looking for new sounds, the static of radios, crushing blenders, and throbbing power tools all found their way into his compositions. He also started playing a "prepared" piano that could be manipulated to make different sounds by a series of structural alterations that allowed the entire instrument to be used in the music, not just the keys. Cage was an endless innovator, and he is seen as one of the pioneers of sampling. He created works for dance with his lifelong partner, Merce Cunningham.

Claude Cahun (1894–1954)

Cahun was a photographer, sculptor, and writer who transgressed gender and conformity to create works that still thrill and push the line of identity. A transgender artist who worked in the height of surrealism in 1930s Europe, they made work mainly for their own enjoyment, and were mostly unrecognized in their lifetime. Cahun took many self-portraits dealing with costume and gender. As Cahun said about their work, "Under this mask, another mask; I will never finish removing all these faces." Cahun's work continues to be a driving influence on artists around the world.

Call Me by Your Name

This 2017 film made the world stand up and cheer for a first gay love and reconsider the uses of peaches. Directed by Luca Guadagnino, and based on the novel by André Aciman, the film stars Timothée Chalamet and Armie Hammer as a pair of unlikely lovers that find each other in the Italian countryside in the summer of 1983. The screenplay was written by famed writer and director James Ivory and was a huge box office hit. Ivory won the Oscar for Best Adapted Screenplay, and the film launched Chalamet as a major star.

Claude Cahun, Casita del Campo, and Maria Callas

Maria Callas (1923–1977) `ICON`

If you're an opera queen, there's one diva that concerns, elates, and fascinates you. *"La Divina"* Callas was one of the most dynamic and groundbreaking performers of the twentieth century. Callas was the acting diva—an artist of serious musicianship and definitive grandeur whose commitment to her art, and her stylish way of doing it, still inspires artists of all types to this day. She started her career in the late 1940s as a soprano with a voice of power and subtlety and a far plumper frame. The acting was always there, but Callas wanted her physical body to match her characters, so she took on a strict dieting regimen and soon became a sleek and stylish trendsetter.

Callas performed in the biggest opera houses in the world, bringing audiences to their feet with rapturous applause. Backstage, the show was said to be even better. Callas was a temperamental star—getting in fights with management, getting fired from the Met, and frightening even the most powerful men in the world. She became an emblem of the jet set, carrying on an affair with shipping tycoon Aristotle Onassis before he went off and married Jacqueline Kennedy. Callas's voice started to falter at the height of her fame, and she performed her last role on stage as the titular Tosca in 1965, retiring from the stage. For the rest of her life there were attempts to regain her stature, but damage had been permanently done to her voice, and in 1977, she died alone in her Paris apartment.

Michael Callen (1955–1993)

Michael Callen was a singer and songwriter who responded to the call of the AIDS crisis by fighting to keep himself and his friends alive. He was diagnosed with AIDS in 1982, and in 1983, Callen wrote the book *How to Have Sex in an Epidemic: One Approach* with Richard Berkowitz and Dr. Joseph Sonnabend. It outlined for the first time safe-sex practices that could lower transmission of the disease. Callen continued to fight hard to end the epidemic, starting many organizations to support its victims all the while

maintaining a prestigious songwriting career. Callen died of the disease in 1993. The Callen-Lorde Community Health Center was named in his and poet Audre Lorde's honor.

Camp

The often-maligned cornerstone of gay art, *camp* is hard to define. Susan Sontag called it "a sensibility that revels in artifice, stylization, theatricalization, irony, playfulness, and exaggeration rather than content." Camp has been a major part of gay art and life since the beginning. It's often cast off as frivolous, but I've always thought that camp has been queer power. By playing into the falseness, the style—by turning it all up to the heights of its ridiculousness—camp can be a powerful tool for drawing attention to social commentary, truth, and insight as long as you look underneath the thin fabulous veneer.

Bobbi Campbell (1952–1984)

Bobbi Campbell

Campbell was the original "AIDS poster boy," and that was how he wanted it. In 1981, after a series of illnesses, Campbell discovered his first Kaposi's sarcoma lesion. Rather than hiding it, he created a poster, showing his community what to look for and where to find help. He posted the pictures at the Star Pharmacy at 498 Castro Street, right in the heart of gay San Francisco. Campbell wrote a column about his own struggle with the disease and fought until the bitter end, speaking outside the Democratic National Convention in 1984, a month before he died.

Truman Capote (1924–1984)

The man of letters with a baby's voice and lisp to boot, Truman Capote hit the literary scene in 1948 with his novel *Other Voices, Other Rooms* and its much-discussed dust-jacket photo. The young Capote, an "enfant terrible" of the literary set, lay sprawled on a chaise lounge, looking seductively into the camera. The photo made Capote an instant star, but it was his enormous talent that kept him there. He followed his debut with short stories, the book to the musical *House of Flowers,* and a stage adaptation of his short story *The Grass Harp.* It wasn't his novella *Breakfast at Tiffany's* but rather his "nonfiction novel," *In Cold Blood*—a true-crime book about the horrific murder of a Kansas family— that solidified Capote's space in literary stardom. At the top of his fame, Capote hosted the legendary Black and White Ball in 1966. This invite-only, masked

affair at the Plaza Hotel in New York honored his friend Katharine Graham. Acceptance by the jet set was always Capote's fondest wish but also his downfall. For years, he cultivated a group of socialites, his swans, like Babe Paley and Slim Keith. But in November 1975, he published a short story, "La Côte Basque, 1965," a chapter from his yet unfinished book, *Answered Prayers,* and spilled gossip he'd been collecting for years on his dearest friends. The story created an uproar and Capote was shunned by most of his former friends. He spent the rest of his life partying and drinking. His output as a novelist and writer shrunk to almost nothing, though he could still make fascinating, if not bizarre, television appearances. Truman Capote died in 1984 of liver failure.

Gia Marie Carangi (1960–1986)

The world's first supermodel was a foul-mouthed, scrappy bisexual from Philadelphia. Gia Carangi started modeling in local publications when, at just seventeen, she moved to New York and signed with the famous Wilhelmina Models. She soon became a favorite of photographers and magazines the world over. But the high life became a little too high for Carangi and she quickly became addicted to drugs and alcohol. After the death of Wilhelmina Cooper, the matriarch of the agency and a close friend, Carangi fell deeper into her addiction. She contracted HIV and died at the age of twenty-six. A movie about her life, *Gia*, shed new light on Carangi's story and kickstarted the career of Angelina Jolie.

Mariah Carey (1969–) ICON

The queen of the "moment," Carey is one of the most honored and revered pop stars of all time. One of the bestselling artists of all time, with hits like "Fantasy," "Always Be My Baby," and the now-iconic Christmas anthem, "All I Want for Christmas Is You," Mariah Carey is a true legend. She's also a queen of shade—her "I don't know her" comment has become a legendary dig. She's beloved in the gay community for giving us so much music, fun, and finally the movie *Glitter*. Thank you, Mariah.

Brandi Carlile (1981–)

Let's face it, when it comes to folk rock, lesbians really know what they're doing. Carlile is a Grammy-winning singer-songwriter who has been touring and promoting the role of queer women in music for over a decade. Carlile began performing in Seattle, and signed her first contract with Columbia Records in 2004. But it was her second album, *The Story*, produced by the legendary T Bone Burnett, that really rocketed Carlile to stardom. The song "The Story" became a standout hit that was featured in commercials by General Motors during the 2008 Olympics and later became an anthem for the series *Grey's Anatomy*. Her most recent album, *By the Way, I Forgive You*, has been her largest commercial success to date. Her memoir, *Broken Horses*, is a New York Times Bestseller, and the audiobook includes Carlile reading and singing some of the music mentioned in the book.

Wendy Carlos (1939–)

An inventor, composer, and pioneer in electronic music, Wendy Carlos is beacon in the music community and a groudbreaking artist for trans musicians and composers. Carlos released a few albums of her electronic takes on the classics but is perhaps most famous for her scores to films like Stanley Kubrick's *A Clockwork Orange*, *The Shining*, and the sci-fi classic *Tron*. She has been an outspoken advocate for the trans community, talking openly about her transition in the late 1970s.

Edward Carpenter (1844–1929)

Say you're a gay socialist interested in social justice and changing the course of human evolution and you think to yourself, "God, I wish I had a mentor." Well, you do! Edward Carpenter was a philosopher, poet, and writer who advocated for social causes and sexual freedom in a time when Victorian mores were in full bloom. He advocated for free love and the rights of women and started opening the door for gay rights. Carpenter lived openly with his lover George Merrill for many years. Their relationship was the basis for E. M. Forster's novel *Maurice*.

Alan Carr (1976–)

The Chatty Man himself, Alan Carr has been delighting British audiences for years with his toothy grin and his sinister giggle. Carr broke into the comedy scene in the early 2000s and quickly proved a favorite with audiences. Carr hosted his own show, *Alan Carr: Chatty Man*, from 2009 to 2016. Carr has also authored two books and is now a judge on *RuPaul's Drag Race UK*.

Casa Susanna

For the cross-dressing gentlemen of the 1950s and '60s, vacation options were limited. Luckily there was a camp run by Susanna Valenti and her wife, Marie. Casa Susanna was a haven for all types of people who loved the act of dressing up in women's clothes, and while some were gay or trans, many were not, including Valenti herself. Casa Susanna was an undiscovered gem in LGBTQ+ history until the mid 2000s, when a box of pictures from the camp in its heyday were found at a New York flea market. The pictures were collected in a book and later adapted into a play by Harvey Fierstein called *Casa Valentina* in 2014.

Casita del Campo

You wouldn't think of a Mexican restaurant as a gay haven for fajitas and frivolity, but then you wouldn't be thinking about Casita del Campo in Los Angeles. The restaurant opened in 1962 and was noted from the beginning for its colorful and vibrant decoration. No wonder the queens stared to flock. In the 1990s, the owners opened an underground theatre known as the Cavern Club and has since become a staple for gay performance in Los Angeles. Hosting such luminaries as Jackie Beat, Dina Martina, Joey Arias, and Sherry Vine, the Cavern Club is a hot spot for gay entertainment in the City of Angels.

The Castro

The Castro is the great gay-borhood of San Francisco that remains the heart of the queer city by the Bay. Or perhaps the "tourist-y" part of gay San Francisco. It was on these streets that Harvey Milk opened his camera shop and ran his political campaigns, and it was here where Bobby Campbell brought his poster talking about KS lesions and getting the word out. The Castro was the center of gay life in San Francisco and the legacy of this special place continues to this day. You'll know the minute you see the huge pride flag at the end of the block you are in safe space, or at least a very gay one. Check out Twin Peaks, a dishy gay bar with great window views, Orphan Andy's for late-night diner fare, or the famous Castro Theatre for new and classic movies, all beginning with a stirring song on the pipe organ.

Willa Cather (1873–1947)

The grand old aunt of American literature, Willa Cather wrote with the honesty of the plains in which she grew up. She began her career as a journalist but found her voice in fiction when she wrote her novel *O Pioneers!* More books followed until she wrote the now-classic *My Ántonia*, a novel about a young man meeting a family of Bohemian immigrants and falling in love with the beautiful titular character. Cather begins the novel with a brief introduction in which she tells the reader that she heard the story from the young man, thus allowing her to use first person in her narration of falling in love. Cather went on to win the Pulitzer Prize for her novel *One of Ours* in 1923. She lived with her partner, Edith Lewis, for thirty-nine years.

Cazuza and Candis Cayne

Constantine Cavafy (1863–1933)
A Greek-Egyptian poet of startling simplicity and gorgeous sensuality, Cavafy wrote in a Greek revival style that often recalled the ancient myths of the Mediterranean. Using myth, and at times the Greeks' feelings on homosexuality, Cavafy was able to express his own sexuality. He worked for years as a journalist, refusing to publish his poetry formally, publishing only in newspapers and magazines. A complete volume of his work didn't appear until years after his death but has since become a staple of the LGBTQ+ cannon.

Candis Cayne (1971–)
The gorgeous trans woman we all aspire to be—I know because I've seen her midday in a grocery store and even then she was flawless. A trailblazing actress and performer who got started as a drag queen in New York City, Cayne became a staple of the New York drag scene in the 1990s with her supermodel looks and her incredible dance routines. Cayne famously became the first transgender actress to become a series regular on network television with 2007's *Dirty Sexy Money*. She continues to bring her magic to stages and screens around the country, with stints on shows like *Grey's Anatomy*, *The Magicians*, and *RuPaul's Drag Race*.

Cazuza (1958–1990)
Brazilian rock star and activist whose story took on legendary status when he came out as HIV-positive in 1989, Cazuza used his platform to talk about tolerance and social justice for LGBTQ+ people in Brazil. He got his start with the rock band Barão Vermelho. When he left the group in the late 1980s, he began experimenting with his musical genre, expanding his audience, and garnering more praise and fans. Cazuza died in 1990

at the height of his fame. A biopic of his amazing life, *Cazuza: O Tempo Não Pára*, was released in 2004.

Cazwell (1972–)

Since 1999, Cazwell has been creating music that not only openly displays his sexuality, but celebrates it. He first broke out onto the scene with his single "The Sex That I Need" in 2003, and followed it up with "All Over Your Face." The video for "All Over Your Face" was so racy in fact that it was banned from Logo TV. Too gay for a gay channel. That's a trendsetter, baby. He continues to make music that would make your mama blush with songs like "Ice Cream Truck," "Unzip Me," and "Loose Wrists."

The Celluloid Closet

This classic documentary by Rob Epstein and Jeffrey Friedman is based on the book and lectures of the late, great cinephile and activist Vito Russo. The film details the hidden queer characters and story lines during the golden age of Hollywood. Russo had fought for years to get the film made, but he died before Epstein and Friedman began making it in earnest. Funding became a problem until Lily Tomlin, a friend of Russo's, stepped in to host fundraising events to make the film a reality. The result is a harrowing tribute to the forgotten queer voices of Hollywood and to Russo himself.

Luis Cernuda (1902–1963)

A Spanish poet who escaped the horrors of the Spanish Civil War, Cernuda was famously part of the Generation of '27, a group of Spanish poets that rose to prominence in the years prior to the war. Cernuda wrote openly about his sexuality in his work. This fact alone could have made him a target for the Fascists, so he left Spain in 1938 and lived the rest of his life in exile. He taught in colleges around the United States and Mexico and his work continues to astonish new readers worldwide.

Carol Channing

Carol Channing (1921–2019) ICON

You know the voice. Your friend does the impression. There was no one quite like Carol Channing, which is perhaps why she became so unforgettable. Channing was a Broadway legend, starring in shows like *Gentlemen Prefer Blondes* and *The Vamp* before her greatest hit, *Hello, Dolly!* It was this role that she would be most remembered for, and which she toured and revived multiple times. With her distinctively garbled voice, big eyes, and bigger blond hair, she was an object of fascination and imitation to the LGBTQ+ community from the beginning. Channing was a mainstay of 1970s variety television, which brought her quirky and endearing style to audiences around the country and world. She loved her audiences, gay or straight, and they in turn showed her the same kind of adoration to the very end.

Tracy Chapman (1964–)

Chapman has been a voice for social change in music for thirty years. Her first hits, "Fast Car" and "Talkin' 'bout a Revolution," took the country by storm in 1988. She won two Grammy awards for her first album. Chapman has always used her music for change and is often called upon to give voice to social issues. Though she's never publicly come out, her relationship with writer Alice Walker in the mid-1990s was well known. Chapman made a comeback of sorts in 1997 with her hit single "Give Me One Reason." She continues to perform around the country, and hopefully we'll get a new Chapman record in the near future.

Charlene (1989–)

The reigning queen of Brooklyn drag, this trans superstar is making waves and showing boobs to crowds across the country. Charlene first hit the Brooklyn drag scene in 2012. She was vocal about her style and transition from the beginning, going so far as to shoot her hormone injections on stage. Known for her wild and carefree style, often stomping it out in Doc Martens, Charlene isn't afraid of going there, usually with as little clothing as possible. In 2018, after comments surfaced from RuPaul about not allowing trans women on *Drag Race*, Charlene was asked by BuzzFeed to respond. In a thoughtful and eye-opening piece, she dissected the comments and yet again proved that trans people have and always will be a vibrant part of the drag community.

Alexander Chee (1967–)

A bright star among the new gay literati, Alexander Chee began his career writing short stories and essays for gay publications. His first novel, *Edinburgh*, was awarded the Lambda Literary Foundation Editor's Choice Award, and his second novel, *The Queen of the Night*, is a historical novel about an opera diva in the late nineteenth century. Chee continues to put forth a voice in literature that is both breathtakingly honest and gorgeously phrased. His 2018 collection of essays, *How to Write an Autobiographical Novel*, is a stunning addition to a career that only promises more brilliance.

Cher (1946–) ICON

The gold standard in gay iconography and the queen of reinvention, Cher has been one of the only artists to have a major hit in almost every decade of her career. She's *Cher*, bitch! Cher has

Cher

been delighting gay audiences since the beginning. From her sexy numbers and even sexier outfits on the *Sonny & Cher Comedy Hour* and *Sonny & Cher Show*, to her acting in serious films like *Silkwood* and *Moonstruck*, to her electronic hits making us all "Believe" in life after love, Cher stands the test of time. She continues to prove herself as an important and vital gay ally and artist with her hilarious Twitter presence, her stint in the *Mamma Mia!* sequel, and the Broadway musical about her life. As is often said of the icon, "at the end of the world, there will be cockroaches and Cher." And I hope those little queer roaches know LGBTQ+ royalty when they see it.

Mel Cheren (1933–2007)

Mel Cheren felt that disco was all well and good, but why couldn't it be gayer? He got his start at ABC records in the 1960s but struck out on his own in 1976 and founded West End Records, a label that produced mostly dance music, with partner Ed Kushins. It was there that Cheren invented the twelve-inch vinyl single to make for longer playing times at parties that went all night. In 1977, Cheren and his former lover Michael Brody created Paradise Garage, a popular disco in New York that operated for ten years. At the onset of the AIDS crisis, Cheren donated his time, money, and property to help his community in crisis, giving office space to the early days of the GMHC. A documentary about Cheren called *The Godfather of Disco* was released in 2006.

Merrie Cherry (1985–)

The reigning drag mother of Brooklyn drag, Merrie Cherry is a drag queen that breathes the reverence of a bright star of the old school but shines with the bravery and the grace of someone on the cutting edge of drag as an art form. (Perhaps you can tell I'm a fan.) Merrie Cherry makes you do that amazing thing that only a great queen can do—she can take a song and perform it in such a way that gives you a very different understanding without ever singing a note. Merrie is one of the founding members of Bushwig, the Brooklyn drag festival, and continues to dazzle a fawning fandom in the borough and around the country.

Justin Chin (1969–2015)

A gay San Francisco poet and essayist who was an expert chronicler of the gay Asian American experience, Chin was born in Malaysia and raised mostly in Singapore until he moved to the States for college. He released just four volumes of poetry in his short life, as well as four semi-autobiographical collections of essays and many solo works for the stage. He died tragically in 2015, after a stroke brought on by complications with AIDS.

Margaret Cho (1968–)

One of the funniest, bravest, and most recognizable voices in comedy, Cho is a champion for anyone who has felt different or out of place. From the beginning, Cho was a trendsetter, from her early days of stand-up to being one of the first Asian Americans to create and star in their own network sitcom, *All-American Girl*. Though the sitcom didn't last, Cho used the ordeal as an opportunity to talk about body positivity and the trials of women of color in Hollywood. But that's what Cho does—she goes there. Whether it's talking about growing up in San Francisco among a thriving-then-surviving gay community or her own bisexuality, Cho's bravery and courage of spirit continues to keep audiences in stitches and tears.

Gay Men's Chorus

There's one in almost every major city in America, and why, you may ask? Because apparently gay men love putting on a show. The Gay Men's Chorus movement began in the late 1970s as a social network of gay men looking to get out there and sing. Choruses popped up in Los Angeles in 1979 and New York in 1980, but they soon spread out to cities like Washington, DC; Atlanta; Chicago; San Francisco; and Philadelphia. Choruses became great organizers for AIDS charities and often used their platforms to raise money to fight the epidemic. Most choruses are still active today and still do a lot of charity work. They've even inspired a host of new trans choruses around the country to join in the fight and the song.

Christine and the Queens

This French art pop group brings a solid focus on lyrics and danceability to pop again. Headed by Héloïse Adélaïde Letissier, the group first drew attention with the single "Tilted" in 2015. The song and video captivated the world, incorporating dance in new and inventive ways—a project that Christine wants to keep as a major part of their performances. As the song started to catch on in America, so too did Christine, who was asked to sing at the season 11 finale of *RuPaul's Drag Race*. The band released a follow-up album, *Chris*, in 2018.

Christopher Street

Named after the famous street in New York on which the gay movement was born, this magazine was started in 1976 by Charles Ortleb. While it was certainly taking on the subject of gay life, the magazine also tried to capture cultural and intellectual life in New York. It published fiction by eminent gay writers and covered politics and art created by gay people. It was a thinking-gay's magazine that published 231 editions before finally folding in 1995.

The City and the Pillar

Gore Vidal's 1948 novel is an early and pioneering gay novel. While it falls into some of the pitfalls of early gay works—usually ending in the death of the gay character—it's a sympathetic and beautiful ride until you get there. Vidal based most of the book on his relationship with the great love of his life, or at least so he claimed—the fallen Jimmy Trimble, who was killed during the Second World War. The book was controversial from the beginning and forced Vidal into writing under pseudonyms after its publication. It has since emerged as a classic in the LGBTQ+ canon.

City of Night

If you're looking for a gay adventure through America, with all the sex, drugs, and jokes you could ask for, look no further than *City of Night*. John Rechy's 1963 novel about hustling in a pre-Stonewall world is a brilliant and poetic exposé of a gay world that was out of sight from the rest of society. Often compared to Jack Kerouac's *On the Road*, this novel still stands as an epic adventure into the gay underbelly of the late 1950s and '60s. The young man is loosely based on Rechy himself. He travels to cities across the United States, like Los Angeles, New Orleans, and New York, meeting the local gay scene in each. The novel even features the 1959 Cooper Do-nuts Riots in which Rechy took part.

Julian Clary (1959–)

Dishy, swishy, and endlessly elegant, Julian Clary is a groundbreaking comedian. One of the first comedians in Britain to perform in a camp style with open acknowledgment of the gay life that went with it, Clary started telling jokes and breaking barriers in the 1980s. Always dressed to the nines and glammed out, Clarey presents as a real person, and has won over audiences with his charm rather than some sort of gay artifice. He's been a hallmark of the comedy and panto scenes in England, and he's also had great success in television. He's hosted many shows and specials and continues to delight audiences throughout the UK.

Montgomery Clift (1920–1966)

There are few actors who ever brooded as well as Montgomery Clift. He was a highly successful theatre actor when Hollywood scooped him up to star opposite John Wayne in the 1948 film, *Red River*. Clift was troubled by Hollywood and often fought over the quality of the scripts he received. He also balked at the strict

Hollywood code that kept him in the closet. He was a close friend of Elizabeth Taylor, whom he met on the set of *A Place in the Sun* in 1951. Taylor often credited Clift with teaching her about acting. In 1956, while leaving Taylor's house, he was involved in a nearly fatal car crash. His face was deeply scarred by the accident, and he underwent a great deal of plastic surgery to regain his smoldering good looks. After his accident, Clift relied more and more on drugs and alcohol. He continued to act, turning out brilliant performances in films like *The Misfits* and *Judgment at Nuremberg*. In 1966, through the help of Taylor, he was signed to do the film *Reflections in a Golden Eye*, the story of a closeted army official and his wife, but Clift died before filming began.

Kate Clinton (1947–)

Yes, there were lesbian comedians before Ellen, and the biggest and best of them all is Kate Clinton. A comic who dived right in and never veered away from her sexuality, Clinton began doing stand-up in 1981, using her perspective as an out and proud lesbian as the centerpiece of her act. Clinton's work is always smart and progressive, like her one-woman shows *Lady Haha*, *Correct Me If I'm Right*, and *Kate's Out Is In*. She has been a hallmark of LGBTQ+ comedy and activism and continues to make work that provokes audiences today.

Clone

Have you ever noticed how some guys date men that look exactly like them? It's usually called twinning, or, in some circles, narcissism, but this trend toward a uniform look traces itself back at least to the 1970s with the invention of clones. The '70s clone had facial hair, usually a moustache, and wore flannels and tight jeans. While styles have changed, the clone mentality has carried on into the modern day. Though there are so many types of people in the LGBTQ+ community, there's still a strong pull toward fitting in. Clones, then and now, just want to be like everyone else.

Club Kids

Club Kids

With wacky and outlandish costumes and personas, the Club Kids of the late '80s and '90s took advantage of going out as a runway for their art. This group of nightclub-going kids, unofficially led by Michael Alig and James St. James, made freakdom seem more than appealing. The group has members that are still making art and fun today, like Amanda Lepore, Richie Rich, and even RuPaul. The Club Kids also hit the airways with legendary appearances on the *Geraldo Rivera Show* and the *Joan Rivers Show*, giving the country a look at the kids who were indeed alright, until they weren't. Alig was eventually sent to prison for the horrendous murder of fellow Club Kid Andre "Angel" Melendez. The story and scene were captured by James St. James in his memoir, *Disco Bloodbath: A Fabulous but True Tale of Murder in Clubland*, and then in the documentary *Party Monster: The Shockumentary*, which was eventually turned into the movie *Party Monster* with Macaulay Culkin and Chloë Sevigny in 2003.

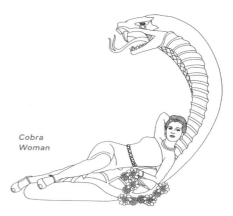

Cobra Woman

Club My-O-My

This popular drag bar in New Orleans operated from the 1930s to the '60s, when it burned down under mysterious circumstances. It was a hot spot for gay clientele, as well as a large swath of straight patrons who enjoyed the female impersonators. Drag performers sang live nightly and entertained the clientele, which often included Hollywood greats traveling through New Orleans. In a city known for sin, Club My-O-My was a hot spot for things still forbidden.

Cobra Woman

This film, starring Maria Montez and inspiring a whole host of camp reinventions, was released in 1944. It's so bad it's good again, then bad, then fantastic.

It's a camp-tastic story of idol worship, true love, and snakes. In the movie, Montez plays two roles: a South American priestess who worships the cobra god and offers him virgin sacrifice, *and* the virgin about to be sacrificed. But how does the priestess choose her victims, you may ask? Through the art of the dance; the Cobra Dance. *Cobra Woman* was an inspiration for drag legend Mario Montez, who took her name from Maria, and outsider director Jack Smith. It was a moment of camp that was passed around and talked about by gay folks for over thirty years.

The Cockettes

There are some performances that are legend, some you had to be there for, some you had to be high enough for. Luckily, the Cockettes gave us all three. This bearded hippie pansexual psychedelic theatre troupe was formed by the illustrious Hibiscus and began as late-night entertainment in a movie theatre in San Francisco on New Year's Eve 1969. From that first night, the group went on to create works of theatre such as *Gone with the Showboat to Oklahoma, Tinsel Tarts in a Hot Coma, Journey to the Center of Uranus,* and the seminal *Pearls Over Shanghai.* The shows highlighted a group of glittered, heavily medicated misfits displaying their talents, or lack thereof. But there were highlights—it was an early showcase of the brilliant singer Sylvester and brought some of John Waters's Dreamland players to the stage, such as Divine and Mink Stole. David Weissman's 2002 documentary about the group has become a primary document in gay theatre and brought the Cockettes to a whole new generation of theatre creators. The works of the original troupe, mainly written by Scrumbly Koldewyn and Martin Worman, are performed by a new company, the Thrillpeddlers, in San Francisco today.

Jean Cocteau (1889–1963)

There was never a closet that could hold Jean Cocteau, but the same could be said about a genre. A poet, designer, illustrator, filmmaker, and playwright, Cocteau was born at the height of the Belle Époque. In his early twenties he began running with the artistic set of Paris, as well as those working with Sergei Diaghilev's Ballets Russes. He began as a poet, but eventually moved to the theatre, writing plays like *Les Parents Terribles* and his anonymous sexual memoir, *Le Livre Blanc.* Cocteau had a long relationship with the actor Jean Marais, whom he used in films like *La Belle et la Bête,* a visually dazzling retelling of "Beauty and the Beast," and the stylized *Orphée.* Cocteau and his work stand as a colossal achievement in French art and influence artists around the world.

Andy Cohen (1968–)

The chipper and charming producer behind the reality engine that is the Bravo network, Andy Cohen got his start in news at CBS but moved to Bravo as a vice president of original programming in 2004. Unlike most TV executives, Cohen appeared in front of the camera. starting with all those *Real Housewives* reunions, of which he is the executive producer, and then on his own show, *Watch What Happens Live with Andy Cohen,* which premiered in 2009. Cohen has released two books and most recently hosted New Year's Eve on CNN with close friend Anderson Cooper.

Colette (1873–1954)

French novelist, dancer, sexual provocateur, and come-what-may bisexual, Colette wrote about love and lust in the careless and freeing French way that sounds almost like American Republicans talking about politics—with a certain gleeful insanity. Colette began writing under the pen name of her then husband, Willy. Her first novels, the Claudine series, became wildly popular and eventually led to the breakup of her marriage and her breakthrough as an artist. Her novel about this time, *The Vagabond*, is a seminal work of feminist fiction. Colette went on to write over twenty novels, as well as columns and articles. She's most famous in America for her novella *Gigi*, which became a movie musical in 1958.

Collectibles

Go into any queen's home and you will see them: stuff, mementos, memorabilia. Gay people love to collect. Some of it is a preservation of the things that were special or influential, others are almost archival in nature, like flyers or posters from gay events. Sure, some could call it hoarding. But in some cases, these collections are the only archives of often ignored gay history.

Compton's Cafeteria Riot

It's August of 1966 and you're a transsexual sex worker on the corners of San Francisco. You're just trying to make a little dough in a world that won't even give you a chance. At the end of a long night, you and your friends go to Compton's, a small cafeteria in the Tenderloin. You'd go to a gay bar, but they don't like your kind around there. Uptight butch queen fakeness, so you're just trying to grab a coffee and get out of these shoes for a fucking minute before you hit the streets again. But then Compton's starts asking you for a service charge, and they don't want you loitering and scaring away all that sweet hobo and drug-

Compton's Cafeteria Riot

addict traffic they're getting at three in the goddamn morning, so they call the po-po on your ass. That's right, and that cop, that dirtbag cop says, "get up," before you've even finished your cup of coffee—coffee that you've paid for, thank you very much—and you've finally had enough, so you hurl that shit right in his pig face. That's how the Compton's riot of 1966 began. Three years before a trans person started the Stonewall Riots, trans girls in San Francisco were standing up for themselves, and all the rest of us, too. Before any of us even knew it. These first recorded riots of trans people fighting police brutality signaled the beginning of the trans movement in San Francisco.

Continental Baths

A bathhouse with a touch of class located under the famous Ansonia Hotel in New York's Upper West Side, this famous gay hot spot opened in 1968. While you could have all sorts of adventures, the thing that set it apart was the entertainment. Shows were performed nightly, and with a roster of talent that included everyone from Minnie Riperton to Natalie Cole to Margaret Whiting, the place was always a hit. However, they are most remembered today for being the birthplace of the Divine Miss M. Bette Midler was the queen of the Continental Baths, with her accompanist Barry Manilow. The Continental Baths were closed by the city in the mid-1980s.

Anderson Cooper (1967–)

This silver fox of CNN has been delivering the news and melting our hearts for decades. Cooper got his start at ABC, even hosting the reality show *The Mole*, but quickly started setting himself apart in his on-location reporting. He went to Bosnia, Rwanda, and Somalia and brought back footage and stories of harrowing courage. He even involved himself in a rescue while reporting in Haiti after that country was devastated by an earthquake. Cooper has tried his hand at many mediums—a daytime talk show, co-hosting New Year's Eve with Kathy Griffin and now Andy Cohen, even a documentary about his mother, the legendary fashion icon and artist Gloria Vanderbilt—and he still remains the best-looking newsman in the game.

Dennis Cooper (1953–)

The dark and provocative horse of gay literature, Cooper dealt with the deeply dark and sexy details of love and lust in his work. He began his career as a journalist and poet, but his novels certainly set him apart. Never afraid of controversy, his George Miles Cycle series of five semi-autobiographical novels have become a staple in the gay cannon, with new novels still coming out. Cooper battled Google in 2016, when the Internet giant deleted his blog along decency guidelines. The story hit all the major outlets, and after some serious negotiations, Google returned Cooper's blog.

The Cooper Do-nuts Riot

This often-forgotten riot was the first recorded uprising of the LGBTQ+ community in the history of the United States. Cooper Do-nuts was located between two gay bars in Los Angeles and a popular hangout for the clientele of either bar to go for a breather. In May of 1959, police came into the shop and started harassing people for their IDs, hoping to catch some of the trans clientele on cross-dressing charges. But the people of the bar rose up, and turned the cops out. The police arrested a few people, but a ruckus ensued, and the detainees were broken out in the melee. All ten years before Stonewall.

Aaron Copland (1900–1990)

Often called the dean of American composers, Aaron Copland studied in Paris with the famous pedagogue Nadia Boulanger but ultimately found that his music wanted to glorify an American sound. He often used hymns and folk songs in his work to expand his thoughts on the lushness of the American landscape. He's most remembered today for his *Appalachian Spring* suite and his *Fanfare for the Common Man*. Copland was a dedicated teacher and conductor who championed the work of other artists. He was also a great writer of lectures and books on the subject of music. As composer Ned Rorem said of Copland, "Thanks to Aaron, American music came into its own."

Jeanne Córdova (1948–2016)

Córdova was an activist and writer who became a beacon of hope and dignity on the West Coast. Beginning in the 1970s, she was always on the front lines of organizing the lesbian and queer community, including the West Coast Lesbian Conference at the Metropolitan Community Church and the first National Lesbian Conference. Córdova helped found the Gay and Lesbian Caucus within the Democratic Party in the 1980s. She was also responsible for the Community Yellow Pages project, which helped people find LGBTQ+ businesses to patronize. Her memoir, *When We Were Outlaws*, was published in 2011 and is a stirring tale of activism and love in the early days of the Gay Rights movement.

Brent Corrigan, née Sean Paul Lockhart (1986–)

The king of the twinks for many years, Corrigan got his start in porn a little earlier than was legally allowed. Making films for Cobra Video, he became an instant sensation. When it was discovered that he'd been performing underage, his videos were pulled. Later when Cobra founder Bryan Kocis was murdered, Corrigan testified for the prosecution. *King Cobra*, a film about the tragedy and the complicated relationship leading up to it, was released in 2016, starring James Franco, Christian Slater, and Garrett Clayton as Corrigan. He went on to perform and direct porn but wanted to make the leap to more mainstream films. He appeared in *Milk* and *Another Gay Sequel* in 2008 and in the 2011 film *Judas Kiss*.

Jayne County (1947–)

The punk rock transgender goddess of your dreams, Jayne County has been kicking ass and taking names for decades. County was punk before punk, and got her start performing in plays of her friend and mentor, Jackie Curtis. County formed Wayne County & the Electric Chairs upon moving to London in 1977. There, she recorded her now-famous track, "Fuck Off." County became Jayne in Berlin in 1979, and since then has been an outspoken and passionate defender of trans rights. Her musicianship and performance style influenced many of her famous friends, including Lou Reed and David Bowie. County continues to make art and music to this day.

Jayne County

Noël Coward (1899–1973)

Noel Coward was prolific in all ways, writing more than fifty plays, countless songs, musicals, short stories, novels, and three volumes of autobiography. Perhaps that's why he was called The Master. Coward was an artist and iconoclast that carved his own path and offered the world a new kind of wit and sophistication that can only be called Coward-esque. He grew up in theatre as a child actor but achieved his first breakout success with his play *The Vortex*, in which he also starred. More plays followed, many of them classics. *Private Lives* with Coward and the actress Gertrude Lawrence has been called one of the greatest performances of the twentieth century. Besides plays, Coward wrote songs like "I've Been to a Marvelous Party" and the ever heartbreaking "If Love Were All." He also wrote the classic film *Brief Encounter.*

Laverne Cox (1972–)

There are many words to describe Laverne Cox: beautiful, poised, capable, grand; but more than anything, she is groundbreaking. Cox got her start in reality TV on *I Want to Work for Diddy*, but she reached a whole new world when she debuted on *Orange Is the New Black* in 2013. On the show, Cox played a transgender woman named Sophia Burset, and her talent and depth in the role were immediately crowd favorites. Cox began doing the talk show circuit, where she presented herself always as a regal woman, living her absolute truth. She was the first transgender woman to appear on the cover of *Time* magazine. Cox continues to act and be a strong voice for trans rights and the queer community.

Crafts

One of my favorite things about the queer sensibility is the ability to take something lost or damaged or discarded and turn it into a work of art. It's been a secret queer power for centuries, but it never gets taken as seriously as perhaps it should be. I like to think of these crafts as queer folk art. They're objects and outfits that tell the story of our tribe, that help us remember and be brave in the face of a world that would rather we forgot. So make that drag queen toilet paper cozy and ball gown out of zip-ties, because queen, you are telling our story.

Hart Crane (1899–1932)

Harold Bloom cites the poet Hart Crane as a true American genius. Hart grew up a son of privilege—his father invented Life Savers—but he felt a calling toward poetry (and boys). He wrote some of his greatest work in Brooklyn, most notably *The Bridge* in 1930. The Brooklyn Bridge figures into a majority of his work. He was not an overnight sensation, and for the greater part of his life he wasn't really seen as a major writer. In 1934, he won a Guggenheim Fellowship and went to Mexico to work, but by then his drinking had gotten out of hand and he ended up engaged to a woman. On the return voyage to New York through the Gulf of Mexico with his fiancée, he made a pass at some of the crew and was beaten up. The next morning after an argument at breakfast, Crane jumped off the side of the boat and was drowned. Tennessee Williams, a long-time devotee of Crane's, wanted to be buried in the same spot where Hart sank to his death.

Joan Crawford (c.1904–1977) `ICON`

What is it that makes an icon like Joan Crawford? The shoulder pads? The eyebrows? A tragic backstory?

Crawford grew up as Lucille LeSueur in a one-horse town where her mother ran a laundry and her stepdad diddled her on the side. She started off as an extra, then a dancer, then a bad girl, then a matron, and a lover. She was style and sophistication, but she was always Joan—slapping people left and right and looking great doing it. You know her today as a kid-beating monster, but for a whole generation of queers, Joan Crawford meant something different. She meant determination. She meant fighting the fight and even if you didn't win it, at least you could look good doing it. Yes, the camp, yes the ax, god knows, and yes the no wire hangers, but before all of that, there was Joan the woman. Her image has been forever changed by the film *Mommie Dearest*, starring Faye Dunaway, but for many fans out there, she's more than wire hangers.

Quentin Crisp (1908–1999)

"Don't keep up with the Joneses, drag them down to your level," once quipped the one and only Quentin Crisp, a self-admitted failure, who did everything from artist modeling to illustration to teaching tap dancing without knowing tap dancing. It wasn't until much later in his life when he wrote his memoir, *The Naked Civil Servant*, that his true fame began. The book was turned into a movie starring John Hurt, and Crisp became a celebrity, and celebrities live in New York. He performed around the city, introducing the world to his rather singular world view and epic purple hair. Much like Oscar Wilde, he was a queen with a quip, and here are a few of his more famous lines:

If at first you don't succeed, failure may be your style.

Fashion is what you adopt when you don't know who you are.

For flavor, instant sex will never supersede the stuff you have to peel and cook.

Quentin Crisp

Dzi Croquettes

This dance troupe of gender-bending glittery drag clowns headed by the legendary Lennie Dale took their native Brazil and the world by storm. Dale was born in Brooklyn and danced in Broadway shows when he was offered solo club gigs in Brazil. He fell in love with the country and decided to stay, becoming a friend and mentor to singer Elis Regina. Dale came up with the idea for Dzi Croquettes as Brazil was gripped in the thralls of military dictatorship in the 1970s. The troupe featured glitter-laden dancers who, under Dale's direction, performed shows about the barriers of gender and sexuality. They toured and made a huge splash in Paris. The group eventually disintegrated under the pressure of performance and eventually the AIDS crisis, which claimed the life of Lennie Dale in 1994. A documentary about the group was released in 2009.

Leigh Crow

A legendary drag king who has been performing for more than three decades under many guises. Crow got their start in San Francisco performing as a lesbian Elvis impersonator under the name of Elvis Herselvis. The act was an instant hit, especially for its deeper implications of a male impersonator taking on such a symbol of masculinity. Crow was not only a hit with the LGBTQ+ community, but also with the adoring fans of the King himself, and has often been invited to conventions celebrating the works of Presley. Crow continues to perform in San Francisco and has become a mainstay of D'Arcy Drollinger's Oasis nightclub.

Cruising

A 1980 crime drama set in the gay underworld of the leather scene in New York. The film was initially controversial for its depictions of gays as heartless killers but in later years has achieved a different status within the community. Written and directed by William Friedkin, the movie starred Al Pacino as an undercover cop out to investigate a series of gruesome murders in the gay community. The film was dogged by protestors and did moderately well, but now stands as one of the most vivid depictions of a vanished leather and S&M scene in New York.

Wilson Cruz (1973–)

For those early-millennial or late gen-Y-ers, Wilson Cruz will always be Rickie Vasquez, the troubled, openly gay kid from *My So-Called Life*. While the show only lasted one season, its impact has long been felt. At the time, Cruz was the first openly gay actor to be playing an openly gay character on network TV. Since then, Cruz has continued to work in shows like *Noah's Arc*, *Ally McBeal*, and *Grey's Anatomy*. He has also become an advocate for gay kids, and has an established a long-standing relationship with GLAAD since 1997.

George Cukor (1899–1983)

Known most of the twentieth century as the great director of the "woman's picture," Cukor had a talent for working with his leading ladies, whether it was Katharine Hepburn, whom he directed many times, or Judy Garland, when he directed her in 1954's *A Star Is Born*. He understood women and got performances out of them that still thrill to this day. He even directed the movie *The Women*. But Cukor was much more than an attendant to leading ladies. He was a visionary director of wit and style. He was fired from *Gone with the Wind*, but so many of his films have become classics. He won his only Oscar for directing the movie musical of *My Fair Lady*. Cukor was also a great socialite in Hollywood, hosting his leading ladies for brunch on Saturday, and then a separate, boys-only brunch on Sunday. Cukor's Sunday gay pool parties became the absolute height of sophistication and sex in gay Hollywood.

Countee Cullen (1903–1946)

A poet of the Harlem Renaissance. Cullen wrote poetry, novels, and plays, but it was his first column, The Dark Tower, for the magazine *Opportunity* that kicked off his literary career. He went on to release *Color*, his first published book, in 1925; *Copper Sun* in 1927; and finally *The Black Christ* in 1929. He was a proud follower of the European traditions of poetry, citing John Keats as a major influence, but Cullen created a bridge in his work to the modern Black experience that was truly all his own.

Alan Cumming (1965–)

Cumming was a long-successful actor on film and stage before he reinvented the role of the emcee in Sam Mendes's production of *Cabaret* in 1998. Cumming won the Tony Award for this career-defining performance, but as has always been the case with an artist of his magnitude, he was just getting started. He continues to work in television and film, in shows like *The Good Wife* and *Instinct*. Cumming has also written a novel and *Not My Father's Son: A Memoir*. He's become a staple of New York theatre, and spread some of his magic into a new club and cabaret space called Club Cumming in the East Village.

Merce Cunningham (1919–2009)

Cunningham was a giant in the field of modern dance whose work expanded the ideas of the communicative body in motion until his death at age ninety. He started dancing with Martha Graham but left the Graham company to pursue his own work in 1944. With his partner John Cage, he wanted to create a company that merged the arts, and they often collaborated with visual artists like Robert Rauschenberg and Bruce Nauman to create pieces that were a delight for all the senses. Cunningham created over two hundred dances and eight hundred experiences—dances made for site-specific pieces of work. For his long contribution to dance, he was awarded a National Medal of Arts and the Légion d'honneur from the French government.

Michael Cunningham (1952–)

Pulitzer Prize–winning author and screenwriter Michael Cunningham is most famous for his novel *The Hours*, later a film with Meryl Streep and Nicole Kidman's prosthetic nose. He has been writing since the early 1980s. His other works, like *A Home at the End of the World* and most recently the critically acclaimed *The Snow Queen*, have earned him a place in the great canon of queer writers.

Jackie Curtis (1947–1985)

"A superstar in a housedress" according to entertainment writer Michael Musto, Jackie Curtis was often seen as "the smart one" out of the trio of Warhol superstars including Candy Darling and Holly Woodlawn. He was a writer, performer, and playwright who took huge chances with his life and

Jackie Curtis

his work. Andy Warhol said of Curtis, "Jackie is an artist. A pioneer without a frontier." Though Curtis appeared in two Warhol movies, *Flesh* and *Women in Revolt*, it was the stage where he found his biggest inspiration. Curtis began working with John Vaccaro's Playhouse of the Ridiculous but eventually began writing his own works, like *Vain Victory* and *Glamour, Glory, and Gold*. He continued to write plays and poetry, mixing gender and social commentary until his death from drugs in 1985. A documentary about his life, *Superstar in a Housedress*, was released in 2004.

Charlotte Cushman (1816–1876)

Charlotte Cushman, often considered the first great actress of the American stage, got her start in opera and light comedy, but when she played Lady Macbeth, her true artistry was on full display. The famous William Charles Macready saw talent in the young actress and told her that England would teach her all that she needed to know to become truly great. Europe also offered her a freedom to be open about her sexuality. Cushman would often tour in men's roles, playing Romeo opposite her sister as Juliet, and the title role as Hamlet. She lived openly with her female lovers and became a staple of the international arts scene. A new biography of Cushman, *Lady Romeo* by Tana Wojczuk, was released in 2020.

Cut Sleeve

A Chinese legend rumored to be about Emperor Ai of Han and his lover Dong Xian tells this story: The lovers lay in bed together, and the emperor awoke in the middle of the night. As he tried to rise out of bed, he found his lover asleep on the sleeve of his silk robe. Dong Xian looked so beautiful in his slumber that rather than wake him up, the emperor cut his own sleeve. The cut sleeve became a euphemism for homosexuality for years. It's a sweet story, but one I wonder about in a modern context. I mean, silk? I'm rolling that girl over.

D

is for . . .

Leonardo da Vinci (1452–1519)

The original Renaissance man of the Renaissance, Leonardo da Vinci was seen even in his time as a genius. He was a painter, scientist, philosopher, poet, the list goes on, and at the end, if included at all, is homosexual. Yes, the painter of the *Mona Lisa* was a mo. Some have even theorized that the portrait was of the artist in drag. No wonder her eyes follow you wherever you go—she's challenging you to look at her beauty. Though there is speculation about da Vinci's sexuality, he was charged with sodomy in 1476. Da Vinci fell in love with his assistants, most notably Gian Giacomo Caprotti, or Salaì, 'the unclean one." (We've all been there.) Homoeroticism comes up in his work more often than not. Sure, *The Da Vinci Code* would have you believe that Christ had a wife, but when looking at the picture under a gay gaze, da Vinci was making a far stronger case for a relationship between Jesus and the slight and effeminate John—often cited in the Bible as his "favorite" and the one "he loved most."

Daddy

A gay term of endearment usually for an older man. But let's face it, it can be anyone over thirty, and it can gauge anywhere from hot to annoying. My rule of thumb: if it is physically impossible for me to be your daddy, you better ask first. And besides, in my case, I'm more of an auntie.

Joe Dallesandro (1948–) ICON

"Little Joe never once gave it away," or so Lou Reed wrote in his 1972 classic "Walk on the Wild Side." But who can be sure? Dallesandro was a heartthrob and hustler of the old school—dark, broody, and gorgeous. Warhol director Paul Morrissey saw something in the enigmatic Dallesandro and wanted to put him in the movies. The role and the opportunity came in 1968 with *Flesh*. In the film, Joe plays a street hustler looking to make money for his lesbian wife's girlfriend's abortion. Out he goes into the world, looking to make money hustling. The film was heralded for its time for its gritty New York feel and open sexuality. It even spawned a trilogy, with the follow-up films *Trash* and *Heat*. Though Dallesandro continued to make films with Morrissey, he also ventured out working with European directors—notably with singer-songwriter-turned-director Serge Gainsbourg in the 1976 film *Je t'aime moi non plus*, opposite Gainsbourg's partner Jane Birkin.

Dancer from the Dance

Whenever I'm asked, "What's the greatest gay novel you ever read?" my answer is always this novel by Andrew Holleran. It's gorgeous and dishy and sexy and so painfully real that it reads like lore rather than a formal novel. Set in the late 1970s, it centers around the gorgeous Malone, a midwestern farm boy who's hot, hot, hot and talked about and envied by the small gaggle of gays in Manhattan's hot scene. The story is ultimately tragic, ending with the famous fire at Everard Baths, but leaves the door open for Malone to survive, somewhere. It's a gorgeous piece of poetry that talks frankly about the realities of gay life. While the world that it speaks of was demolished by the AIDS crisis, there are so many truths about the lives of gay people that ring through on almost every page. "Now of all the bonds between homosexual friends, none was greater than that between friends who danced together. The friend you danced with, when you had no lover, was the most important person in your life; and for people who went without lovers for years, that was all they had."

Lee Daniels (1959–)

A major voice in Hollywood who continues to challenge the aesthetic and the barriers still put in front of actors and creators of color, Daniels broke out with his first major project, *Monster's Ball*, in 2001. The film won Halle Berry an Oscar and launched his production company, Lee Daniels Entertainment. Since then, he has continued as a producer, director, and writer, bringing forth films like *Precious* and *The Butler*—both of which he directed—and television series like *Empire* and *Star*. He continues to be a proud voice for gay creators of color in Hollywood, and has a strong relationship to LGBTQ+ charities and the fight against AIDS.

Darcelle XV

Darcelle XV (1930–)

There are hard working queens in the world, but few have been at it for as long as Darcelle. In 2016, Darcelle XV was cited by *Guinness World Records* as the oldest working drag queen at age eighty-six. Born Walter Cole, Darcelle came out in 1969 and began his gay life with his partner Roxy Neuhardt. The two bought the club the Showplace in

Portland, Oregon, that later became known simply by the name of its owner, Darcelle XV. In 2010, Darcelle released his memoir, *Just Call Me Darcelle*, co-written with Sharon Knorr.

Candy Darling (1944–1974)

"The pretty one" of Andy Warhol's trio of drag queens in the late 1960s and early '70s, Candy was born in Forest Hills, Queens, but from an early age dreamed of being a movie star like Kim Novak or Joan Bennett. Greenwich Village offered Candy an escape and a chance to truly be herself. She met Jeremiah Newton in 1966, and the two became friends and roommates for the rest of Candy's life. In 1967, Candy met Andy Warhol while she was appearing in her friend Jackie Curtis's play, *Glamour, Glory, and Gold*. Warhol and his director, Paul Morrissey, started putting Candy in their movies—first in *Flesh*, and eventually writing *Women in Revolt* for her in 1971. Candy went on to perform in other independent films like *Klute* with Jane Fonda and *Lady Liberty* with Sophia Loren. She modeled for major magazines and appeared in Tennessee William's off-Broadway production of *Small Craft Warnings*. Candy died of cancer in 1974, but was a fashion plate till the very end. Pictures of her taken by Peter Hujar are some of her most remembered images and were used for the album art of Antony and the Johnsons' album *I Am a Bird Now*. A documentary on Candy's life, *Beautiful Darling*, was released in 2010.

Ram Dass (1931–2019)

When you think of LSD, most people think of Timothy Leary, but many forget that working alongside him was Richard Alpert, who later became the spiritual leader and guru Ram Dass. It was Leary's experiments with LSD and other mind-altering substances that led Alpert to seek a more spiritual path. That journey led him to India, where he formed a close relationship with Hindu guru Neem Karoli Baba. Baba gave him the name Ram Dass, which means "servant of god." Dass became a devotee of Baba and brought his teaching on spirituality to the United States with the now-classic book *Be Here Now*. Dass taught for many years and wrote many books. In 1997, he suffered a massive stroke that left him paralyzed, but he continued to teach and be an inspiration to millions around the world.

Daughters of Bilitis

The first lesbian political organization in America was formed in San Francisco in 1955 by Del Martin and her partner Phyllis Lyon. The club was originally seen as a place to hang out apart from the bar scene, but soon the group saw they could do so much more. They started a magazine called *The Ladder*, generated mostly by readers' content. Playwright Lorraine Hansberry wrote several short stories for the magazine. But that was just the beginning of the engagement that the Daughters of Bilitis wanted to have. They were creating a dialogue about the rights and lives of women, something they had done for fourteen years by the time feminism in the United States started to rise. Some early feminists like Betty Friedan thought that lesbians were a liability to the movement, but the Daughters of Bilitis were a tough crew, and even after *The Ladder* shuttered after a fourteen-year run, many of the members continued their work for the rights of women and lesbians.

Angela Y. Davis (1944–)

You've probably seen a hipster or two with a T-shirt that says "Free Angela," but maybe never knew who Angela was. Angela Y. Davis is an icon of resistance. She began studying Marxist theory in college at Brandeis University, and continued working with a Marxist paradigm as her involvement grew with the Black Panthers and Black freedom movement of the late 1960s. Her membership in the Communist Party USA made her a target in 1969, when then-governor Ronald Reagan tried to have her barred from teaching anywhere in California. In 1970, Davis purchased firearms for personal security guards. Those guns were later used in an armed takeover of a Marin County courtroom. Davis was arrested and tried for conspiracy to murder. For two years, she fought the case and

eventually was acquitted, but her time in the prison system made her a strong advocate for the plight of incarcerated Americans. Since the 1970s, Davis has been a voice of hope and change for countless communities, and one that has never shied away from controversy. In 2019, Davis was awarded the Fred Shuttlesworth Human Rights Award by the Birmingham Civil Rights Institute, but the award was later rescinded because of Davis's support of a free Palestine. After public outcry, the rescind was rescinded.

Bette Davis and Angela Davis

Bette Davis (1908–1989) ICON

A diva of the highest form and an actress of endless ability and pathos, Bette Davis was a different kind of movie star. Not seen as conventionally pretty, Davis saw herself as a character actress suiting her look and attitude to each of her characters' unique journies. She had a tough time starting out, as the studios didn't know what to do with her. But in 1934, *Of Human Bondage* brought on the star status of Davis.

Her star continued to rise in movies like *Jezebel, Dark Victory*, and one of my personal favorites, *Now, Voyager*, where she plays a frumpy old spinster tortured by her wicked mother. After a transformative experience in a sanitarium, she goes on a cruise, meets and falls in love with a married man, and yells her mother to death. Perhaps her most iconic role though came in *All About Eve*, where she plays aging actress Margo Channing. Davis represents something special to the LGBTQ+ community—a drive to be accepted on one's own terms, to take oneself to the edge of oblivion, and with sure will and talent, to do it all with style. She's an icon for the individual, and for the force that refuses to let up, which is why she continues to draw in a queer audience to this day.

Vaginal Davis (1976–)

A pioneering performance artist, creator who has thrilled and challenged audiences for more than forty years, and a genderqueer artist before such a term existed, Davis has always been at the forefront of gender as performance, deconstructing our history to find a new truth. Davis was one of the founders of the homocore punk movement in the 1980s, performing "terrorist drag" and playing with bands like Afro Sisters, PME, and Black Fag. But she found she was "too gay for the punk scene and too punk for the gay scene." Davis was also one of the early pioneers of the queercore zine movement, putting out work like *Fertile La Toyah Jackson*, which was seen as a classic even at the time of its printing. Davis hosted events like Bricktop, a weekly salon based the work of Ada "Bricktop" Smith—the lesbian proprietress of Bricktop, a famous salon and bar in Paris in the 1920s. Davis continues to make performance work and visual art that is on the cutting edge of gender.

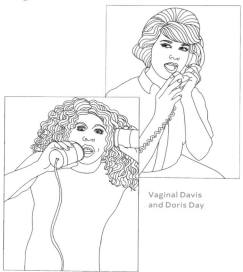

Vaginal Davis
and Doris Day

Doris Day (1922–2019) ICON

This plucky blonde who delighted audiences for decades still holds the record for being one of the highest-grossing movie stars in history. With her sultry sounds and her perky good looks, Day was more of a talent than she is often given credit for, and certainly more of a gay icon. Her film version of *Calamity Jane*, in which she played the title character and sang the song "Secret Love," endeared her to a host of young gay women. Her later comedies with Rock Hudson, complete with slight little winks toward homosexuality, lightened the mood in the early '60s. While her wholesome image may have made her palatable for most of America, she was never afraid to take a stand for what she thought was right. Whether it was her numerous animal charities or her public support of co-star Rock Hudson as he struggled with AIDS, Day proved that she was a star in each and every use of the term.

Mercedes de Acosta (1893–1968)

Mercedes de Acosta was always interested and in many cases in love with some of the most thought-provoking women of the early twentieth century. Though she saw herself more as a poet and writer, de Acosta is much more remembered for who she slept with than what she wrote. She had them all, including silent film star Alla Nazimova, dancer Isadora Duncan, and actress Eva Le Gallienne. But most famously she had a deep relationship with film star Greta Garbo. The two had a fiery affair that lasted a number of years, but their letters have been suppressed from the public even until this day. In 1960, de Acosta wrote her memoir, *Here Lies the Heart*. The memoir is deeply coded, and barely mentions homosexuality, but as Alice B. Toklas once said of her, "Say what you will about Mercedes, she's had the most important women of the twentieth century."

Alexis del Lago (1938–)

Glamour never looked so good as it does on Alexis del Lago. A darling of the downtown New York art scene, Alexis del Lago is a grand dame right out of the movies she idolizes. She was a collaborator with artists Jackie Wilson and Holly Woodlawn, a muse to Warhol and Mapplethorpe, and a staple of the Pyramid Club. Born in Puerto Rico, del Lago came to New York in the 1960s and almost immediately found her way downtown working with theatre artists in search of a performer who could fit those larger-than-life roles. Del Lago was up for the challenge. In the 1980s, she made the transition to cabaret under the direction of writer and lyricist Scott Wittman. Del Lago eventually left New York for Los Angeles, where she resides to this day.

De Profundis

It's essentially the longest love letter ever written. While Oscar Wilde was serving his two-year sentence of hard labor for gross indecency, he wrote to his former lover, Bosie, a.k.a. Lord Alfred Douglas. The first half is mostly a rehash of everything that went wrong. It's repetitive in parts because Wilde was only allowed the paper for certain amounts of time, so he never got to read what he'd previously written. The second half continues on a religious bent, where he imagines Jesus as a romantic artist and an archetype for suffering. It's Wilde at his most brilliant and intimate. He was handed the complete manuscript after he left jail, but didn't revisit the work before he died in 1900. Robbie Ross—Wilde's first lover, executor, and someone who genuinely hated Bosie—published the work shortly after Wilde's death, cutting out all references to Bosie. The text was restored in the 1960s, and an annotated version of the text was published in 2018.

Death Becomes Her

This 1992 camp classic starring Meryl Streep and Goldie Hawn has become a hallmark for the LGBTQ+ community. Maybe it's because of the two leads' obsession with beauty that drives them to drink the elixir of life that hits so close to home. Or it could be the hilarious infighting between Streep and Hawn, both of whom ham it up in the best ways. Or maybe it's simply the need for a glamour even as time and spray paint betray us all that makes this film a queer classic. Whatever it is, we all still keep going back and may we always. Sempre vive!

Death in Venice

This 1912 German novella from Thomas Mann tells the story of a great author, Gustav von Aschenbach—said to be based on composer Gustav Mahler—who travels to Venice to cure his writer's block. While there, he falls hopelessly in love with the beautiful boy Tadzio. It's a tale of love and obsession where the two main characters almost never speak, and has become a hallmark of the queer literary canon. It was adapted into a film by Visconti in 1971 starring Dirk Bogarde, an opera by Benjamin Britten in 1973, and a ballet by John Neumeier and the Hamburg Ballet in 2003.

Flotilla DeBarge

One of the great ladies of the New York drag scene, Flotilla DeBarge brings a sense of camp and no-nonsense fun to everything she does. She has performed alongside some of the greats, like Joey Arias and Charles Busch. She's also been in quite a few films, playing roles in *To Wong Foo, Thanks for Everything! Julie Newmar*; *Marci X*; and *Angels in America* for HBO. In 2006, DeBarge was arrested for assault after getting into a fight with a man and hitting him with her high heel. But all that is far behind her, and these days you can still find DeBarge telling it like it is and singing for the people all over New York. A true artist of immense talent, Flotilla DeBarge is a pioneering legend of drag.

Frank DeCaro (1962–)

This queen of kitsch has been delighting audiences around the country for decades. DeCaro got his start writing for the *Detroit Free Press*, but eventually his wit and sense of camp helped him find his way to *The Daily Show with Jon Stewart*. DeCaro was the first gay correspondent on the show from 1996 to 2003. After *The Daily Show*, he found his way to SiriusXM, hosting his daily radio show with co-host Doria Biddle from 2004 to 2016. He continues to entertain with his stand-up, touring with Lisa Lampanelli and writing books like *The Dead Celebrity Cookbook* and his memoir, *A Boy Named Phyllis*. His newest book, *Drag*, is a compendium of the history of drag and a great tome on the art form.

Ellen DeGeneres (1958–)

Ellen DeGeneres is an iconoclast who's opened the door for millions of people to be themselves and dance their way to happiness. An icon who is on a first-name basis with all of America, for the last fifteen years, Ellen has been the major force behind daytime TV, but her legacy goes back much further than that. DeGeneres started doing stand-up in the 1980s and proved too big a hit, playing the *Tonight Show* and starring in her own comedy specials. This success led to her own show, *Ellen*, in 1994. At the height of her and the show's popularity, Ellen, the character and the comedian, came out in 1997. She was the first openly gay woman to appear on the cover of *Time* magazine. Her sitcom was canceled just a year later, and she struggled to find new footing in Hollywood. In 2003, she rebounded with the *Ellen Show*. Today, Ellen is more popular than ever and she's done everything from hosting the Oscars to voicing the fish Dory in the Pixar film *Finding Nemo* and its sequel *Finding Dory*. In 2020, allegations of bad behavior and toxicity in the workplace plagued Ellen and her show. Though she apologized for the behavior, the damage was done and Ellen announced the end of her show in 2022.

Samuel R. Delany (1942–)

For a whole generation of readers, Samuel R. Delany has been pushing the levels of the mind and the barriers of the universe as we know it. He first came to prominence publishing short stories in the 1960s, and published his first novel, *The Jewels of Aptor*, in 1962. He continued publishing almost a book a year, gaining Hugo nominations for his novels *Babel-17*, *The Einstein Intersection*, and *Nova*. His most popular work, *Dhalgren*, was published in 1975. It speaks of a postapocalyptic midwestern town of Bellona, surrounded by the now-destroyed United States. His works continually deal with sexuality, and he never shies away from gay content. He received a place in the Science Fiction and Fantasy Hall of Fame in 2002, and the Brudner Prize from Yale University for his contributions to gay literature.

Lea DeLaria (1958–)

You may know her as Big Boo from the hit Netflix series *Orange Is the New Black*, but there's a lot more to Lea DeLaria. She started performing in the 1980s, and became the first openly gay comic to perform on late-night television in 1993 on *The Arsenio Hall Show*. For many years, DeLaria was the go-to lesbian for network television and independent movies, but she truly stepped into her own stardom with the 1998 Broadway revival of *On the Town*. DeLaria is also an accomplished jazz singer, who continues to tour the country with her cutting-edge comedy and her swingin' beats, but DeLaria's charms do not end there. She's an outspoken advocate for the LGBTQ+community, and thank goodness for her.

Stormé DeLarverie (1920–2014)

She was the butch lesbian who threw the first punch at Stonewall. Though contemporary storytelling would have you believe that Marsha P. Johnson or Sylvia Rivera started the infamous Stonewall Riots, according to eyewitnesses and DeLarverie herself, she was the one who threw the infamous first punch. DeLarverie had worked for years as an emcee and singer, presenting as male for traveling female impersonation troupes. DeLarverie, who always presented male and self-identified as a butch, was at the Stonewall for a drink. When cops raided the place, she'd had enough. DeLarverie was a courageous and early pioneer for LGBTQ+ rights, and though often overlooked for her role, DeLarverie should be remembered as a lifelong champion for her people, before and after the riots she started.

Stormé DeLarverie

Desert Hearts

This 1985 movie, based on the novel *Desert of the Heart* by Jane Rule, tells the story of a university professor played by Helen Shaver, waiting on her divorce in Reno. While there, she meets the young Cay Rivvers, an outspoken and daring sculptor. The two quickly develop feelings for each other and fall in love. The film did very well with US and UK audiences, and is often cited as one of the first films to deal with lesbianism in a positive light.

Sergei Diaghilev (1872–1929)

There's a strong argument to be made that modernism, as it grew to be identified in the twentieth century, was a fire lit by the Ballets Russes, and the man who built the Ballets Russes was

Sergei Diaghilev. Diaghilev started organizing art shows highlighting Russian art in 1905, but his true brilliance came into being in 1909 with the Ballets Russes. He assembled the greatest Russian dancers of the period: Anna Pavlova, Tamara Karsavina, and Vaslav Nijinsky, who was also his lover. For the next twenty years, the Ballets Russes, under the direction of Diaghilev, created some of the most brilliant and collaborative work in the world with music by Stravinsky, Debussy, and Prokofiev; art and sets by Kandinsky, Picasso, and Matisse; and choreography by Nijinsky, Fokine, and Massine, who was *also* Diaghilev's lover. It also started the career of the young George Balanchine. Though Diaghilev died in 1929, his impact in so many realms of art can still be felt to this day.

Mario Diaz (1971–)

Party promoter, actor, and club owner—there's little that Diaz hasn't done. Mario Diaz was a mainstay of 1990s New York, where he started party promoting and curating with friends like Jackie Beat and Sherry Vine. In the aftermath of AIDS, New York seemed to have lost some of the edge it once had in the sex-fueled heights of the 1970s and '80s. Diaz wanted to bring some of the debauchery back. He reopened the Cock, a down and dirty, sleazy-but-good time bar where fun could be had by all.

It was up-front about its backroom action, and brought back a flavor of what had been lost in the years since the AIDS crisis. After years of throwing some of the best parties in New York, Diaz decided to try his luck in the City of Angels, where he continues to get people dancing and feeling all kinds of sexy with his parties BFD and Full Frontal Disco. A documentary about Diaz and his work, *Club King*, was released in 2014.

Emily Dickinson (1830–1886)

The woman in white, the belle of Amherst, Emily Dickinson has become a legend and a mystery all her own. But it has only been in recent years when certain truths about her life have begun to emerge. For so long, she has been seen as a slight and frustrated woman who lived at home, baked cakes, and wrote her poems on envelopes to save on paper. While all these things are true, there's also the case to be made that Dickinson was an active and humorous bisexual woman who was passionate about the life and the love she created. Love letters originally thought to be written to a male friend have later been found to be written to her sister-in-law, Susan, with whom she had a long-standing affair. It's always the quiet ones.

Marlene Dietrich (1901–1992) `ICON`

All glamour. All smoke and mirrors. Nitrate film was invented for the mystery that was Marlene Dietrich.

Bisexual with a vengeance, Marlene Dietrich pushed the boundaries of sex and respectability on and off screen. Making her first splash internationally with the film *The Blue Angel* in 1930, Dietrich became a film star around the world and a force to be reckoned with. Famous for wearing a tuxedo, she invented herself as legend. And this invention continued even after she left film. She was a singer in spirit more than voice, but sold the image of herself around the world as a chanteuse in a beautiful gown. With numbers arranged by the very young Burt Bacharach, Dietrich continued her personal style and grandeur on stages across the globe—a goddess in soft light, squeezed in a latex sheath for the perfect silhouette, giving you the experience of a lifetime.

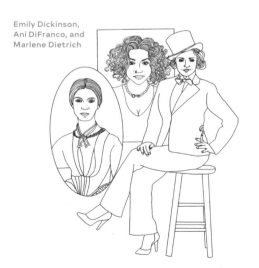

Emily Dickinson, Ani DiFranco, and Marlene Dietrich

Ani DiFranco (1970–)

If you were an angsty teenager in the 1990s, chances are you got real into Ani DiFranco, but to write her off as merely an artist of angst would be a grave mistake. DiFranco started making music in 1989, when she started her own record company, Righteous Babe Records, and released her self-titled debut the following year. From the very beginning, DiFranco set herself apart with her distinctive staccato guitar style and lyrics that cut to the essence of heartbreak and righteous anger. Throughout the 1990s, DiFranco rode the wave of strong female artists, but set herself apart with her open bisexuality and her commitment to social issues. Her live double album, *Living in Clip*, went gold, and in 2009 she was awarded the Woody Guthrie Award for her commitment to social change.

Asia Kate Dillon (1984–)

A nonbinary actor who has broken barriers for nonbinary performers on mainstream television, Dillon began acting before coming out as a nonbinary person, achieving success in the New York theatre scene. When they did come out around 2015, Dillon began using *they* pronouns and continued to work in theatre and film, getting a big break playing Brandy on *Orange Is the New Black*, and then Taylor Mason, a nonbinary character, on Showtime's *Billions*.

Dinah Shore Weekend

If you're a lady looking for a chance to get away, free yourself up around early April so you can head to the Dinah Shore Weekend in Palm Springs, California. A five-day weekend event catering to the lesbian community, the Dinah, as it's affectionately known, began in 1991. Named after the famous singer and talk-show host Dinah Shore (who herself was not gay), it all began as a golf event but soon became a sprawling lesbian free-for-all with dancing music and endless fun. To this day it's considered one of the largest lesbian events in the world.

Christian Dior (1905–1957)

His name still stands for class and sophistication, even though he has been dead for more than sixty years. Dior began his career in fashion in 1942, working for Lucien Lelong, and creating a name for himself in couturier circles. In 1946, he was invited by Marcel Boussac to work for the house of Philippe et Gaston, but Dior wanted to create a name for himself. On December 8, 1946, the house of Dior was born and the women of the world were given a new understanding of glamour. Dior was a master of silhouette and form. His first collection was called "Corolle," which meant a circle of flowers, as Dior always thought of giving his clients the features and pleasures of a flower. From years of working with fabric rations, Dior revolutionized the bodice, giving women the tight, slimming waist that became a staple throughout the 1950s. Dior instantly became a fashion star and reinvigorated Paris as the couture capital of the world.

Beth Ditto (1981–)

In every generation, there comes a voice that knows how to rock, and for the modern day that voice belongs to Beth Ditto. Sultry, soulful, and full of grit, Ditto is instantly recognizable and undeniably great. Ditto started singing in the late 1990s, after moving to Washington State in 1999 and immersing herself in grunge influences. In 1999, she formed the band the Gossip with Nathan "Brace Paine" Howdeshell and Kathy Mendonca. With Ditto's booming vocals, the band quickly set themselves apart and recorded their first album, *That's Not What I Heard*, in 2001. The band's first major hit, "Standing in the Way of Control," hit the airways in 2006 and led Gossip to sign with Sony Music. Ditto was pushed into the limelight and started bringing her vocals and southern charms to stages around the world. In 2012, she released a memoir co-written with Michelle Tea, *Coal to Diamonds*. In 2016, Ditto parted ways with the Gossip and released her first solo record, *Fake Sugar*, in 2017.

Disclosure: Trans Lives on Screen

Trans people have had a complicated history with film. Most often portrayed by non-trans actors, their identity has been used as a punchline or a sinister revelation. This documentary, released on Netflix in 2020, seeks to dispel these hurtful tropes and to talk to real trans actors and directors about the way trans people are seen, and how trans stories can be told when finally trans people are in charge of their telling. The film is directed by trans filmmaker Sam Feder and features interviews with Laverne Cox, Jen Richards, Yance Ford, and many more. It also tells the story of Sandra Caldwell, a pioneering trans actress, who hid her identity for many years. It is a celebration of the trans experience and a call to trans artist to tell their own stories.

Divine

Divine (1945–1988)

The first drag superstar, Divine was born Harris Glenn Milstead in Baltimore, Maryland. She met John Waters as a teenager, and it was Waters who gave her her name. "Divine: the most beautiful woman in the world, almost." Divine became Water's friend and muse, starring in his earliest films *Roman Candles*, *Eat Your Makeup*, and *The Diane Linkletter Story*. Divine most often performed in drag, trying to look like her idol, Elizabeth Taylor. Waters and Divine continued making films together, and had their breakout hit with 1972's *Pink Flamingos*. A cult classic to this day, Divine's character wants to be the "filthiest person alive."

The film was a hit of the midnight movie circuit and launched Divine as counter-culture hero. She began to perform onstage with the Cockettes in San Francisco and in New York in plays by Tom Eyen. More films followed, from the seminal *Female Trouble*, in which Divine plays Dawn Davenport and her own rapist, to the bigger-budget and "odorific" *Polyester* opposite Tab Hunter. She began to cross over into the music scene, releasing dance songs in the late 1970s. Divine and Waters both found mainstream success with the 1988 film *Hairspray*, in which Divine plays Mrs. Turnblad and Arvin Hodgepile. While in LA to film an episode of *Married . . . with Children*, Divine died of a massive heart attack. Since her death, she has maintained a legendary following and continues to offer inspiration to drag queens and misfits alike. Divine was very famously used as the inspiration for Ursula, the sea witch in the Disney animated film *The Little Mermaid*.

Tim Dlugos (1950–1990)

Dlugos wrote the colloquial poetry of a generation of gay men who experienced the first flush of freedom after the breakthrough of Stonewall, only to see the life they had finally claimed ripped away by AIDS. He came to New York in 1976, and soon found friends and compatriots on the burgeoning art scene of the Lower East Side. He was a long-time friend and confidant of writer Dennis Cooper, all the while writing his own unique poetry dealing openly and frankly with his life as a gay man. Dlugos died of complications from AIDS in 1990. A major collection of his works, *A Fast Life*, was published in 2010 and won a Lambda Literary Award.

Xavier Dolan (1989–)

This actor, writer, and filmmaker is one of the youngest and most famous auteurs in the world. A favorite at Cannes, Xavier made a splash there in 2009 with his first movie, *I Killed My Mother*. Dolan wrote, starred in, and directed the film, all at the age of twenty. He followed it up with 2010's *Heartbeats* and 2012's *Laurence Anyways*. He has a unique style, with influences ranging from French New Wave to Scorsese, and his output is still constant and lauded. In 2015, Dolan sat on the jury at Cannes, and his most recent projects, *The Death and Life of John F. Donovan* and *Matthias & Maxime*, have both been met with critical praise and a host of awards.

Drag

Drag is the act of wearing clothes usually assigned to another gender for performance. Since the beginning of time, I think, queer people have always participated in drag. It's many things—clowning, glamour, beauty, empowerment—but it all boils down to expression, a chance to cast off the shackles of gender and get to be the person you always wanted to be. Whether that's a pageant queen or a drag king, drag has given our community a chance to change the paradigm when talking about gender and opportunities for performers of all ilks to take the stage and, in some way or other, share their truth. Drag queens and kings have been our sages, our heroes, our hopes, boldly or foolishly or glamorously going to places we couldn't go without them. Drag is a time-honored tradition of transformation, transference, and transcendence. It's not a form of gendering minstrelsy, as some have accused it of being. It's a chance to glorify in the profane and revel in the forbidden. So, tip those queens and kings, because they are doing the good work and we need them now more than ever.

DragCon

A drag conference thrown by *RuPaul's*

Drag Race that celebrates all that is drag—or at least all that has merch—DragCon is a fairly new phenomenon, starting in 2015. The convention was a chance for fans of the show to meet their idols from the series and to find out more about drag. It's become an annual event on both the East and West Coast and attracts a large cross section of the LGBTQ+ community, as well as a lot of young girls, who see drag queens as the glamorous beings of our dreams.

Dragstrip 66

A monthly party started in 1993 by Mr. Dan, a.k.a. Gina Lotriman, and Paul Vitagliano, it brought the best drag and performance art in the Silver Lake area of Los Angeles to one place for almost twenty years. Held in the basement of the Mexican restaurant Rudolpho's, Dragstrip 66 hosted the famous and the infamous, from Jackie Beat and Joey Arias to Varla Jean Merman. It was *the* queer event in Los Angeles until it was forced to leave the space in 2004. A "frockumentary" about the legendary party is currently in the works.

Dragula

This alternative-drag competition show is created and hosted by the Boulet Brothers. The brothers, who take on the darker and scarier side of drag to begin with, wanted to give a showcase for this style of drag. It originally aired in 2016 on the Hey Qween network on YouTube, but after the show's popularity, the Boulet Brothers created an expanded version to air on Canadian network OutTV and other platforms. The show has been distributed by multiple companies from World of Wonder to TV One.

Drew Droege (1977–)

Ask any gay comedian in the country who one of the funniest people in the world is and the name Drew Droege will inevitably be on their lips. Droege is that rare combination of smarts and slapstick that all comes from his genuine power as an actor. Skilled in improv and trained at the Groundlings, Droege has appeared in film, television, and stage. He had a major breakthrough with his *Chloe* web series, where he impersonates an only slightly exaggerated version of the actress Chloë Sevigny. Droege continues to bring his work to audiences everywhere, most recently with his off-Broadway solo play *Bright Colors and Bold Patterns.*

D'Arcy Drollinger (1969–)

The modern doyenne of San Francisco performance who bring his sense of camp and sex appeal to performance and parody, Drollinger has a long history of performance, but found his home in 2015. That's when Drollinger, along with co-owner Heklina, created a great performance space, the Oasis for LGBTQ+ artists in San Francisco. Drollinger not only curates the acts, but also brings his own plays—like *Champagne White and the Temple of Poon*, and *Disastrous!*—as well as parodies of *The Golden Girls*, *Sex and the City*, and *Buffy the Vampire Slayer*. Drollinger is also the creator of Sexitude, a body-positive, sex-positive workout that brings all the booty to the floor.

Zackary Drucker (1983–)

Drucker hit the art scene after graduating from CalArts in 2007, creating work with trans artist Amos Mac and then Rhys Ernst. An outspoken advocate for trans rights, Drucker worked as a consulting producer on Amazon's *Transparent* and on the E! reality show *I Am Cait*, starring Caitlyn Jenner. In 2015, Drucker worked on a documentary about her own life, *This Is Me*. Drucker and Ernst's work *Relationship* was featured in the Whitney Biennial and released as a book in 2016. Drucker continues to make work, executive producing the documentary series *The Lady and the Dale*, about trans pioneer and con artist Elizabeth Carmichael in 2021 and an biopic about the life of Candy Darling.

Martin Duberman (1930–)

A playwright, biographer, historian, and novelist, Duberman has always been at the forefront of social justice movements, coming out in an essay in the *New York Times* in 1972. He's written extensively about LGBTQ+ subjects, and has also been a voice for other oppressed peoples. Duberman was chosen by Paul Robeson's son to write a major biography on the civil rights leader and artist. He wrote one of the greatest books on the Stonewall Riots, as well as plays about social justice, and has been candid about his personal life as a gay man in the early days of gay liberation. Duberman continues to produce work on gay themes, most recently his biography of Michael Callen and Essex Hemphill, *Hold Tight Gently*, and his biographical novel about the life of Roger Casement, a gay Irish revolutionary, was released in 2018.

Isadora Duncan (c.1877–1927)

The grand goddess of modern dance, Isadora Duncan lived life on a grand scale. Born in San Francisco, Duncan began her career dancing on stage as a child where, even then, she hungered for her own course of expression. She rejected the artifice and tricks of ballet, and drew inspiration from Greek myth and images to create a form of physical expression. Duncan moved to London in 1898, where she began dancing for private hosts interested in her reinvention of dance. She married theatre designer Gordon Craig, with whom she had two children. Both children died in an automobile accident in 1913. She later married Russian poet Sergei Yesenin, who was eighteen years younger than her. They were separated in 1924, and a year later Yesenin killed himself. Duncan continued to dance for many years, but as she got older, the work dried up. Duncan was killed in a strange accident while riding in an open car. Her long scarf was caught in the spokes of the back wheel of the car and she was strangled to death.

Jeremy Dutcher (1990–)

Dutcher is a two-spirit Indigenous singer and musician living and working in Canada. His intense vocals and

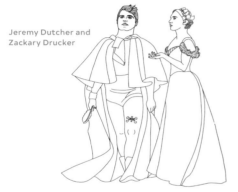

Jeremy Dutcher and Zackary Drucker

interplay with Native music have made him an international sensation. Dutcher's first album, *Wolastoqiyik Lintuwakonawa*, released in 2018 in his Native language of Wolastoq, utilized old recordings of other Native speakers to build a continuum between Dutcher and his vibrant past. The album was awarded the Polaris Music Prize in 2018 and the Juno Award for Indigenous Music Album of the Year in 2019. Dutcher is an outspoken advocate for the rights of LGBTQ+ and Indigenous peoples.

Dykes on Bikes

At the beginning of every New York Pride Parade, the rev of engines lets you know it's time to get crazy. Founded in 1976 by Soni Wolf, it officially began at San Francisco Pride. Dykes on Bikes have always been out there, way in front, to prove yet again that women don't need to be anything but the fierce powerful warriors they are. Over the years, dykes have opened their ranks to the entire LGBTQ+ community. Though they've been criticized for keeping their name, Dykes on Bikes still prove that they're not here for your approval. They're here to ride.

Dynasty

The '80s prime-time soap opera that taught the world about shoulder pads and cat fights, *Dynasty* tells the tale of the Carringtons, a Colorado oil oligarchy. The family is headed by Blake, played by John Forsythe, and his new wife, Krystle, played by Linda Evans. Trouble really gets stirred up when Blake's first wife, Alexis, played by the one and only Joan Collins, arrives in season two. Things get even hotter with the appearance of Dominique Deveraux, played by Diahann Carroll, in season four. Besides being the campiest of the camp, *Dynasty* was also one of the first shows in prime time to tackle homosexuality, with a story line about Blake's son Steven, played by Al Corley, being gay. I personally believe the show can be used as a teaching tool, because it's essentially *White Privilege: The TV Show.* Watch a couple of episodes and then turn to yourself and say, "They get away with a lot of this because they're white."

is for . . .

The Eagle

The Eagle is a chain of gay bars that aren't united by a franchise, but still have a bit of a brand. The first Eagle opened in 1970 in New York. The original bar was named after an eagle's nest, telling its clientele that from the high vantage point they could see what's coming, and that in the Eagle, you were safe. Since then, the name has stuck and spread. Though most gay bars known as the Eagle seem to be on brand—a little leathery, a little rougher, a little dirtier, in the good sense—they are only united by lore and a clientele that still looks to them as a place to get down to it.

John Early (1988–)

A comedian and actor who has a style and a way with characters that are all his own, Early started performing around New York, making his name as the host of *Showgasm* at Ars Nova. Early made the transition to television with shows like *Wet Hot American Summer: First Day of Camp* and his own episode of the Netflix sketch show *The Characters* in 2016. Since then, he's appeared in several films and television shows like *Search Party*, where he plays the vain and slightly evil Elliott, and *At Home with Amy Sedaris.* No wonder *Esquire* called him "comedy's secret weapon."

Ernestine Eckstein (1941–1992)

One of those figures from LGBTQ+ history who continues to seem like a badass, Eckstein worked with the civil rights movement in the 1950s and used this training and strategy to inform her work with the LGBTQ+ movement. She was a leader in the Daughter of Bilitis in New York in the 1960s, even going so far as to appear on the cover of the June 1966 issue of *The Ladder.* In the 1970s, as the feminist movement started to gain momentum, Eckstein was again on the front lines, organizing and lending her voice to the rights of all oppressed people. She organized the Black Women Organized for Political Action (BWOPA) in the early 1970s, and worked with them until 1980.

Edward II (1284–1327)

The gay king of England's preference for his favorite nobleman, Piers Gaveston, led to his abdication and eventual death. Edward was so hated that it is said that his enemies killed him by inserting a hot poker in his anus. The story became the stuff of legend, and was first taken up by gay playwright Christopher Marlowe in his play *Edward II*. The play was later used as the basis for the film *Edward II* by Derek Jarman and starring Tilda Swinton.

Ethyl Eichelberger (1945–1990)

Once in New York, there was an artist of amazing height—not just in her work, she was also very tall! Ethyl Eichelberger was an original. A classically trained actress, Eichelberger came to New York to give camp some room to grow. She worked with Charles Ludlam quite a bit, and also found space in the club scenes, especially at the Pyramid Club, to perform her own unique work. She introduced her character Minnie the Maid there, a smart-talking working girl with an accordion whose tales of woe and wonder captivated audiences. She wrote plays for herself based on classical mythology with her own camp underpinnings, proving herself a dynamic performer as well as an interesting social critic. She worked commercially on HBO's original children's program

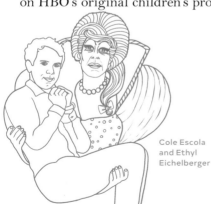

Cole Escola and Ethyl Eichelberger

Encyclopedia and appeared on Broadway opposite Sting in *The Threepenny Opera*. Eichelberger contracted AIDS, but kept her diagnosis a secret. Eichelberger took her own life at her home in Staten Island in 1990.

Billy Eichner (1978–)

Frightening us and making us laugh with his particular brand of assaulting comedy that never lets up on the laughs or the energy, Eichner started performing in New York, with his live show, *Creation Nation: A Live Talk Show* at Ars Nova. From there, Eichner granered more praise and television appearances until finally truTV signed him up for *Billy on the Street*. The show featured Eichner's particular brand of guerilla-style street questioning and became a runaway hit. Eichner parlayed this success into the series *Difficult People*, which he wrote and starred in with friend Julie Klausner. Since the success of two shows running concurrently, Eichner seems unstoppable. Eichner starred in the live-action remake of *The Lion King* and is writing and starring in a romantic comedy project with Judd Apatow. It will be a Hollywood first, to have a gay actor write and star in a gay story. It seems Eichner's in-your-face-style will make him a major player in entertainment.

Bret Easton Ellis (1964–)

Ellis is an author who's not afraid to go there, and his tenacity to take on the serious and the dark is a recurring theme in his work. Ellis's first novel, *Less Than Zero*, was published in 1985 and followed the lives of the young and the dissatisfied in Los Angeles. There were drugs and sex and rock and roll, and also critical acclaim. Ellis followed it with *The Rules of Attraction* and the now-classic *American Psycho* in 1991.

Ruth Charlotte Ellis (1899–2000)

Ellis grew up among former slaves in Tennessee and came out in 1915, when she was fifteen years old. In the 1920s, she moved to Chicago and met her life partner, Ceciline "Babe" Franklin. The pair moved to Detroit in 1937. Ruth and Babe's house became a bastion for gay and lesbian people in Detroit for most of the century. Ellis was an outspoken proponent of gay rights for most of her life. A documentary on her life, *Living with Pride: Ruth C. Ellis @ 100*, was released in 1999. The Ruth Ellis Center in Detroit still operates today as a center for LGBTQ+ people and homeless queer youth.

Julian Eltinge (1881–1941)

At one time, there was a Broadway theatre named for a drag queen. I'm speaking, of course, of Miss Julian Eltinge. A female impersonator from his days as a military cadet, Eltinge just would not put down the dress and continued right on up to Broadway. At the height of his powers, he was thought of as the clear rival to leading lady Lillian Russell. Eltinge was enormously popular—so popular, in fact, that they

named a theatre for him on Forty-Second Street. The Julian Eltinge Theatre is now an AMC movie theatre, but the façade remains the same. Think how profound that sounds. Eltinge worked in Hollywood, but his heart remained in the theatre until he died in 1941, just days after a club date.

Julian Eltinge

Brian Epstein (1934–1967)

Often called "the fifth Beatle," without Epstein there would be no Beatles as we know them today. Born into a family of wealthy merchants, he wanted more from his life. He attended the Royal Academy of Dramatic Art in London, but eventually went back to work for his father in the record department. On a lunch break from work in 1961, he heard the Beatles play at the Cavern Club and wanted to manage them. With Epstein's help, the group went on to became world famous. He later started the career of close friend Cilla Black. Epstein struggled with his sexuality and died of a drug overdose at the young age of thirty-two.

Erasure

This synth-pop duo consisting of Andy Bell and Vince Clarke has been making music since the 1980s. Their biggest hit, "Chains of Love," hit the Billboard Top 20 in 1988, but they'd been making music for years before that. They've had many hits, including the song "A Little Respect," which was featured heavily in the first season of HBO's series *Looking*. Andy Bell provides the vocals for the duo and has always been out and up front about his sexuality and his HIV-positive status. Together, the duo has recorded over fifteen albums and sold over 25 million records worldwide.

Cole Escola (1986–)

A genius. There I said it. But I assure you I'm not the only one. Cole Escola started making videos with friend and writer Jeffery Self as the VGL Gay Boys. The videos became so popular that the two sold the idea as a show to Logo network. *Jeffery & Cole Casserole* premiered in 2009 and was called a cult classic by *Vice* magazine. When *Casserole* ended after two season, Escola moved on to solo shows and guest starring with friends like Bridget Everett. They were cast in Hulu's *Difficult People* with Billy Eichner and *At Home with Amy Sedaris* as neighbor Chassie Tucker. With major profiles in the *LA Times,* and slew of projects from Showtime's *Ziwe* to a writing gig on HBO Max's *Hacks*, Escola is emerging as a mjor new talent on the comedy landscape.

Melissa Etheridge (1961–)

If you were a lesbian when you heard the song "Come to My Window," you knew exactly what Melissa Etheridge was talking about. Since her debut in 1988 and first flashes of commercial success, Etheridge has been making music with a lot of grit and meaning. A skilled guitarist and songwriter, Etheridge won a Grammy for her song "Ain't It Heavy" in 1993 and an Oscar for her song "I Need to Wake Up" from the film *An Inconvenient Truth* in 2007. She has been an outspoken activist for LGBTQ+ families and rights throughout her career, and added cancer to her long list of causes after she survived a bout with breast cancer in 2004.

Everard Baths

On West Twenty-Eighth Street in Manhattan, these baths were a place for men to meet and congregate for almost a hundred years. Not the nicest or the chicest of the bathhouses, the "Everhard" Baths, as they were commonly called, offered a place for a schvitz and schwish, if you know what I mean. It was the place to go for generations of gay men, flourishing to a full hilt in the 1970s. The baths caught on fire in 1977 and nine men were killed. Though the

Everard was rebuilt, Mayor Ed Koch closed all the baths in 1986.

Rupert Everett (1959–)

A British actor and writer whose wit and good looks have made him an enormous star, Everett had his first big hit in the play *Another Country*, about the Cambridge Five—a group of students who became Soviet spies in the 1950s. He immediately grabbed attention, and even released an album of pop songs called *Generation of Loneliness*. In 1989, he wrote a novel called *Hello Darling, Are You Working?* which was effectively his coming-out letter. Everett is now openly bisexual. He garnered huge praise playing opposite Julia Roberts in the romantic comedy *My Best Friend's Wedding* and has continued to work in the theatre and film. He was nominated for an Olivier for his portrayal of Oscar Wilde in the play *The Judas Kiss* in 2013. He again played Wilde in the film *The Happy Prince* in 2018.

Tom Eyen (1940–1991)

A darling of downtown Manhattan, writing plays at hot spots like the Caffe Cino and La MaMa long before Broadway came calling, Eyen became famous for his high sense of camp set among his sparkling wit and style. He wrote over thirty-five plays at La MaMa in the '60s and '70s and worked with stunning artists like Divine and Jackie Curtis. He also gave actress Bette Midler her first job in his play *Miss Nefertiti Regrets* in 1965. Eyen is most remembered today for writing the book to the musical *Dreamgirls*, for which he won the Tony Award.

F is for . . .

The Factory

Owned by Andy Warhol, the Factory, as it was commonly known, became a place of queer visibility in the 1960s art scene in New York. Being around the enigmatic Warhol made stars of queer artists who were able to make work and make names for themselves by association. For some the relationship was exploitive, especially as Warhol began to move into filmmaking, using this group as his stars. For others it was a chance to be among the *beautiful* people of the era. The most famous of the early superstars would probably be Edie Sedgwick. The lovely gamin, with the short blonde hair and movie-star good looks, became the girl of the moment. But the fast-paced and drug-filled life eventually led to her tragic demise in 1971 at the age of twenty-eight. There were other superstars: Brigid Berlin, also known as Brigid Polk, and Billy Name, who worked as Warhol's assistant and actually painted the Factory its legendary silver color; he became a great photographer in his own right.

There was Ondine, a talkative queen who was great with the funny quips. There was Mary Woronov and Viva, who both went on to become writers. Warhol's films always had gay representation, but as Warhol moved toward narrative filmmaking, these superstars, including Taylor Mead, provided the gripping dialogue and excitement. In movies like *Chelsea Girls* (1966), *The Nude Restaurant* (1967), and *Lonesome Cowboys* (1968), it's the superstars, with Meade and Viva in particular, who provided a lot of the dialogue and the personality to these films. After Warhol was shot in 1968, he moved away from the wild days of the silver Factory.

Fag Rag

Produced out of Boston in 1971, this gay magazine was an attempt at both lifting and lowering the conversation. A magazine for fags, it had a heavy dose of sexual content and letters from the readership, and also reached out to the artists of the day. Writers from Allen Ginsberg and John Rechy to Gore Vidal

Fag Rag

and John Wieners all contributed to making *Fag Rag* not only a document of the time, but also a treasure trove of gay sex and artistry. Started by a group of gay writers in Boston, Larry Martin, Charley Shively, and John Mitzel formed the Fag Rag Collective. A precursor to *BUTT*, *Hello Mr.*, and even *Gayletter*, *Fag Rag* ran from 1971 until the early 1980s.

Faggots

This novel by Larry Kramer was published in 1978 and met with controversy at the time. Kramer wrote about one man's pursuit of love in a world bent on sex and drugs and fun. At the time, it was seen as sex negative—a stigma that Kramer wore into the '80s when he started calling for the use of condoms or abstinence at the beginning of the AIDS crisis. But it is this debate that started to happen at the end of the 1970s that has been lost a bit since the overwhelming tide of AIDS. The '60s started a sexual revolution that the '70s took to the next level, but by the end of the decade, people were asking questions about our spirits and our hearts, and Larry, like it or lump it, was trying to address this issue in his work. It's still something we're all trying to figure out.

The Faggots & Their Friends Between Revolutions

This poetic, spiritual novel about the power and wisdom in difference, written by Larry Mitchell in 1977, is poetic and funny and has been treasured by radical queers all over the country since its initial publication. The book sees faggots as almost a different breed of people, free from norms and clichés, and imagines a world of queer utopia. It remained out of print for many years, but thankfully a free online version was available. In 2019, the book is reissued to inspire a new generation of readers.

Falcon Studios

They make the movies that make you . . . well, do whatever it is you do while watching porn. Founded in 1971 by Chuck Holmes, Falcon became a staple of the gay-porn industry. With breakout films like *The Other Side of Aspen* in 1978, Falcon Studios redefined the genre of gay erotica and, for a long time after that, set the standards. As the business grew, so did Holmes's power as a major political and charitable donor. The LGBT Center in San Francisco is named for Holmes. A documentary about Holmes and the beginning of Falcon, *Seed Money: The Chuck Holmes Story*, was released in 2015.

Ronan Farrow (1987–)

A muckraker of the old school, Ronan Farrow graduated from Bard College at the tender age of fifteen, and since then he has been working with and writing about people in power and questioning how they use it. Farrow worked for the Obama administration, working with Secretary of State Hillary Clinton and the State Department. After the White House, Farrow started concentrating on his writing.

He has written for the *Wall Street Journal*, the *Los Angeles Times*, and he even had a guest spot on NBC's *Today*. But it is his reporting about sexual abuse that truly sets Farrow apart. In 2017, he wrote his first piece about the Harvey Weinstein sex scandal in the *New Yorker*, and the world paid attention. For this work, Farrow was awarded the Pulitzer Prize.

Rainer Werner Fassbinder (1945–1982)

Filmmaker, playwright, and actor, Fassbinder was a visionary, not just in the theatre, which he began at the age of eighteen, but in film, where his gifts fully began to develop. In his fifteen-year career, he made over forty works for film and television, all with the touch of gay, gawdy genius that still inspires directors searching for their own voice. Fassbinder was bisexual, but his queerest works are some of his most haunting. His last film, *Querelle*, based on the book by gay genius Jean Genet, is a work of hot, hot brilliance with penis towers and Jeanne Moreau to boot.

Faster, Pussycat! Kill! Kill!

Go-go dancers run amuck in this fast-paced camp classic directed and written by Russ Meyer. With a star turn by Tura Satana as the infamous Varla, the film is a gripping and hilarious joyride with some bad girls out for a good time. While not successful when released in 1965, it has since become a

Faster, Pussycat! Kill! Kill!

cult classic and left its mark on filmmakers like Quentin Tarantino.

The Favourite

If you're looking to see Emma Stone get pushed in the mud or Olivia Colman eat a lot of cake, this 2018 dark comedy will not disappoint. *The Favourite* details the lesbian love affairs of the often-overlooked Queen Anne of England. Starring Olivia Colman as sad and lonely Anne, the film details the real-life rivals for her hand. In one corner, the brilliant and cunning Sarah, Duchess of Marlborough, played by Rachel Weisz. In the other, the downtrodden but conniving Abigail Hill, played by Emma Stone. Directed by Yorgos Lanthimos, this stunning film was almost universally praised, winning many major awards, including the Best Actress Oscar for Colman.

Frances Faye (1912–1991)

Faye was a rollicking cabaret singer who electrified audiences with her brassy voice and her kicking beats. But hidden among the fun were her jabs and nods to the queer family around her. Faye started performing and writing songs in the 1930s and actually wrote the song "Well All Right," which became a hit for the Andrews Sisters. Faye was a favorite in the late '50s and '60s, always hinting at her queer identity and often including the name of her lover, Teri Shepherd, in her songs. Shepherd discussed their relationship in Bruce Weber's film *Chop Suey* in 2001. Faye was also a major influence on and friend of the bisexual singer Peter Allen. Faye's recording of "Frances and Her Friends," a song about the mixing up of couples of all sexes and identities, was used in the first season of *The L Word*.

Fortune Feimster (1980–)

Fortune Feimster moved to Los Angeles in 2003 to pursue a career in comedy and soon became a fixture of the scene. She made her television debut in 2010 with *Last Comic Standing*, which opened her up to a whole new audience, and eventually found her way to *Chelsea Lately* with Chelsea Handler. When Handler moved to Netflix with her show *Chelsea*, Feimster was all too happy to come along for the fun. Her impressions of Ann Coulter and Sarah Huckabee Sanders became the clips to talk about. Feimster continues to make audiences laugh around the country as she appears in more and more hilarious roles on television and in films, as well as her many specials on Netflix.

David B. Feinberg (1956–1994)

In the history of gays, there's always that real snarky friend—the one sitting on the side with the best comments and the shadiest reads. It's a time-honored tradition of our people. And the line of this elevated snark was perhaps perfected in the works of David B. Feinberg. He was a wit and writer whose first novel, *Eighty-Sixed*, debuted in 1989 and won the Lambda Literary Award for Gay Men's Fiction. The fact that Feinberg wrote comedic novels during the height of the AIDS crisis might sound impossible, but he somehow made it work. He's a writer of such genuine insight and wit that the saddest part of his works is that there's just not more of it. His follow-up book, *Queer and Loathing*, all about living with HIV, is as beautiful and funny as it is harrowing. As Feinberg wrote, "There's a part of me that knows that I'll never die. There's a part of me that knows better."

Leslie Feinberg (1949–2014)

Feinberg described herself as "an anti-racist white, working-class, secular Jewish, transgender, lesbian, female, revolutionary communist." Her first novel, *Stone Butch Blues*, has become a seminal LGBTQ+ text and with good reason—it's stunning. Blurring the lines between trans and lesbian, she lives in the ambiguity and thrives. Here's one of my favorite quotes from the book: "You're more than just neither, honey. There are other ways to be than either-or. It's not so simple. Otherwise there wouldn't be so many people who don't fit." This role of fitting and not fitting was central to so much of Feinberg's work. She wrote extensively about the trans experience, which she defined as all "people who cross the cultural boundaries of gender." A kinder, gentler understanding of trans that I feel more and more we need today.

Michael Feinstein (1956–)

A pianist and singer who's holding the flame for the Great American Songbook, Michael Feinstein started playing in piano bars in Los Angeles, where he was able to meet some of his idols, like Rosemary Clooney, and eventually work with a personal mentor in Ira Gershwin. From there, Feinstein took on the curation of the Great American Songbook, researching and archiving some of the greatest achievements by a legendary group of composers and lyricists. His recordings of many of these works have become standards all their own. Feinstein continues to perform and record, reinventing and revitalizing the great standards of American music.

Female Trouble

Perhaps the gayest of movies by John Waters, which is saying something, and starring Divine as the troubled and troubling Dawn Davenport, *Female Trouble* is a camp classic of the highest order. Though Waters would certainly achieve higher heights with successes like *Hairspray* and *Serial Mom*, this film stands out as the pinnacle of his early career. And the costumes. Everything Divine wears here is just that—divine. Besides the camp and the horror, it's the quote from Aunt Ida, played by the one and only Edith Massey: "The world of the heterosexual is a sick and boring life." I couldn't agree more, Edith. I couldn't agree more.

Jesse Tyler Ferguson (1975–)

Most famous for his role as Mitchell on *Modern Family*, for which he received five consecutive Emmy nominations, Jesse Tyler Ferguson got his start on stage. He was a tried-and-true talent of off-Broadway, first hitting it out of the park with the revival of *On the Town* with Lea DeLaria, and finally making his debut in the stellar *The 25th Annual Putnam County Spelling Bee*, in which he played Leaf Coneybear. Ferguson was a standout from the beginning, and when Hollywood came a-calling, he was ready to take the leap. Following his unrivaled success on TV, Ferguson returned to the theatre in the hilarious *Fully Committed* in 2016. He and his husband, Justin Mikita, led the Tie the Knot effort to raise awareness and support for LGBTQ+ marriage in 2013.

Jack Ferver (1979–)

A dancer, writer, and actor whose work explores the rich legacy of queer art and its place within his emotional life, Ferver is recognizable from some more mainstream work—a recurring character on *Strangers with Candy* and a notorious commercial for Starburst—but it's his dance work that has earned him high praise from the *New York Times* and audiences that clamor for his work. *Mon, Ma, Mes* and *I Want You to Want Me* both received rave reviews from the *Times* for the deliciously witty work that takes darkness and transforms it into light.

Fez

So much of New York is gone, and one place that people still miss and talk about is the Fez. Right under the Time café in the East Village, Fez was a stomping ground for some of the most brilliant performers and artists. A starting place for Kiki and Herb, Joey Arias, and Sherry Vine, and others, it was also an early venue for artists like Rufus Wainwright.

Patricia Field (1942–)

Some people have style and some have vision. Patricia Field has both. Field opened her famous boutique in New York in 1966 and for fifty years it was the place to find fashion, art, and the people that create them both mixing and mingling. Her sense of style and fun came to national attention when she was asked to do the costumes for *Sex and the City*. Field gave Carrie her iconic looks, including her namesake necklace. Since then, Field has continued to make people look and feel fabulous in series like *Ugly Betty* and *Younger*. Field was nominated for an Oscar for her work on *The Devil Wears Prada*.

Danny Fields (1939–)

Fields is the gay daddy of the punk movement. As the *New York Times* said, "You could make a convincing case that without Danny Fields, punk rock wouldn't have happened." He got started in music journalism, but found his place among the gay scene of Warhol's Factory and formed close bonds with the Velvet Underground. He was hired as a publicist for Elektra Records, which first put him in contact with the Doors. Fields saw the punk scene burgeoning at places like CBGB and persuaded Elektra to sign Iggy and the Stooges. He also discovered the Ramones at CBGB and became their manager for several years. Since leaving music, Fields has continued to write and started telling the treasure trove of stories he has in the documentary *Danny Says*, released in 2015.

Harvey Fierstein (1954–)

He truly doesn't get enough credit, but for a whole generation of theatre-going people, Harvey Fierstein has been the gay voice of a generation. He began his career in downtown New York City in plays with folks like Jackie Curtis. He started writing his own work, not shying away from the gay experience, but diving right into it. Fierstein wrote *Torch Song Trilogy*, which became a huge hit on Broadway, winning him a Tony for Best Actor and Best Playwright. Fierstein also wrote the book to the Jerry Herman musical *La Cage aux Folles*, and in 1983, both shows were running concurrently. On top of all this treasure we have to thank him for, he also brought us Estelle Getty, who played his mother in *Torch Song Trilogy*. Fierstein continues to work and charm his way into the hearts of America, whether as Mrs. Turnblad in *Hairspray* or the playwright of *Kinky Boots*.

Finocchio's and Harvey Fierstein

Finocchio's

San Francisco's drag nightclub first opened as a speakeasy named the 201 Club in 1929. When Prohibition was repealed in 1933, they changed the name to Finocchio's after its owner Joe Finocchio, who thought female impersonation was funny. Apparently, so did his wife, and from 1933 to 1999, the club had drag shows almost every night of the week. It became a major destination in the '40s and '50s when they put out beautiful brochures advertising their entertainers and catering to a fancy Hollywood clientele. After Joe's death in 1998, his wife closed the club because of increasing rent and dwindling audiences. A beacon of glamour and glitz, Finocchio's remains a thing of legend from a bygone and much more closeted era.

Fire Island

A little home away from home, just a train and a ferry ride away every summer with every other queen you know and can't stand. Fire Island is a long and peopled isle rich in history. Artists and gay folks have flocked to this little isle for almost a century, and it still holds so much of its luster. Fire Island is also a house divided, and in some ways a perfect illustration of the two forces at work in the gay community at all times. On one side you have the Pines, the dishy, pricey Pines, where lawyers and doctors and moguls abound. It's very classy, with just a hint of the seedy in a "who spilled poppers on my Egyptian cotton sheets" kind of way. You dine at home in the Pines, and perhaps go to a tea dance to see what Andy Cohen's up to. Cross the great divide through the Judy Garland Memorial Pathway, or the "Meat Rack" as it's commonly called, which I find both disrespectful and inaccurate, and you're in Cherry Grove. A little flashier and a little tackier, here people are out for a good time. Mostly straight people, but we deal. There's life and energy in Cherry Grove, whether it be at Cherry's, which has the best sobering-up food anywhere on the Eastern Seaboard, or at the Ice Palace, which offers you the finest in drag queens and underwear parties. It's campier. It's sillier. It's a little more off the cuff, but at times it's just a lot more fun because it doesn't take itself so damn seriously.

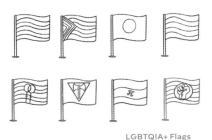

LGBTQIA+ Flags

Flags

We as a community love a flag and believe everyone deserves one. Or at least everyone in our community deserves one. The rainbow flag was first used in San Francisco in 1978 and was designed by Faerie Argyle Rainbow, Gilbert Baker, and James McNamara. Many flags have followed, with the trans flag, designed in 1999 by Monica Helms. There's a bisexual flag, a bear flag, and a gender queer flag. Basically, if you're something in the LGBTQ+ umbrella, we want you to have a flag. And if you don't, we'll get you one. In recent years, there have been debates about the rainbow flag, and many have wanted to add brown and black stripes to include people of color. My personal favorite is the all-inclusive flag, designed by Daniel Quasar in 2017.

Janet Flanner (1892–1978)

A writer with a sharp wit and even sharper observation, Janet Flanner started out in New York, hanging out with the Algonquin Round Table, but she found a far more heady horizon in the Paris of the '20s. It was there that Flanner wrote her column, Letter from Paris, under the name Genet, filling in the intellectual audience at home of all the fun they were having abroad. During the Second World War, she turned toward journalism, writing an in-depth profile on Hitler and eventually covering the Nuremberg trials. Her *Paris Journal, 1944–1965* won the National Book Award in 1966 and still stands as one of the best records of the wild period. Flanner continued to cover national events with her particular brand of biting realism almost until her death in 1978.

Flawless Sabrina (1939–2017)

Jack Doroshow, or as she was more commonly known, Flawless Sabrina, was the star of the 1967 film *The Queen*, a documentary about a drag contest two years before Stonewall. Sabrina was the hostess with the mostess, before and after the film, but throughout her long life she was the mother hen to a whole generation of gay and trans artists and friends. She was a supporter of so many wonderful people, working up to the end of her life with new artists like Zackary Drucker. Flawless read tarot cards, and it was always my dream to have her read mine. I heard she often hid personal advice among the cards. For a year, she told everyone whose cards she read to get off their laptop. Maybe it was advice we all needed to hear, cards or no. Flawless lived a long and beautiful life—always active, always funny, always wise—and even though she's left us, I like to think of her still watching all over of us, with all her wit and wisdom.

Bruz Fletcher (1906–1941)

One of the most prolific and talented performers to come out of the "Pansy Craze" of the early 1930s, Bruz Fletcher was an accomplished pianist and composer whose wit and way with a lyric made him a treasured entertainer, and whose career ended far too soon. He was known for his "sissified"

way through a song, and for his double and triple entendre. His song "My Doctor" was an audience favorite for his five-year residency at Los Angeles' Club Bali, but it's his ballad "Drunk with Love," that he may be most remembered for. The song was later sung by Frances Faye, and it tells of the sad end to a love affair. Fletcher himself had a sad end. As tastes changed, Fletcher's style of sophistication and sexual subversiveness fell out of style and he took his life at age thirty-five.

Wayland Flowers and Madame

Wayland Flowers and Madame (1939–1988)

It's true what RuPaul says: "Everyone loves puppets!" And everyone loved Wayland Flowers and Madame. A mainstay of 1970s variety-show television, Flowers and his foulmouthed puppet Madame entertained the nation with jokes just skirting the line of obscene. Madame went there, and often left audiences in peals of laughter. Flowers had developed his routine with Madame in gay cabaret clubs in New York, and soon caught the attention of television producers. Wayland Flowers and Madame made their television debut on *The Andy Williams Show* in 1970. Flowers and his old-broad puppet, styled after the famous Gloria Swanson, became a hot commodity on TV. They were a solid replacement for Paul Lynde on *Hollywood Squares*, and eventually got their own show, *Madame's Place*, which ran for fifty-one episodes in 1982. After Flowers's death of complications from AIDS, Madame was auctioned off and can still be seen around the country with a series of new handlers.

Folsom Street Fair

The world's largest outdoor BDSM and Leather festival takes place in San Francisco, and remains one of the wildest weekends in the world. The fair was started in 1984 and since then has only grown in popularity and scope. It has everything—flogging demos, rope-tying workshops, cotton candy— you know, fair stuff. It's a celebration of kink in a city that for many years celebrated a freedom to do exactly whatever you wanted to do. Folsom has spawned other festivals in New York, Folsom Street East; and in Toronto, Folsom Fair North, but the original fair is still a sight to see.

Charles Henri Ford (1908–2002)

A man of many talents and many stories, Ford was a writer, filmmaker, and visual artist. His first novel, *The Young and Evil*, written with Parker Tyler, was published in 1933 and is one of the earliest accounts of homosexual life in the twentieth century. Gertrude Stein compared the book to Fitzgerald, and it stands today as an early and unapologetically gay narrative. Throughout his long life, Ford was always part of the avant-garde. With his partner, the painter Pavel Tchelitchew, Ford created circles of artistry that included everyone from Salvador Dalí to Andy Warhol and Marcel Duchamp. His diaries, *Water from a Bucket*, published in 2001, are a wonderful and wicked read of his time as an artist among artists.

Tom Ford (1961–)

Elegance looks like a lot of things, but it often resembles something involving Tom Ford. A designer, film director, and writer, Ford continues to find new ways to make the world look beautiful. He got his start working for Chloé and Perry Ellis in the United States, and then found himself at the head of Gucci and Saint Laurent. Ford revitalized these brands and brought his particular brand of sexual elegance that's always set his work apart from his contemporaries. He launched his own line in 2006, and has since established himself as a designer for the stars, and even First Lady Michelle Obama. Ford expanded his vision in 2009 with his directorial debut of the film *A Single Man*, based on the Christopher Isherwood novel and starring Colin Firth and Julianne Moore. He released his second film, *Nocturnal Animals*, in 2016.

María Irene Fornés (1930–2018)

Fornés and her work are hard to characterize. She was a playwright, performer, and director, whose plays about humanity and the puzzles we often are to each other have confronted and affected audiences for over fifty years. Fornés became a leading voice of the off-off-Broadway movement in the 1960s. She won Obie Awards for her plays *Promenade* and *The Successful Life of 3*. Fornés was also shortlisted for the Pulitzer Prize for her play *And What of the Night?* Her work is always cited for its originality and tremendous depth of thought. In her long and storied career, she won nine Obies and was praised by other playwrights like Tony Kushner and Edward Albee.

E. M. Forster (1879–1970)

Perhaps the great gay uncle of the English novel, Forster was nominated for the Nobel Prize for Literature sixteen times during his lifetime. He came out of the distinguished Cambridge University and quickly found himself among a group of artists and freethinkers that would eventually be known as the Bloomsbury Group. Forster published his first novel, *Where*

E. M. Forster and María Irene Fornés

Angels Fear to Tread, and while well received, it wasn't until his novel *A Room with A View* in 1908 and finally his *A Passage to India* in 1924 that he found his greatest success. In the '30s and '40s, he worked with BBC Radio, and after *A Passage to India*, he didn't write any more novels. Or at least that's what the public thought. After Forster's death, his lone novel dealing with homosexuality, *Maurice*, was published in 1971 and instantly hailed as a masterpiece. Forster's book *Howards End* was the basis for the gay play *The Inheritance* by Matthew Lopez, which opened on Broadway in 2019.

Michel Foucault (1926–1984)

A world-renowned philosopher who dealt with how societies are formed around knowledge and power, Foucalt took long views of history, while also delving into the immediate in his work. His first book, *Madness and Civilization*, published in 1961, was a study in how society defines madness both as a tool for its own protection and a system to define sanity within the realms of its control. In his work *The History of Sexuality*, published in 1976, Foucault argued that even sexuality was in some ways based on cultural influence. This, along with much of Foucault's work, has been credited with starting the study of queer culture.

Daniel Franzese (1978–)

Most famous as everyone's favorite gay best friend, Damian in *Mean Girls*, Daniel Franzese has become so much more than too gay to function. He has starred in many other projects, including *Recovery Road* and HBO's *Looking*, and has also taken up the call of activism. He uses his status as a celebrity to push for charitable causes, becoming an ambassador for the Elizabeth Taylor AIDS Foundation as well for Lambda Legal. Besides his activism and acting, Franzese tours the country as a hilarious stand-up comedian.

Fried Green Tomatoes

Based on the novel by Fannie Flagg, this feel-good movie about murder, fried food, and racial injustice just makes you sigh and believe in love. This is one of those movies that reminds you of a simpler time, or at least gets you to put down the laundry and kill some time on a Sunday. The film tells the story of two female relationships in different times. In the modern age,

Kathy Bates forms a friendship with an older woman at a nursing home played by Jessica Tandy. Tandy tells of her life in a small whistle-stop town and the "friendship" between the tomboy Idgie Threadgoode, played by Mary Stuart Masterson, and her more uptight and proper friend Ruth, played by Mary-Louise Parker.

The Front Runner

This novel by Patricia Nell Warren, published in 1974, was the first book with an openly gay story line to become a *New York Times* #1 Best Seller. It tells the story of Harlan Brown, a college professor accused of sexual misconduct with a male student. The book is told in flashbacks to Brown's earlier life in a luscious prose. It's a coming out of sorts, and also deals with complexities in gay relationships. After its success, Warren, a lesbian herself, wrote many more books about gay male relationships, including *The Fancy Dancer* and *The Beauty Queen*.

Stephen Fry (1957–)

A comedian of genius, Fry's erudite observations have set him apart as a beloved storyteller and teacher around the world. Fry got his start as part of the comedy team Fry and Laurie. Working alongside Hugh Laurie, Fry became a staple of the British comedy scene, and since those days has continued his ascent to the pinnacle of British culture. From his tenure as the host of the hit panel show *QI*, to his stunning turn as Oscar Wilde in the film *Wilde*, Fry shows that when it comes to almost any artistic challenge, he is ready for the task. Fry has also turned his enormous intellect to writing three memoirs and, most recently, a retelling of the Greek myths. An outspoken and compassionate atheist, Fry has often defended the right not to believe while stressing a greater humanism and compassion for the entire human race.

Fun Home

This autobiographical graphic novel by Alison Bechdel broke the rules of the genre and ushered in a new period of serious storytelling with pictures. Bechdel tells the story of her own coming out, while detailing the struggle her father had dealing with his own homosexuality. This struggle eventually led to his death. The book was a *New York Times* Best Seller when it was released in 2006. It has since been adapted into a musical by Jeanine Tesori and Lisa Kron, which won the Tony Award for Best Musical in 2015.

Funny Girl

Well, hello, gorgeous. The movie that first gave us Barbra Streisand, *Funny Girl* is a perennial favorite for its lush cinematography and gorgeous musical numbers. Originally set on the stage in 1964 with songs by Jule Styne and lyrics by Bob Merrill, the show made Barbra a huge star. Streisand lights up the screen in the 1968 film, based on the life of the legendary comedian Fanny Brice and directed by William Wyler. The movie won Streisand an Oscar for Best Actress.

G is for . . .

Hannah Gadsby (1978–)

This "anti-comedy" comedian made an international hit with her stand-up special *Nanette* in 2018. The Netflix show caused quite a stir, and a sea of think pieces, but at the heart was Gadsby. She's a skillful and emotional storyteller with a wit and vulnerability that takes her audiences on a journey to darkness and back to light again. *Nanette* made Gadsby an instant star in the United States, though she'd been a respected comedian in her native Australia for a number of years. Her new show *Douglas* debuted in 2019, and further confirms Gadsby as a master of this new form of confessional comedy she's inventing.

Juan Gabriel (1950–2016)

When it comes to Mexican pop music, there are few people who have hit the same heights with the same amount of style and feeling as Juan Gabriel. A cultural phenomenon in Mexico, but also around the Spanish-speaking world, Gabriel scored countless hits and his albums sell in the millions. Juan Gabriel is seen as one of the most successful musical artists in Mexican history. Though he never spoke openly about his sexuality, his flamboyaance onstage and his sense of the dramatic made him an icon to the Spanish-speaking LGBTQ+ community.

Greta Garbo (1905–1990) `ICON`

Before there was Dietrich, before there was Davis or Crawford or Hepburn, there was only one. And that was Garbo. A brilliant, moody film actress, Garbo exuded sex and sadness that lit up the silent movies and then moved moodily into talkies. She was an international sensation, with huge hits in the silent era like *Torrent* and *Flesh and the Devil* in 1926. Sound pictures like *Grand Hotel* in 1932 and *Camille* in 1936 proved that Garbo could still hold an audience rapt with the sound of her voice. She even played veiled lesbian characters like Queen Christina of Sweden. She retired from film in 1941, at the age of thirty-five. She wanted to be alone, and for the most part she remained so. For years, she could be spotted walking around Manhattan in a hat and galoshes, window shopping but never really buying anything. Garbo died in 1990 at the age of eighty-four.

Judy Garland (1922–1969) `ICON`

The greatest of all gay icons, Judy Garland stands apart. With a voice that, even as a child, told of an emotional depth well beyond her years, Garland captivated her audiences and made them feel a connection with her. That special bond built her a fan base that honored and treasured her for the majority of her life and beyond. But what is it that makes her the greatest of gay icons? Well, some have said it started with her biggest breakout role, that of Dorothy Gale in the iconic *The Wizard of Oz*. When Judy sings the now-classic "Over the Rainbow" among the sepia-toned boringness of Kansas, she touches on a longing for magic that to this day can touch the heart of anyone hoping to belong. Or maybe it was the flash of her later roles—the glorious Technicolor delights of *Meet Me in St. Louis* or the show-stopping bombast of *A Star Is Born*. Perhaps it's her tragedy, as a child star raised on a steady diet of amphetamines that eventually led to her untimely death at forty-seven. Or maybe it's her love of the gay people from the beginning. It's known that Garland's father was a homosexual, and so were at least two of her four husbands. She loved her gay fan base and remained devoted to them during her lifetime. Or perhaps it's something far simpler. Garland, at her best, told the truth: Life is hard, a trial, a struggle, but even in that it can still be beautiful. Garland, far from a tragic icon, is a beacon of hope that lifted everyone

Judy Garland

who could see or hear her out of their own troubles to a place over that rainbow. It's a powerful thing to behold, even to this day. A gift like Judy comes once in a lifetime, and when it's gone, there's a sadness that is hard to express. Some say this sadness led to the Stonewall Riots, which took place a few days after her death in 1969. But even in death, Garland was able to transform that sadness into something strong and powerful. That's the remarkable power of Judy Garland: bravely, evenly, defiantly transforming the sorrow of life to something heroic and courageous. Something that lifts us all back over the rainbow, to a place where we all belong.

Jean-Paul Gaultier (1952–)

Gaultier is a brilliant designer and perfumer whose love of the risqué and couture have made him an international star. He has made his name with slick and sexy designs, giving Madonna her famous cone bra and making the now-iconic "mec" design for his signature men's fragrance, Le Male. His work has been heralded around the world for his brilliant use of texture, and as a creator he continues to astound and amaze the fashion world with his daring design. In 2011, a major exhibition of Gaultier's work toured the world, showcasing his enormous breadth and depth of talent.

Mary Gauthier (1962–)

This singer-songwriter has taken the road less traveled many times, but each venture out has led her to something marvelous and new. For many years, Gauthier cooked Cajun food in Boston, of all places, and played music on the side. But her talent for music soon outweighed her abilities with grits, and with the release of her early albums like 1997's *Dixie Kitchen* and 1999's *Drag Queens in Limousines*, Gauthier established herself as a songwriter with something new and vital to say. Her playing and vocals led themselves to the storytelling for which Gauthier is a master. Her newer albums, like *The Foundling* in 2013 and *Trouble and Love* in 2014, achieved great commercial success, and 2018's *Rifles & Rosary Beads*, co-written with veterans and their families, gave Gauthier a long-overdue Grammy nomination.

Roxane Gay and Jean-Paul Gaultier

Roxane Gay (1974–)

Gay is a novelist, essayist, and social commentator of enormous skill, wit, and insight. If you don't believe me, follow her on Twitter. Her first book, *Bad Feminist*, hit stores in 2014 to rave reviews. This collection of essays heralded the coming of a great intellectual mind, which Gay showed in her following releases, like the novel *An Untamed State* in 2014 and a collection of short stories, *Difficult Women*, in 2017. Her 2018 memoir *Hunger* addresses Gay's struggles with weight and body issues. In 2021, it was announced that Gay would start her own imprint at Grove Atlantic Publishing, bringing voices of underrepresented writers to larger markets.

Gay Bars

Bars are different for gay people. They're not the friendly atmospheres of a TV show like *Cheers*. They're havens from a world that doesn't understand or approve, meeting houses for the fight for liberation or even just a theme party, places were people may not know your name but certainly know what you're looking for. For decades, bars have been the meeting places and hubs for LGBTQ+ people. Looking back at our history, bars play a more prominent role than in the history of any other people. These were the realms of our possibility and continue to offer community and freedom to a diverse community looking for a place to be. There's a reason why the gay-rights movement began at a bar.

Gay City News

One of the last bastions for gay news in the country, this free local paper in New York has offered news and opinion to the LGBTQ+ community since 1994. It grew out of need, after one by one other gay publications folded during the AIDS crisis. The paper still provides commentary, gay arts and culture, and news affecting the LGBTQ+ community at large.

The Gay Deceivers

A little like trying to get your grandmother to get your pronouns right—irritating, but hopefully a little funny—*The Gay Deceivers* is a very problematic, gay-themed comedy released the same year as 1969's Stonewall Riots. It's rife with stereotypes but also quite a few laughs. The film tells the story of two friends, Danny and Elliot, who try to get out of the Vietnam draft by pretending to be gay. They move into a gay apartment building and try to blend in. Essentially it's an earlier version of Adam Sandler's *I Now Pronounce You Chuck & Larry*, from a simpler, more fashionable, and less bro-y time.

Gay New York

Published in 1994, George Chauncey's study of the gay world of New York in the early twentieth century is required reading for anyone interested in gay history. Charming, daring, and utterly informative, Chauncey delves not only into the history of men who had sex with men, but also into the communities and lives they built for themselves long before the Stonewall Riots.

Gay Sunshine

No, it's not an energy drink. It's a journal of gay liberation started in the 1970s by Winston Leyland. The magazine was a collection of art, fiction, and essays that attracted some of the biggest and brightest LGBTQ+ figures of the period. One of its great features was its interviews with luminaries like Allen Ginsberg, Christopher Isherwood, and Gore Vidal. These interviews were so popular that they were collected into two anthologies during the 1970s. The magazine was in operation for almost twenty years and was a hallmark for LGBTQ+ art and literary aficionados.

David Geffen (1943–)

A music mogul and philanthropist who has produced some of the greatest American music of the twentieth century, from Joni Mitchell and Elton John to Linda Ronstadt and Bob Dylan, Geffen has amassed an empire that reaches into all forms of media. Besides being a music tycoon, Geffen was also a founding member of Dream-Works. With his enormous wealth, Geffen has chosen to give back to the LGBTQ+ community in substantial ways. He promotes the arts with the David Geffen Hall at Lincoln Center and the Geffen Playhouse in Los Angeles. He has also given funds to promote the training of doctors with the David Geffen School of Medicine at UCLA.

Genesis P-Orridge (1950–2020)

P-Orridge was a trans artist, musician, poet, painter, and activist who has had a long and storied career on the outskirts of mainstream music and art. Making industrial chaotic music that spoke to the rage and unrest in London during the height of the punk movement, they used their voice to speak out against the establishment and a host of its evils. They formed the band Throbbing Gristle in 1975, which now has legendary status and is seen by many as the godfather of industrial music. After the breakup of the band in 1981, P-Orridge took on the Pandrogeny Project with their partner, Lady Jaye, taking on body-modification surgery to begin to resemble one another until Jaye's death in 2007. P-Orridge continued to make art—visually and musically—with strong leanings to the occult and a deeper understanding of the follies of gender. In 2021, their memoir, *Nonbinary*, was released to critical acclaim.

Jean Genet (1910–1986)

If you're a down-and-out degenerate of the oldest gay order, you may feel out of place in the modern paradigm. Where are the criminals? Where are the badass, kick-ass, take-no-prisoner queers? Well, look no further than French novelist and playwright Jean Genet. He was a bad kid—a real bad kid—who was in and out of jail for most of his young life. It was during a prison term in 1943 that he wrote his first, and perhaps most famous, novel, *Our Lady of the Flowers*. All about a tragic queer prostitute named Divine—think about it—and her pimp lover Darling Daintyfoot. Genet sent the novel to Jean-Paul Sartre, who called it "the epic of masturbation," and Jean Cocteau, who both recognized its genius and helped Genet get it published. When Genet got in trouble again, Cocteau and Sartre petitioned the French government to overlook it and release him, which they did. Genet went on to write more novels, like *Querelle* in 1947 and *The Thief's Journal* in 1949. He also wrote plays, like *The Maids* and *The Balcony*, which have become classics. In all of Genet's work, he explores crime, lust, and social injustice. He was a firm supporter of civil rights, not only with his play *The Blacks*, which played off-Broadway with James Earl Jones, Cicely Tyson, Maya Angelou, and Lou Gossett Jr., but also as an outspoken supporter of the Black Panther movement.

Rudi Gernreich (1922–1985)

Austrian-born fashion designer Gernreich splashed onto the fashion scene with his provocative "monokini" in 1964. Though he had been a designer and fashion influencer for years prior, this bikini without a built-in bra was a huge success. As an experimental designer, Gernreich who felt as though fashion could be a vehicle to raise social consciousness. He was also a founding member of the Mattachine Society, an early LGBTQ+ rights organization. He was much lauded during his lifetime for his forward-thinking designs, and in the years after his death, he continues to be a major influence on designers looking to experiment with new forms.

Masha Gessen (1967–)

Gessen is an investigative journalist and author whose outspoken opposition to Vladimir Putin and his treatment of the LGBTQ+ community earned them the title of "Russia's leading LGBTQ+ rights activist." Throughout their career, Gessen has written for other publications about the inner workings of the Russian government. Their work has been featured in the *New York Times* and they are a regular contributor to cable news. Their books on Putin and his tyranny have offered keen insight into one of the world's most notorious and criminal regimes.

André Gide (1869–1951)

Gide was a Nobel Prize-winning French author who was one of the world's first major writers to deal with homosexuality from a personal and private viewpoint, and to illustrate the complexities of same-sex love. Gide is most remembered for his personal books like *The Immoralist* and *The Counterfeiters*, and his autobiography, *If It Die*, which show him as a searcher looking for meaning in a life unchartered by mainstream culture.

John Gielgud (1904–2000)

The most glorious voice to speak the words of Shakespeare in modern history, Gielgud was an actor of legendary status during his lifetime. Often seen as the only rival to Laurence Olivier, Gielgud was all beauty and sound, whereas Olivier was bravura and passion. Gielgud, much like his rival, was dedicated and obsessed with his profession, often directing, coaching, and always endlessly working on his craft as an actor. Though he is mostly remembered as the foulmouthed butler in the *Arthur* movies of the 1980s, for which he won an Oscar, they are merely the tip of the iceberg for a career that lasted over seventy years and reached heights rarely seen in any lifetime.

John Giorno (1936–2019)

A poet, writer, performance artist, and visual artist deeply influenced by the Beat Generation, Giorno had a spontaneous freewheeling style that perfectly endeared him to the radical art and politics of the 1960s. From his projects like Dial-a-Poem in 1967, where people could call in to hear a poem read live, to his experimentations with electronic music and sound saturation in the 1970s, Giorno was endlessly seeking new ways to create the poetic experience into something more visceral and immediate. This experimentation eventually led him to visual media, making large, colorful, and eye-catching works from some of his most famous phrases and poetic motifs, like, "Life is a Killer," and "I want to cum in your heart."

Nikki Giovanni (1943–)

Giovanni is a true legend of the Black arts movement of the 1960s, who is often called the "Poet of the Black Revolution." Giovanni has worn many hats in her long and storied career: poet, children's author, talk show host, social commentator, educator and even Grammy nominee. Her poems are visceral, using contemporary language to express the truths of Black lives as they happen. Her live readings of her work are awe-inspiring, and bring the listeners the full breadth of her work. For her work and activism, Giovanni has become one of the most awarded writers in modern literature and continues to be a champion for the lives and arts of Black people.

Gigi Gorgeous (1992–)

A YouTube star who guided a whole generation through her transition in funny and often touching videos, Gigi, then Greg, started posting makeup tutorials in 2008 and gained a major following for her free and easy manner and her expert painting tips. In 2013, Gigi announced her transition publicly and found a lot of support. A documentary about her journey to YouTube stardom and her coming out as trans, *This Is Everything*, was released in 2017. Since her transition, her fan base has grown and so has her popularity. She's made many appearances in music videos and television and she continues to be a vocal and encouraging voice for trans people everywhere.

Allen Ginsberg (1926–1997)

Ginsberg was a poet, writer, and activist who was the heart and soul of the first Beat Generation. He was one of the first Beat writers to be published, and he fought hard to see his friends Jack Kerouac and William Burroughs in print as well. His poem "Howl" became a seminal American text, calling back to the free verse of Walt Whitman and bringing it into the modern paradigm. Ginsberg was, almost from the beginning, unabashedly queer, writing about sex and men with tenderness but also brute force. He brought graphic gay sex into poetry, but that was not all. Virulently antiwar, Ginsberg wrote against the military-industrial complex and its evils all over the world. A great precursor to the hippie movement of the 1960s, he joined the peace movement as guide and mentor. Ginsberg became committed to Buddhism and the peace movement, even testifying in the famous Chicago 8 trial on behalf of the protestors. Throughout his life, he was a committed advocate of social change. Like Allen, I wish we would all put our "queer shoulder(s) to the wheel."

Girls Will Be Girls

Girls Will Be Girls

This 2003 independent film, written and directed by Richard Day, has become an underground classic. With a drag cast that includes Varla Jean Merman, Coco Peru, and Jack Plotnick as the evil has-been Evie Harris, *Girls Will Be Girls* is a quotable classic with a huge cult following. Set in modern-day Los Angeles, the story follows these three drag queens as they look for love and fame in the sinister world of Hollywood. With more twists and turns than a colonoscopy, this movie has it all. It's a hilarious romp that checks all the boxes of a camp classic. It's raunchy, racy, and hilariously obscene.

Barbara Gittings (1932–2007)

"Out" before out was a thing to be, Barbara Gittings formed and ran the New York chapter of the lesbian group Daughters of Bilitis and edited their magazine *The Ladder*. She worked with Frank Kameny to protest the US government over discrimination of LGBTQ+ employees in the '60s. She fought the American Psychiatric Association to remove homosexuality from a list of mental disorders. Gittings said her job was to remove the shroud of invisibility about homosexuality. She at times admitted to being a lesbian separatist, which I love. If the lesbian community ever goes off to build their own world, I wonder if I could tag along, just to revel at the organization.

Wilhelm von Gloeden (1856–1931)

Von Gloedon was a German pioneer in the early days of photography as an art form. His photos of young men in classical poses are still controversial for their use of male sexuality and the adoring way in which von Gloeden captured them. He was born into an aristocratic family, and it's his life in Italy and his love for the culture and people there for which von Gloeden is most remembered. His works, mostly of young nude or semi-nude young men, were considered risqué during his life—if not outright pornography—which made him a scandalous and sought-after figure.

Ari Gold (1974–2021)

Gold was a pioneer in gay pop music who produced music that dealt openly and overtly with his sexuality since the 1990s. Since the beginning, Ari Gold's work was deeply autobiographical—not only dealing with his sexuality, but also his Jewish heritage. He wrote about his life in one-man shows, which detail his rise in the music industry, but it's his club anthems that have earned Gold a fawning and eager fan base. With dance hits like "Wave of You," Gold has kept us dancing for years. Ari died tragically in 2021, after a battle with cancer.

The Golden Girls

What is it about a sitcom about four older women living together in Miami that makes gays lose their minds with delight? The answer is long and varied, but the truth is that since it debuted on NBC in 1985, *The Golden Girls* has become a hallmark of gay culture. Instantly quotable and hilarious, this comfort food of a sitcom has delighted the community for decades.

The Golden Girls

Set in Miami, it tells of four friends: the slutty and sultry southern belle, Blanche Devereaux, played by Rue McClanahan; the innocent and idiotic St. Olaf native, Rose Nylund, played by Betty White; the sarcastic and stoic Dorothy Zbornak, played by Bea Arthur; and the punchy and pugnacious mother of the group, Sophia Petrillo, played by Estelle Getty. The show follows the ladies through friendships, dating, and the importance of the family you find for yourself. Perhaps it's this last topic that touches a gay audience. The show always knew it had a gay following and often included gay story lines, from Blanche's gay brother to Rose's AIDS scare. *The Golden Girls* is a classic, and there's hardly a city in this country where episodes aren't performed in loving tribute by a group of drag queens to a warm and willing audience.

Jewelle Gomez (1948–)

Gomez is a poet and playwright who has been writing and creating theatre and literary work for more than forty years. Her most famous work, *The Gilda Stories*, was published in 1991 and seen as a trendsetting book when it came to supernatural lesbian fiction. Perhaps this is why Gomez refers to herself as the "foremother of Afrofuturism." Her work is rooted in a deep understanding of race and the sexual history of our American past and has been featured in many collections. She is a regular contributor to the *San Francisco Chronicle* and the *Black Scholar.*

Marga Gomez (1960–)

Gomez is a playwright and comedian whose solo plays about love and loss have inspired and informed a generation of performers and fans alike. She originally started in stand-up and made her way onto HBO's *Comic Relief* and Comedy Central. But a desire to explore her stories more fully led her into solo plays. Her works, like *Not Getting Any Younger* and *Lovebirds*, deal openly and honestly with her struggles and her triumphs, and have been almost universally lauded. For her role as a storyteller and a pioneering artist in the Latina LGBTQ+ community, Gomez has been honored by GLAAD and by her hometown of San Francisco.

X González (1999–)

González is a Parkland massacre survivor whose strength to stand up to the government who failed them and their classmates on gun reform made them a national figure in 2018. González , then Emma, attended Marjory Stoneman Douglas High School in Parkland, Florida, when, on February 14, a gunman came into the school and killed seventeen students with a semi-automatic weapon. González's stunning speech about gun control in the wake of the tragedy went viral. Their "We call B.S." was heard around the world and ushered the young González into the national spotlight. Since the shooting, González has continued their advocacy for gun reform, and has also taken up other causes like the rights of women and advocacy for the LGBTQ+ community.

Ricky Ian Gordon (1956–)

He reinvented the art song for the modern day. Gordon's songs like "A Horse with Wings" and "Once I Was" have become standard fare in both classical music and musical theatre for a new generation. His opera work also has astounding breath and scope, from his 2007 *The Grapes of Wrath*, adapted from the novel by Steinbeck, to his personal *Morning Star* in 2015. Gordon is defying and redefining an age-old art form along decidedly American lines.

Lesley Gore (1946–2015)

The singer of our codependence, this good girl with the broken heart lit up the charts in the 1960s. While outwardly always waiting for a guy to treat her right, privately Lesley Gore was only waiting on the right lady. She had hits with songs of painful and dire breakups, like "It's My Party" and "Judy's Turn to Cry," but it's her great anthems of female independence like "You Don't Own Me" that still get people up on the dance floor to this day.

Nathan Lee Graham (1968–)

There's something perfectly purr-fect about performer and actor Nathan Lee Graham. Perhaps it's his style, which is considerable, or his stunning vocals, or maybe it's his comedic timing. Most likely it's a combination of all three. Graham has been capitvating and delighting audiences from stage and screen for decades. A cabaret singer par excellence, Graham was in the original production of Michael John LaChuisa's *The Wild Party* with his idol, Eartha Kitt, but he's also proven himself as a dramatic actor, starring in the original off-Broadway production of Tarrell Alvin McCraney's *Wig Out!* On screen, he's played Todd, Will Ferrell's side-kick in both the *Zoolander* films, and Frederick in *Sweet Home Alabama*, and delighted audiences on the CW's *Katy Keene* as the often flamboyant Francois.

Ariana Grande (1993–) ICON

A pop diva whose stunning vocals in an age of overproduction are a balm and a joy to many, Grande grew up as a performer, making her Broadway debut at fifteen in the Jason Robert Brown musical *13*. From there, she began releasing songs on YouTube and grew a steady following. In 2012, she was cast on the Nickelodeon show *Victorious*, and this began her big ascent to pop stardom. Her first album, 2013's *Yours Truly*, debuted at no. 1 in the United States. Since then there have been a steady stream of hits, like "thank u, next" and "God is a woman," making Grande one of the most played artists in the world, with a host of LGBTQ+ fans. She herself is a vocal champion and supporter of the community, and her brother Frankie Grande, also a performer and singer, identifies as gay himself.

David Greenspan (1956–)

An actor and playwright whose work revels in theatricality, but never shies away from insight, Greenspan has mined his personal life in works like *Principia*, and also the grand classical tradition like his *Old Comedy after Aristophanes' Frogs*. He was the book writer for a musical version of Neil Gaiman's *Coraline*. For his work as a playwright and actor, Greenspan has been awarded countless awards, but also a special Obie for his Sustained Achievement in 2010.

Garth Greenwell (1978–)

This author, critic, poet, and teacher wears many hats, but he's most widely known for the critically acclaimed novel *What Belongs to You*, published in 2016. It's loosely based on Greenwell's own experience while teaching in Bulgaria and takes a fresh look at the relationship between the hustler and the hustled. His latest novel, *Cleanness*, was a finalist for the Lambda Literary Award.

Grey Gardens

When you're worried you and your mother might be codependent, watch *Grey Gardens* to relax a little. The 1975 cinema vérité classic of the Maysles brothers has become a hallmark of the gay world and made stars of its subjects, Big Edie and Little Edie Bouvier Beale. Cousins of First Lady Jacqueline Kennedy, the Beales are living in squalor in their East Hamptons home, Grey Gardens, when Kennedy and her sister Lee Radziwill are asked to intervene. Radziwill asks the Maysles to film the Beales to make a movie about the Bouvier family, but it turns out the Beales were too interesting to simply be a part of the movie. They had to be the whole show. The film has fascinated and haunted people for decades, spawning a musical in 2006 and an HBO movie in 2007.

Miss Major Griffin-Gracy (1940–)

Miss Major Griffin-Gracy

Miss Major, as she is affectionately known, is a survivor of both Stonewall and the infamous Attica Prison riot. A longtime advocate of the LGBTQ+ community, Miss Major has always been on the front lines of the queer movement. Besides being at the Stonewall Riots, Miss Major was on the front lines of the AIDS crisis, organizing the folks of San Diego to fight back and support those suffering with the disease. She worked as a sex worker and was incarcerated for burglary at Attica Correctional Facility. In 1971, when the riots broke out, Miss Major was there, fighting for the rights of her fellow prisoners. Prisoner rights has been a lifelong cause for her. She has worked with the Transgender Gender-Variant & Intersex Justice Project since 2016. A documentary about her extraordinary life and activism, *Major!*, was released in 2015.

Grindr

A gay social app, first launched in 2009, Grindr identifies other members in an approximate area and lists their sexual likes and dislikes. Though originally seen as a hookup app, Grindr has moved into different arenas in recent years, now offering video programming and other forms of social interaction. I can't wait for the day when people say they're on Grindr for the shows—are you with me?

Thom Gunn (1929–2004)

A gay poet of intense honesty and vision, Gunn wrote harrowingly of the AIDS crisis in his seminal *The Man with the Night Sweats* in 1992. Gunn was an English-born poet who emigrated to the United States in the 1950s. He was originally associated with what was called the Movement, a group of young writers working after the Second World War, but Gunn's work soon ventured into territory all its own. Moving to San Francisco, he chronicled the heady days of gay sex and drugs with a keen eye for detail and emotion. With the coming of the AIDS crisis, Gunn wrote about the enormous despair and need for love in any way one could find it. His work remains deeply personal but ultimately human and accessible.

Tim Gunn (1953–)

The master of "making it work," Gunn was the original fashion consultant on the reality hit *Project Runway*. While the show was seen as a vehicle for Heidi Klum when it debuted in 2004, it was Gunn who soon emerged as a break-out star all his own. With his cool demeanor and sonorous voice, Gunn became a favorite of the casts and fan base alike. His popularity turned the rather shy teacher from Parsons into an international star and enabled Gunn to take on many other projects and opportunities. But through it all, Gunn returned to *Project Runway* until 2018, when both he and Klum decided to leave the show. Since then, Klum and Gunn have started a new show on Amazon called *Making the Cut*, which premiered in 2020.

H is for...

Reynaldo Hahn (1874–1947)

Hahn wrote and conducted the music of the Belle Époque in Paris. He was originally from Venezuela but moved to Paris at the age of three and soon showed himself to be a musical prodigy. He performed a great deal, playing the piano and singing at eight and soon composing his own songs. He composed popular songs using the words of poets Victor Hugo and Paul Verlaine and became one of the most popular composers and conductors of the period. He also became one of the most respected music critics of the time. It was his attention to detail and to deep understanding that influenced the work of his young lover, Marcel Proust, to go on to write his now famous *Remembrance of Things Past*.

William "Billy" Haines (1900–1973)

Billy Haines's is one of those rare Hollywood stories where the good guy wins in the end. He was discovered in 1922 and signed to make movies. Haines was an affable boy-next-door-type with a sweet charm that made audiences around the country fall in love with him. He had his biggest hit in 1926's *Brown of Harvard*, and it looked like everything was going right for Haines. The fact that Haines was a homosexual was an open secret in Hollywood, but when the studios started to ask Billy to be more secretive about his private life, Haines refused. He retired from acting in 1935 and opened an interior design business with his longtime partner, Jimmie Shields. Haines and Shields became a favorite of Joan Crawford, but all of Haines's former Hollywood friends clamored to have the duo decorate their homes.

William Haines and Radclyffe Hall

Rob Halford (1951–)

Halford is the lead singer of heavy-metal mega band Judas Priest. Known for his trademark style of black leather and studs, from the beginning Rob Halford has been bringing a little bit of the gay into the world of heavy metal. When Halford came out in 1991, he thought he would lose a lot of fans from the metal community, but his talent and stamina have kept him a favorite. No wonder his nickname is "Metal God."

Radclyffe Hall (1880–1943)

Often considered the grande dame of lesbian fiction, Radclyffe Hall grew up in England and always identified as a gay woman. She had a series of affairs with women but wrote most of her early novels with only hints about her sexuality. Her greatest-known work, *The Well of Loneliness*, published in 1928, was Hall's first novel to deal openly with lesbianism, referring to her main character, Stephen Gordon, as an invert. The book was immediately controversial and was banned in the United States for many years. For Hall, it was an exposé on the dignity and right of homosexual love to flourish in the world. As Hall writes in *The Well*, "If our love is a sin, then heaven must be full of such tender and selfless sinning as ours."

Todrick Hall (1985–)

There's little that singer, actor, director, and choreographer Hall can't do, and he's been doing it all for quite some time. Hall first came to the national stage as a contestant on *American Idol*, but it was his parodies and original music on YouTube that catapulted him into an international figure. It was there that Hall's panache for making a complete vision of images and music first took hold. Many of his early videos were typical Internet fare, showing off his strong vocals and cultural references to Disney and *The Wizard of Oz*. With his concept and visual albums like *Straight Outta Oz* and *Forbidden*, Hall truly came into his own. Touring the world, and collaborating with RuPaul and Taylor Swift, Hall continues to earn fans and likes with a talent that takes his fans to higher heights with every project.

David Halperin (1952–)

Halperin is a queer theorist that concentrates his work on gay and queer studies and their presentation in the media and culture. In 1991, Halperin and Carolyn Dinshaw co-founded the *GLQ: A Journal of Lesbian and Gay Studies*. Haplerin has been a strong and outspoken voice for the study of queer history and the ways in which this history is gathered and studied. His works include *One Hundred Years of Homosexuality* and *What Do Gay Men Want?* His *How to Be Gay* is seen as a strong statement about the value and contribution of gay culture. But he is also quick to point out that while still popular, it has lost its power at moving the culture forward.

Halston (1932–1990)

A fashion designer who made the 1970s look sleek and chic on the world stage, Halston began making hats for the wealthy and famous—he designed Jacqueline Kennedy's famous pillbox hat—but eventually moved into the world of clothing design in the 1960s. He classic-yet-sporty American design made him a favorite of the fashionable and his sense of fun made him a famous feature on the disco circuit. With close friends like Liza Minnelli and Bianca Jagger, Halston became a feature of the Studio 54 set. He eventually sold his line and then tried to create a line for JCPenney in the 1980s but the years of partying and poor business decisions eventually caught up with him. Halston died of complications from AIDS in 1990. In 2021, Ryan Murphy produced and wrote a dramatic series about the legendary designer with Ewan McGregor playing Halston.

Barbara Hammer (1939–2019)

Hammer was a groundbreaker when it came to experimental cinema and portraying lesbian story lines. After studying film at San Francisco State University, Hammer came out and went on an adventure to make movies about the queer lives all around her. Her 1974 film, *Dyketactics*, is often considered one of the first lesbian films in the United States. Hammer continued to make films throughout her life, becoming a powerhouse of avant-garde and gay film. She was an outspoken champion for other queer and female filmmakers throughout her

lifetime. Her films have been shown and respected all over the world. New York's MoMA did a retrospective of her work in 2010. After Hammer was diagnosed with ovarian cancer in 2006, she battled it for the next twelve years. When finally there were no more options, Hammer turned her illness into art and began a lecture on "The Art of Dying," which she performed at the Whitney Museum of Art in October 2018. Hammer died of her cancer in March of 2019.

Mabel Hampton

VOICESOFNEWOMEN

Mabel Hampton (1902–1989)

At the height of the Harlem Renaissance, among the enclave of male queer voices, Mabel Hampton was a shining light for queer women of color in the artistic movement. Hampton got her start as a dancer, but as she got older, she began to clean houses for wealthy white families in New York. During all this time, she saved countless archival documents and ephemera detailing the lives of queer women of color in a society and an age that would often overlook their accomplishments. Hampton contributed her papers to the Lesbian

Herstory Archives and in her late seventies and eighties became an outspoken icon of LGBTQ+ history. At the 1984 Pride Parade in New York, Hampton said, "I, Mabel Hampton, have been a lesbian all my life, for eighty-two years, and I am proud of myself and my people. I would like all my people to be free in this country and all over the world, my gay people and my black people."

Lorraine Hansberry (1930–1965)

To be young, gifted, and Black was a phrase put forth by this writer and playwright, and can be most effectively used to describe her. Hansberry grew up in an upwardly mobile Black family in Illinois. When her father, Carl Augustus Hansberry, tried to buy his family a house in Chicago's South Side, he and the entire family were met with racial harassment that eventually led the Hansberrys to take their case all the way to the Supreme Court in 1940. Hansberry would take some of this experience as inspiration for her greatest work, *A Raisin in the Sun.* Hansberry got her start writing for the Black newspaper *Freedom* in 1950. It was through her work at *Freedom* that she met and married Robert Nemiroff, a songwriter and political activist. Nemiroff encouraged her to write for the theatre. When *A Raisin in the Sun* debuted on Broadway in 1959, it was an instant classic, winning the New York Drama Critics' Circle Award

and catapulting Hansberry into the national spotlight. She also adapted her play for the 1961 film version starring Sidney Poitier, who had starred in the play on Broadway. Hansberry had lesbian relationships throughout her life, and wrote about her desires in a number of anonymous essays for the lesbian magazine *The Ladder.* Hansberry died at the age of thirty-four from pancreatic cancer.

Keith Haring (1958–1990)

You can see his work on T-shirts, mugs, and even stamps all over the world, but artist and activist Keith Haring got his start on the subways of New York. Haring grew up in Kutztown, Pennsylvania, but found his place in the world in New York City when he moved there in 1976. He began creating his unique cartoon-based work on the subway system, and his individual, radiant baby tag became a thing of legend before people even knew his name. He became a big part of the graffiti scene in New York but wanted to move into more formal settings. His work began to be recognized internationally in the early '80s, and Haring traveled the world, painting all sorts of murals and art pieces while staying true to his cartoon and gay roots. In the height of the AIDS crisis, Haring lent his talents to AIDS activism. He became an art-world darling, working with Andy Warhol, one of his heroes, and the incredible Grace Jones, who was a longtime muse. Haring was diagnosed with AIDS in 1988 and continued to lend his voice to ending the epidemic until his death in 1990.

E. Lynn Harris (1955–2009)
One of the most successful writers of his generation, E. Lynn Harris had ten consecutive books on the *New York Times* Best Seller list. Harris's first novel, *Invisible Life*, self-published in 1991, dealt with bisexuality in the Black community and dived deeply into the world of the "down-low," where men would live outwardly heterosexual lives but have homosexual affairs on the side. It was a theme Harris would revisit in many of his later works. He sold copies of this first book out of his car, and later, when he signed to Doubleday, it became a *New York Times* Best Seller. Harris continued to write about queer sexuality in the Black community and to garner more and more praise for his work, including a James Baldwin Award and three Blackboard's Novel of the Year Awards. His memoir, *What Becomes of the Brokenhearted*, was published in 2003. Harris died suddenly at the age of fifty-four after a heart attack.

Jeremy O. Harris (1989–)
This actor and playwright made a splash on Broadway with his brutal and controversial *Slave Play*. Harris has been writing brilliant and thoughtful work for much longer than that. He got his start as an actor with the Steppenwolf Theatre Company in Chicago but quickly turned his talents to writing. His *Slave Play* was first seen in 2017 and eventually put on at New York Theatre Workshop under the direction of Robert O'Hara. The play was almost universally heralded, and so was Harris. His style and willingness to talk brilliantly about his work and the world have made him a favorite for magazines. While *Slave Play* opened at NYTW, another of Harris's plays opened at the Vineyard. That play, *Daddy*, with Alan Cumming and Hari Nef, was also a huge success and did much to establish Harris as a writer to watch. *Slave Play* eventually made its way to Broadway, where it played for a seventeen-week limited engagement.

Neil Patrick Harris (1973–)
From child actor to Broadway star to *How I Met Your Mother* and beyond, Neil Patrick Harris has a long and storied career with many more stories yet to come. He started out getting small roles on television and in film before landing a series of his very own, 1989's *Doogie Howser, M.D.*, in which Harris played a young genius who becomes a teenage doctor. After the success of *Doogie*, Harris took a break from TV and found further success on. There he played a host of roles, from the Emcee in *Cabaret* to the Balladeer in *Assassins*. But it was his turn in the 2014 revival of *Hedwig and the Angry Inch* that brought him his first Tony Award. Harris returned to television in the

very successful series *How I Met Your Mother*, where he played Barney Stinson, a very randy heterosexual.

Patti Harrison (1990–)

A comedian and writer shaking up the world of comedy with her funny and insightful jokes and her representation of trans people, Harrison describes her stand-up as being an "evil shitty person" on stage. Her talents have landed her all over the landscape, with appearances on shows like *High Maintenance*, *Shrill*, and *Full Frontal with Samantha Bee*. Harrison made the leap to the big screen in 2021 with the independent film *Together Together*, starring opposite funny man Ed Helms.

Lorenz Hart (1895–1943)

Hart was one of the most prolific lyricists of the Great American Songbook. Without him, we wouldn't have songs like "My Funny Valentine," "Blue Moon," or "The Lady Is a Tramp." With music by his writing partner, Richard Rodgers, Hart wrote some of the most memorable songs in the American canon. Hart and Rodgers met at Columbia University and almost immediately started writing together, though temperamentally they couldn't be more different. Rodgers was steady and reserved, where Hart was more boisterous. Hart struggled with depression and alcoholism; much of his drinking had to do with his discomfort with his own homosexuality. The team got their first great success in writing the score for *The Garrick Gaieties* in 1925. From then on, Rodgers and Hart went on to write twenty-six musicals for Broadway, introducing songs like "Where or When," "Bewitched, Bothered and Bewildered," and "With a Song in My Heart," to name just a fraction of their output. The team finally broke up in 1943 and Hart died not long after. Though Rodgers is often remembered for his hopeful musicals with Hammerstein, the music he wrote with Hart has a sexy, sleek sophistication that has never been repeated.

Harry Hay (1912–2002)

The faerie godfather of the gay rights movement, Harry Hay was a constant and controversial voice for LGBTQ+ equality. Perhaps *equality* is the wrong word, because Hay sought more than a simple equality—he actually sought for LGBTQ+ people to find their own voice and lifestyle without an assimilation with heterosexual life. Hay got his start as an actor but quickly found that his passion for politics was stronger than his lust for the stage. He got involved with the early days of the socialist party in the United States. Taking on these ideas about organization, Hay was one of the founders of the Mattachine Society, one of the first organizations in the United States fighting for the rights of homosexuals. After years with the organization, Hay left to pursue more radical avenues for

Hedwig and
Harry Hay

gay liberation. After meeting his life partner, John Burnside, Hay decided to found the Radical Faeries with John and Don Kilhefner in 1979. This movement was Hay's way of reconnecting to our "sissy" selves outside the bar culture so prevalent in the 1970s. Hay stayed involved with the Faeries and gay politics until his death in 2002.

Todd Haynes (1961–)

Haynes is a queer director and screenwriter who has taken on the epic and the "woman's" picture and won with a gorgeous eye for style and character. He also had an ability to reintroduce queer narratives into the larger world of cinema. He got his start with a student film called *Superstar: The Karen Carpenter Story* in 1987. The short experimental film was done mostly with Barbie dolls and told the tragic story of 1970s singer Karen Carpenter. From there he made his big-screen debut with 1991's *Poison*, which received heaps of praise and enabled him to make *The Velvet*

Goldmine in 1998, which was a huge hit that year at the Cannes Film Festival. From there, Haynes returned to a love of the costume epic, with 2002's *Far from Heaven*, a remake for television of the novel *Mildred Pierce* in 2011, and 2015's *Carol*. Haynes continues to present queer stories with the truth, honesty, and glamour that are the best Hollywood has to offer.

Heathers

A dark comedy about high school with quotable lines like "What's your damage, Heather?" and "Fuck me gently with a chainsaw," *Heathers* has become a camp favorite. This cult-classic film starring Winona Ryder and Christian Slater debuted in 1988. And while its subject matter about a murderous teen rampage at a high school may seem deeply disconnected from the modern era of school shootings, *Heathers* stands up as a daring critique on teendom and the pursuit of fitting in.

Hedwig and the Angry Inch

Everyone knows the wig—the huge, blond Farrah wig, played out to its camp conclusion. It's as memorable as the winning performance of John Cameron Mitchell in the role he wrote and created. Mitchell also directed the musical film. *Hedwig* originally began as an off-Broadway runaway hit and made the transition to the screen look beautiful. Hedwig was a young boy in East Germany who met a handsome American GI. The American convinces

Hedwig to get sexual reassignment surgery so they can marry and head to America together. Hedwig does, but the surgery does not go well, leaving Hedwig with their "angry inch." Hedwig is left alone in America to find some love on their way to rock stardom. *Hedwig* built a strong cult following over the years for its singable songs and beautiful message about self-love. Its cartoon section, illustrating the song "The Origin of Love," is perhaps one of the most tattooable moments in film across the LGBTQ+ community.

Heels on Wheels

A traveling band of queer femmes bringing art and anarchy to a town near you, the Heels on Wheels crew, founded by Damien Luxe and Heather Ács, were a group of queer femme performers who traveled by van and spread the word about queer visibility and representation. The group always had a changing roster, finding new talent and voices to expand its representation and outreach, but the principles of daring and honesty remained at its core. Luxe and Acs wrote about their experiences and curated a book, *Glitter & Grit*, which won a Lambda Literary Award in 2015.

Heklina

A mother of San Francisco drag who has been slaying them for decades with his bawdy humor, Heklina started the show *Trannyshack* at the Stud in 1996, where it was a huge hit for many years. While the name later became controversial—the show was renamed *Mother*—Heklina's talent as a performer and producer was never in doubt. Heklina continues to be a major force in San Francisco drag, working with Peaches Christ in his productions, and with D'Arcy Drollinger and his productions at Oasis.

Essex Hemphill (1957–1995)

Hemphill was a poet and activist whose work continues to challenge and charm audiences today with its questions about masculinity and the dignity of queer Blackness. He started the *Nethula Journal of Contemporary Literature*, hoping to give more attention to exciting voices in the Black community. His poetry was published extensively, but it was his work with filmmaker Marlon Riggs that is most often remembered today. Together, the two collaborated on the documentary *Tongues Untied* in 1989 and *Black Is . . . Black Ain't* in 1992. Hemphill became a fierce activist during the AIDS crisis, and much of his work is reflective of his fight for the love of his community. His powerful and impassioned verse still shocks readers, though a major republishing of his work has not appeared since his AIDS-related death in 1995.

Jerry Herman (1931–2019)

If you have a Broadway diva, and that diva needs an entrance and an eleven o'clock number, you need Jerry Herman. The king of the hummable, crowd-pleasing tune, Herman has written some of Broadway's biggest hits. He started writing songs for off-Broadway revues, where he met future collaborators like Charles Nelson Reilly and Phyllis Newman. His first major success was 1964's *Hello, Dolly!* with Carol Channing. He followed this up with *Mame*, starring Angela Lansbury. After *Mame*, Herman wrote musicals with beautiful scores like *Dear World, Mack & Mabel,* and *The Grand Tour*, all of which failed to live up to his blockbusters. It was 1983's *La Cage aux Folles*, written with Harvey Fierstein, that put Herman back on the map and solidified his legendary status. For his contribution to the musical theatre, Herman has won two Tony Awards and the Kennedy Center Honor.

Patricia Highsmith (1921–1995)
Death, intrigue, and the dark rumblings beneath the surface all figure into the works of the secretive writer Patricia Highsmith. Her first novel, *Strangers on a Train*, was a huge success in 1950 and was adapted into a movie by Alfred Hitchcock. After *Strangers*, Highsmith wrote about her sexuality in *The Price of Salt*, under the pen name Claire Morgan, and pushed the art form of lesbian fiction forward not only by her brilliant and personal writing, but also in the simple fact that the

book ended happily. It was much later turned into the film *Carol*, starring Cate Blanchett. Highsmith's greatest literary achievements are often seen to be her Ripley novels. She created the sinister and charming Tom Ripley in her 1955 novel, *The Talented Mr. Ripley*. She would go on to write five Ripley novels in all. The first three would be adapted by Anthony Minghella for his 1999 film of the same name starring Matt Damon, Jude Law, and Gwyneth Paltrow.

Murray Hill
Showbiz, baby. He's the king of the one-liner and a throwback to the great acts of the 1950s and '60s, when the martinis were dry and the jokes were a little blue. Murray Hill is a drag king extraordinaire, whose slick yet down-on-his-luck performing style has made him a legend in the field. A king of the Lower East Side and East Village, Hill has toured the world as a host and emcee for many burlesque shows—most famously for Dita Von Teese. His style is warm and gregarious, and while being a mainstay of New York at Joe's Pub within the Public Theater, he's also appeared on television, most recently in a music video for Countess Luann of *The Real Housewives of New York City* franchise.

Magnus Hirschfeld (1868–1935)
You may think Dr. Ruth was the first little German doctor wanting to know

all about your sex life, but you'd be missing out on the infamous Magnus Hirschfeld. He was one of the first champions for gay and transgender rights in the world. Hirschfeld was horrified by the suicide of seemingly healthy and vibrant people who could not reconcile their homosexuality with society as a whole. He started writing pamphlets on the subject of homosexuality in the late 1890s and actually brought a bill before the Reichstag in 1898 trying to repeal Paragraph 175, a law that made homosexuality a crime. He was an outspoken supporter of the rights of women and pushed for a cultural reexamination of homosexuality. In 1919, Hirschfeld opened his Institut für Sexualwissenschaft in Berlin. The institute housed Hirschfeld's extensive collection of sexual artifacts and research and also became a safe haven for homosexual and trans people to learn about themselves and their history. The institute became a target of the Nazi Party and was burned to the ground in 1933. Hirschfeld died in exile in France in 1935.

HIV/AIDS

The human immunodeficiency virus initially was thought to first find its way into the human population in 1981, but contemporary research has unearthed much earlier cases. The disease, then unknown, was first mentioned in a *New York Times* article on July 3, 1981, detailing the mysterious death of a number of gay men from a rare form of cancer. Over the next few years, the numbers of cases and deaths began to rise, though little was done in the mainstream media or the political field to draw attention to the growing epidemic. During the 1980s and '90s, millions of people would die from this devastating disease. While the deaths began to slow with the advent of retroviral drugs in the 1990s, the AIDS crisis is still that—a crisis. The advent of Truvada has slowed the rise of infection to a steady rate, but new cases are still part of the community to this day. You may be wondering why HIV/AIDS would be part of a conversation of LGBTQ+ culture, but this disease has left an indelible mark on the LGBTQ+ community. Besides killing a whole generation of artists at the height of their powers, it also killed an audience for whom they wrote and created. But as is always the case with LGBTQ+ people, we made the hurt into something beautiful, and artists began writing and making work about their experiences. AIDS has left its mark and continues to be a source of great pain, but also great triumph, for the community. HIV/AIDS may not be going anywhere for the time being, but neither is our community's commitment to live with dignity and strength in defiance of this horrible disease.

David Hockney (1937–)

An English painter who taught us how to see LA., Hockney has captivated the world with his strong sense of color and stunning portraiture. He attended the Royal College of Art in London during the swinging '60s, and it was in London that Hockney first came in contact with the then thriving pop art scene. In 1964, Hockney moved to Los Angeles, and it was there that he truly begin to create some of the work that would later define him as a painter. His portraits of chic friends and neighbors around their swimming pools—and at times, just the pools themselves—gave Hockney an individual voice as a painter of supreme insight into human relationships and also a master when it came to the subject of light. He never shied away from his homosexuality and gave his gay subjects the same standing and prominence as he did with heterosexual sitters. Since his early days, Hockney has experimented in a host of artistic mediums, including photography, printmaking, collage, and even new technologies that can create the vivid landscapes of our dreams.

Alan Hollinghurst (1954–)

One of the most acclaimed gay writers in modern history, Hollinghurst has become known for his epic gay novels, which place gay characters both in a historical context and as a vital part of the modern world. His first novel, *The Swimming-Pool Library*, was published in 1988 and praised by critics. He followed it with *The Folding Star* in 1994, *The Spell* in 1998, and *The Line of Beauty* in 2004. *The Line of Beauty* won Hollinghurst the Man Booker Prize and was adapted into a miniseries for the BBC in 2006.

Hollywood Babylon

A camp and dishy classic written by experimental filmmaker Kenneth Anger, *Hollywood Babylon* is all about the trashy underbelly behind the glitz and the glamour of Hollywood in its heyday. First published in 1959, the book took aim at many of the biggest scandals and stars of Hollywood and was an instant bestseller, if not a respected piece of nonfiction. The reviews were not good, and in some cases the book got things wrong—Lupe Vélez didn't die in her toilet—but it has become a classic for LGBTQ+ people looking to know the hidden truth behind the Hollywood Story.

Vladimir Horowitz (1903–1989)

Few have achieved the light touch and brilliance that Vladimir Horowitz brought to his playing. That is why even today he is seen as one of the greatest pianists to have ever lived. Horowitz was born in Ukraine and very early on displayed a gift for music. He began training with some of the greatest teachers in Kiev. Horowitz played his first solo recital in 1920 and caused a sensation. He began to tour

Russia, first making it to the West in 1925 and playing his first concert at Carnegie Hall in 1928. From that concert forward, Horowitz was one of the biggest classical music performers in the world. He was a passionate player who excelled with Beethoven and Rachmaninoff, thrilling audiences with his emotional coloring and technical skill. But this passion came at a price. Horowitz struggled with his sexuality and depression throughout his life. Though he married Wanda Toscanini, daughter of the famous conductor, Horowitz was known to many as a homosexual. In the 1960s, he attempted to use psychotherapy to alter his sexuality, and in the 1970s underwent electroshock therapy. With breaks throughout his career to deal with his mental well-being, Horowitz continued to perform until his death in 1989.

Horst P. Horst (1906–1999)

A predecessor to Mapplethorpe in the realm of light, Horst Paul Albert Bohrmann, also known as Horst P. Horst, was a fashion photographer. Horst is known for his exquisitely planned lighting and illumination of his subjects and their style. He originally wanted to be an architect, but after moving to Paris in the 1930s, he became the assistant to fashion photographer Baron George Hoyningen-Huene. He soon showed promise and began his long association with *Vogue* magazine, taking his first

photographs for French *Vogue* in 1931. He befriended the famous and the infamous of his period and photographed many of them, from Noël Coward to Bette Davis. His stylistic use of light and his clarity of insight into his subjects make Horst's work stand out in a period of glorious black-and-white photography. He was a favorite at *Vogue* for decades and continued to work with the magazine until he retired in 1991.

Whitney Houston (1963–2012) `ICON`

The voice of a generation, Whitney Houston was the Queen of Pop, because unlike some other performers of whom that could be said, Whitney Houston had a voice that comes but once in a lifetime. It was lyrical and swift, with an agility and phrasing that can rarely, if ever, be matched. Whitney came on the scene in the early 1980s, with hits like "How Will I Know" and "I Wanna

Whitney Houston and David Hoyle

Dance with Somebody" that skyrocketed her to fame. But it was her 1992 soundtrack to *The Bodyguard* that affirmed her place in musical legend. Houston struggled with drugs and alcohol, and rumors about her own sexuality were prevalent in her early career. She was said to have had a long-time affair with her assistant Robyn Crawford. Houston married singer Bobby Brown and fell further into addiction. She finally succumbed to her addiction in 2012.

Ivo van Hove (1958–)
Using subtext to create violent and often visually brilliant ways of reimagining older works, Hove has a keen eye for design. The Belgian-born director started writing and directing his own works in his native country, working as artistic director for multiple theatres before assuming the directorship of the Toneelgroep Amsterdam in 2001. He has specialized in reimaginings of theatre classics, stretching the boundaries to find new attempts at meaning. He began presenting his work off-Broadway in the late 1990s, winning Obie Awards for his takes on *More Stately Mansions* by Eugene O'Neill and *Hedda Gabler* by Henrik Ibsen. His greatest success outside the Netherlands came with 2015's *A View from the Bridge* by Arthur Miller. He continues to present bold and innovative works of theatre classics, most recently with Miller's *The Crucible* and the musical *West Side Story.*

Brittany Howard (1988–)
The raw vocals and sultry seduction of Brittany Howard's sound is unmistakable. It was one of the main factors that put her and her band, Alabama Shakes, on the charts in 2012 and blew the band up with the release of their second album, *Sound & Color*, in 2015. Howard has sung everywhere from *Saturday Night Live* to Lollapalooza with Paul McCartney. In 2019, she announced a solo album, *Jaime*, which has let fans into a deeper side of her artistry and made us all only hungry for more.

David Hoyle (1962–)
With his outlandish costuming and punk-inspired makeup, David Hoyle has created a look and tone all his own. A wise wit in the tradition of Wilde, Hoyle creates weird and wonderful works in cabaret, comedy, and film. Originally performing under the character name of the Divine David, an "anti-drag queen," Hoyle became a bright spot on the landscape of British television in the late 1990s. The price of this success left Hoyle a bit depleted and he returned to his home in Manchester to deal with his mental health. Hoyle returned to performing and television in 2005. He's become a mainstay of the Royal Vauxhall Tavern in London, where he debuts his original shows like 2009's *Dave's Drop-In*,

and 2012's *The Ugly Spirit.* Hoyle's also moved into the realm of filmmaking, writing, directing, and starring in 2010's *Uncle David.* His work is known and enjoyed for his deep political satire and cutting wit, as he takes aim against a consumer society bent on its own destruction. A proud and brilliant voice in the fight for LGBTQ+ rights, Hoyle also advocates for mental health in and out of the community.

Rock Hudson (1925–1985)
The great heartthrob of the 1950s and 1960s, Hudson was a man's man who defined tall, dark, and handsome for a generation. He achieved star status with 1954's *Magnificent Obsession.* He continued with a string of hits like *One Desire* and *All That Heaven Allows* in 1955, but Hudson's true crowning as a star came in 1956 with *Giant*, opposite Elizabeth Taylor. The two would remain friends throughout Hudson's life. His sexuality was always whispered about, even at the height of his fame, which caused him to enter into a disastrous marriage with Phyllis Gates, the secretary of his agent, Henry Willson, in 1955. The marriage ended in divorce after three years. Hudson is most remembered today for his work with Doris Day in a series of romantic comedies, like 1959's *Pillow Talk*, 1961's *Lover Come Back*, and 1964's *Send Me No Flowers.* In the 1970s, he made the transition to television with the huge hit *McMillan & Wife*, which ran from 1971 to 1977.

He joined the cast of *Dynasty* in 1984, but by then signs of Hudson's AIDS diagnosis began to show. As rumors swirled about his condition, he was supported by lifelong friends Doris Day and Elizabeth Taylor. Hudson died of complications from AIDS in 1985, and it is said that it was his death that directly led to Elizabeth Taylor's crusade against AIDS.

Holly Hughes (1955–)
Hughes has been a performance artist and teacher for over forty years and was one of the famous NEA Four. Her work is often autobiographical and she has a poetic sensibility that she often undercuts or bolsters with humor. One of her most famous works, *Clit Notes*, explores her own sexual awakening in a society that she views as oppressive. Her work has always had a deep political leaning, and long before she became the subject of the politics, she and three other performance artists who proposed grants from the National Endowment for the Arts were vetoed. Following the election of Donald Trump, Hughes created new works lambasting the misogynist in the White House.

Langston Hughes (1902–1967)
One of the most treasured writers of the twentieth century and a major figure in the Harlem Renaissance, Hughes was widely respected for his poetry, which focused on Black life and elevated Black artforms, like the blues, to stand on an equal footing with the

forms of European writers. One of Hughes's most famous poems, *Harlem*, asks, "What happens to a dream deferred?" and is often quoted to this day in reference to Black life in America. A strong proponent of civil rights, Hughes was an outspoken activist for the rights of Black people in the United States and around the world. Much has been speculated about Hughes's sexuality; during his lifetime he was often assumed to be a homosexual, but to this day there's very little proof. Queer artist and filmmaker Isaac Julien made his now classic *Looking for Langston* in 1989 to explore Hughes's legacy as a Black LGBTQ+ artist.

Langston Hughes

Peter Hujar (1934–1987)

Often considered one of the greatest photographers of the twentieth century, Peter Hujar was known for his brilliant use of light and the reserved hilarity he captured in some of the greatest personalities of his time. Originally a commercial photographer, Hujar always wanted to chronicle the vibrant gay life that was going on around him. He started taking portraits of friends and lovers like David Wojnarowicz, Fran Lebowitz, and Ethyl Eichelberger. One of his most famous portraits, *Candy Darling on Her Deathbed*, was used as the cover art for Antony and the Johnsons' album *I Am a Bird Now*. Hujar died of complications from AIDS in 1987.

Alberta Hunter (1895–1984)

Chirpin' the blues was a term used in the 1920s for softer-sounding singers than the boisterous Bessie Smith or her "Moaner" contemporaries. Alberta Hunter was one of those singers—soft, yet hard when she needed to be, with a sweet voice that had all kinds of sunshine in it. She sang in bordellos and nightclubs and formed a following so strong that she was able to be a signed headliner at the Panama Club for five years. She toured Europe for the first time in 1917 and found the European lifestyle and sense of freedom for Black artists more to her speed. She recorded for all the major American labels during the 1920s, but by the late '20s, she relocated to Europe for an extended stay. She returned to the States before World War II and continued to perform, but when her mother died in 1957, she decided to leave the business. She worked as a nurse until retiring in her eighties and making a celebrated comeback to music in the late 1970s. Her later recordings are some of the most beloved in her long and storied career.

Tab Hunter (1931–2018)

When it comes to clean-cut heart-throbs, it's hard to beat Tab Hunter. With his chiseled good looks, affable smile, and presence, Hunter made most of America's teenage girls swoon with lust, and a few of its boys. He made his film debut in 1950 and quickly attracted a lot of attention. He signed with Warner Bros. in 1955 and also started to release music. He had two big hits with the songs "Young Love" and "Ninety-Nine Ways." Hunter was a teen idol for most of the decade with big movies like *Battle Cry*, *The Sea Chase*, and *Damn Yankees*. He even tried his hand at Broadway playing opposite Tallulah Bankhead in Tennessee Williams's *The Milk Train Doesn't Stop Here Anymore* in 1964. In the 1980s, he had a mini revival, being cast in John Waters's *Polyester* opposite drag superstar Divine, and then shepherding another project with Divine in 1985's *Lust in the Dust*. Later in life, Hunter was open about his sexuality and his time in Hollywood, writing his memoir *Tab Hunter Confidential*. He talked about his relationship with *Psycho* star Anthony Perkins, and with his partner of thirty-five years, Allan Glaser.

Juliana Huxtable (1987–)

A performance artist, writer, and DJ who infuses her work with a stunning portrayal of life and love as a trans woman of color, Huxtable breaks the paradigm of the merely confessional by creating work and environments in which audiences are forced to confront their own truths. Huxtable's work has been featured at the New Museum in New York, as well as Project Native Informant in London. Huxtable is the author of two books, 2017's *Mucus in My Pineal Gland*, a book of poetry, and 2017's *Life*, a bilingual science fiction novel written with artist Hannah Black.

I is for...

Imperial Court

Imperial Court

One of the largest LGBTQ+ groups in the world, the Imperial Court was founded in San Francisco in 1965 by José Sarria. Used to connect communities around the country, the organization was founded to raise money for LGBTQ+ charities and causes. Each court in each area crowns its own monarchs as a symbol and titular head for the organization. The court system holds pageants and fundraisers, but their main objective is uniting the local community around charities that need their support. Diamonds and duty. It's not a bad setup.

In the Life

For twenty years, this was a show—on public television of all places—dedicated solely to the lives and stories of LGBTQ+ people. Created by John Scagliotti in 1991, it was a news and special-interest show that told stories from and for the LGBTQ+ community. It premiered in 1992 and ran until finally signing off in 2012. It is the longest-running LGBTQ+ show in television history, and garnered huge acclaim. With a myriad of hosts from Harvey Fierstein to Kate Clinton, *In the Life* is a milestone and a beautiful time capsule for our history and stories.

Indigo Girls

This singer-songwriter duo of Amy Ray and Emily Saliers produced a series of hits and continues to draw a wide and loyal fan base to this day. Ray and Saliers met in college and began performing together, releasing their first album, *Strange Fire*, in 1987. Their unique sound of tight harmony and interesting and honest lyrics made them stand out in the 1980s music scene, and as the '90s approached, the Indigo Girls became a band to pay attention to. With songs like "Closer to Fine" and "Galileo," the Indigo Girls were raking in the hits. Their self-titled album in 1989 went platinum, and they continued with a flurry of hit records from 1992's *Rites of Passage* to 1994's *Swamp Ophelia*. Both Ray and Saliers are gay, and their sexuality is an intrinsic part of their music. They continue to release albums and solo projects, tour to packed houses, and are outspoken activists for LGBTQ+ rights, the environment, and the rights of women.

William Inge (1913–1973)

No one has ever written with more brilliance or more heart about the quiet desperation that lives in people from the Midwest than William Inge. Throughout the 1950s, he was head-to-head with his friend and rival Tennessee Williams for America's favorite playwright. He wrote his first play in 1947, but his first hit was 1950's *Come Back, Little Sheba*. The play was a major success, and so was the movie adaptation in 1952. A string of hits followed with 1953's *Picnic*, which won Inge the Pulitzer Prize, and *Bus Stop*, which became a star vehicle for Marilyn Monroe. He finished the decade with another hit in *The Dark at the Top of the Stairs*. In 1961, Inge won an Oscar for his original screenplay *Splendor in the Grass*, starring Natalie Wood and Warren Beatty and directed by Elia Kazan. He also wrote novels during this period, but there had trouble finding an audience. Inge struggled with alcohol and depression throughout his life and finally took his own life in 1973.

International Male

While some boys ogled *Victoria's Secret*, other boys went right for *International Male*, the mail-order catalog that provided men with just enough scintillation to be legally and tastefully slipped in their mailbox any day of the week. Starting publication in 1970, the catalog was a treasure trove of hunky chiseled men wearing almost laughable attempts at casual wear—even for the period. Sheer taffeta camisoles over leather pants, oversized sweaters in lavenders and pinks. The clothing on view was an attempt to get American men, mostly gay men, to step outside their comfort zone and try something daring and outrageous. But then came the underwear section. All varieties and styles, none very practical, but all very sexy. The catalog became a staple of gay life for many years and featured the early modeling work of famous faces like Shemar Moore, Reichen Lehmkuhl, and Cameron Mathison. A documentary about the impact of the early days of the magazine, *All Man*, directed by Bryan Darling and Jesse Finley Reed, was released in 2020.

It's a Sin

Russel T. Davies has brought so many gay stories to television, but 2021's *It's a Sin* may be his most personal, and with the biggest launch in Channel 4's history, it may be his most successful. The show tells the story of a group of friends finding their way in London of the 1980s. Starring Olly Alexander of the band Years & Years, *It's a Sin* chronicled the early days of the AIDS crisis in London, shedding light on the fears, misinformation, and ultimately the coming together of a community fighting for its life. *It's a Sin* is a harrowing but often hilarious look at young people dealing with life-and-death consequences just as life is beginning.

Christopher Isherwood as Sally Bowles

Christopher Isherwood (1904–1986)

We couldn't ever "come to the cabaret" if it weren't for Isherwood. A giant in LGBTQ+ literature, his works are universally heralded as some of the best writing of the twentieth century. Isherwood was born in England but found the atmosphere there too stifling for his budding sexuality. So with his friends W. H. Auden and Stephen Spender, he went to Berlin. In the Weimar period, Berlin was known as a center for artistic and sexual experimentation—or as Isherwood so brilliantly put it, "Berlin meant Boys." While in Berlin, he met actress and cabaret singer Jean Ross, who would later become the model for his character Sally Bowles. Though he did not write openly about his sexuality in his Berlin novels, *Mr Norris Changes Trains* in 1935 and *Goodbye to Berlin* in 1939—now known as *The Berlin Stories*—his sexuality exists in hints and details throughout. He went on to fill in the gay parts the stories left out in his book *Christopher and His Kind* in 1976. *The Berlin Stories* were first adapted for the stage as the play *I Am a Camera* in 1951. The play was later adapted to the musical *Cabaret* in 1966. Isherwood continued to write novels and for the movies in the 1950s. It was in Los Angeles during this period that he met his life partner, artist Don Bachardy, in 1953. Despite a thirty-year age difference, the two remained partners until Isherwood's death in 1984. A documentary about their life together, *Chris & Don*, was released in 2007.

James Ivory (1928–) and Ismail Merchant (1936–2005)

The longest-running partnership in independent film history, James Ivory and Ismail Merchant created a world and style of beautiful filmmaking around classics by E. M. Forster. The two met in 1956, at a showing of James Ivory's documentary *The Sword and the Flute*. The two became partners in life and in business, forming Merchant Ivory Productions. Throughout their career, they produced more than forty films, often working with the writer Ruth Prawer Jhabvala. Their films are marked by a brilliant sense of taste and attention to detail. Some of their biggest successes came with literary adaptations and period pieces. Their 1985 adaptation of Forster's *A Room with a View* was a huge hit starring Helena Bonham Carter and Maggie Smith. The film was nominated for Best Picture and won three other Oscars for Best Adapted Screenplay, Best Art Direction, and Costume Design. They followed it by adapting Forster's only gay novel, *Maurice*, in 1987. The team went on to create hits like *Howards End* in 1992 and *The Remains of the Day* in 1993. The team worked and lived together until Merchant's death in 2005. Following the death of his partner, Ivory continued to work in film, winning an Oscar for his adapted screenplay for 2017's *Call Me By Your Name*. James Ivory became the oldest person to ever win an Oscar at age eighty-nine.

J is for ...

Paul Jabara (1948–1992)

The man behind disco hits like "It's Raining Men" from the Weather Girls, Jabara was a performer and personality that lit up the disco era with his great sense of play and camp. He got his start as a performer on Broadway in shows like *Hair* and *Jesus Christ Superstar.* Jabara fell in love with the dance beats of disco and found that he had a knack for writing. He wrote the music for the first disco musical, an infamous flop, *Rachael Lily Rosenbloom*, which closed in previews. Jabara began writing for the young Donna Summer, and the two became friends. Jabara released his first solo album, *Shut Out*, which included a duet with Summers. He went on to release three more solo records and became a staple on *American Bandstand* for his outrageous sense of fun. His biggest success came with the song "Last Dance," written for Donna Summer to sing on the *Thank God It's Friday* movie soundtrack. The song went on to win the Oscar and Golden Globe for Best Original Song. As the disco lights faded, so did Jabara. He died of complications from AIDS in 1992.

Marc Jacobs (1963–)

A staple of American fashion for almost three decades who continues to push the barriers of fashion-forward looks and stylish creation, Jacobs grew up in New York City and began winning awards for his design while still in high school. In 1983, while attending Parsons School of Design, he met his business partner Robert Duffy and they started their first line together. In 1986, he designed his first line under his own label, Marc Jacobs. That lead to working with the Perry Ellis line, but Jacobs always wanted to have his own unique vision out in the public. In 1997, Jacobs was chosen as creative director of Louis Vuitton. He brought a breath of fresh air into the company, collaborating with popular musicians and artists to modernize the classic Vuitton look. In 2001, Jacobs introduced the ready-to-wear line, Marc by Marc Jacobs. In 2013, Jacobs left Vuitton to concentrate fully on his own lines. Jacobs is a supporter of many charities, including his "Protect the Skin You're In" campaign to fight against skin cancer. Jacobs continues to be an inspiration in American design, combining his vision of multiple styles and influences in a way that always looks purely American and fabulously Jacobs.

Derek Jarman (1942–1994)

The word *visionary* gets tossed around, but it is the most fitting when it comes to this designer, film director, writer, and activist. Derek Jarman gave the world new ways to see and understand stories they knew, and some they'd overlooked. In 1976, he made his first feature, *Sebastiane*. The film was an erotic retelling of the story of St. Sebastian with a script all in Latin. He followed it up with the punk-fantasia *Jubilee* in 1977 and *The Tempest* in 1979. His films became known for their visual opulence and mixture of styles and references. In 1986, Jarman made *Caravaggio*, a biopic of the famous Italian painter, and found a muse in Tilda Swinton. It was her film debut. They went on to make the surreal *The Last of England* in 1987, *War Requiem* in 1989, and *Edward II* in 1991, in which Jarman adapted Christopher Marlowe's script to reflect the modern plight of the gay community in its fight against AIDS. Jarman was diagnosed with HIV in 1986 and became an outspoken advocate for the LGBTQ+ community and AIDS research. His final film, *Blue*, in 1993, is a personal statement about the end of life, as Jarman had lost his sight. Throughout Jarman's career, he kept extensive diaries and wrote about his artistic process and the political landscape around him. Jarman died in 1994 of complications from AIDS.

Marlon James (1970–)

Perhaps one of the most respected novelists in the modern cannon. Marlon James continues to leave his readers spellbound with his stunning accounts of Jamaican lives. James is a native Jamaican and writes about his homeland, examining the history, examining the history of his birthplace in ways that have not yet been given voice in modern fiction. Since his critically acclaimed debut *John Crow's Devil* in 2005, James has continued to build momentum with multiple awards for his novels, *The Book of Night Women* released in 2009, *A Brief History of Seven Killings* in 2014, and most recently 2019's *Black Leopard, Red Wolf*, which was a finalist for the National Book Award for Fiction.

Lady Java (1943–)

It often takes a drag queen to get things done, and when it came to breaking not only the color barrier, but the gender barrier in Los Angeles in the 1960s and '70s, it took trans icon and performer Lady Java. Lady Java began her transition at a young age and began performing as a female impersonator under the name Sir Lady Java. She was a wildly successful act, but in 1967 when police started raiding her performances, Lady Java took to the street and the courts. She picketed outside comedian Redd Foxx's LA club, with the support of Foxx himself, and called on the ACLU to help her file

Lady Java

suit against the LAPD. Though Java's case was eventually thrown out of court, the flimsy statute on which she was arrested was overturned in 1969. Lady Java continued to perform until the 1980s, when a stroke limited her from appearing onstage.

Karla Jay (1947–)

An activist and writer who has been there since the beginning, fighting the good fight in the feminist movement, Jay was part of the so-called Lavender Menace, a group of gay women within the feminist movement that leaders like Betty Friedan thought would give the wrong impression of what feminism was all about. Jay and her contemporaries were undeterred and continued their fight for the rights of women and LGBTQ+ people. Jay has written several books, memoirs, and historical essays that tell lesbian and LGBTQ+ stories in bold and exacting ways.

Jazz Jennings (2000–)

A reality star and LGBTQ+ activist who came out as transgender while still a young child, Jazz became the face of trans children around the world when she started making videos for YouTube. These videos eventually led to her own reality show, *I Am Jazz*, in 2015. On the show, Jazz is completely candid about her life as a trans woman. Dating, love, transition surgery, and the acceptance of family and friends are all part of Jazz's journey, which she shares with her public. Jazz has become an out and proud advocate for the LGBTQ+ community and is never afraid to address issues concerning transition and the challenges facing trans youth.

Jobriath (1946–1983)

Glam rock took a gay turn when it turned to the superstar that was Jobriath. At a time when Bowie was lighting the way to an androgynous future, Jobriath, born Bruce Wayne Campbell, was being touted as the next big thing. As Jobriath's manager, Jerry Brandt put it, "Elvis, the Beatles, and Jobriath." Jobriath was signed to a two-album deal by David Geffen and went into the studio to record his first album, the self-titled *Jobriath*. Billboards touted the coming of a new rock god, and everyone prepared for the world to change in the wake. When the final album was released, most reviews were good, but many reviewers were turned off by the extremity of the marketing campaign and turned against the record. Sales were slow, and only got slower when Jobriath starting appearing publicly. While other rockers could play the game of are-they-or-aren't-they, he was a little too open for America to accept. His second album appeared in 1974, *Creatures of the Street*, but sales dipped and the legend that was Jobriath was no more. He changed his name to Cole Berlin and became a piano-bar performer, living in the rooftop apartment of the Chelsea Hotel. He died of complications from AIDS in 1983.

Jobriath and Elton John

Elton John (1947–)

Often seen as the grand high queen of the gay cultural scene, and with good reason, Elton John is one of the most successful musicians and composers of the twentieth century, with most of the major music awards under his belt, a knighthood, a Kennedy Center Honor, and even a Disney Legends Award. He also has an international AIDS charity that continues to raise millions of dollars for the fight against HIV and AIDS. He's been out and proud for a very long time, all the while maintaining an enormous popularity and following around the world. With his outlandish costumes and driving beats, he was the highest-grossing singer-songwriter of the 1970s, with hits like "Rocket Man," "Tiny Dancer," "Your

Song," and "Bennie and the Jets," to name a few. The hits kept coming in the 1980s, and so did a newfound openness about his homosexuality. John first came out as bisexual in 1976, then came out again as gay in 1988. A songwriter of enormous talent, John went on to conquer the musical with his film soundtrack to Disney's *The Lion King*, which then transferred to Broadway to become one of the longest-running musicals in Broadway history. He's followed it up with hits like *Aida* and *Billy Elliot*. There are a multitude of moments to remember in the illustrious career of Elton John, from his tender rendition of "Candle in the Wind" at the funeral of his dear friend Princess Diana to his final tour, launched in 2018, as John decided to leave live performance behind. There's a good reason why Elton John is thought of as not just gay royalty, but as a superstar of music around the world.

Jasper Johns (1930–)

There are few artists who have delved into an understanding of what America is with such subtle insight and brilliant simplicity as Jasper Johns. A titan in the art world who has smoothly transitioned between abstract expressionism to pop art to neo-Dada, Jasper Johns has continued to reveal and reinvent himself in the art world. Johns grew up in Augusta, Georgia, and moved to New York in 1954, where he met artist Robert Rauschenberg. The two fell in love and began a partnership that lasted for many years. Though they were outwardly closeted to the macho art world of the 1950s and '60s, the two were very close and often critiqued each other's creations as both pushed the limits of the abstract expressionism. Johns painted his most famous work, *Flag*, that first year in New York but continued to push himself outside the realms of what painting could do and be in the post–Second World War world. He's made work in many arenas, such as sculpture and printmaking, but it is his painting that continues to draw attention and admiration.

Marsha P. Johnson (1945–1992)

The patron saint of Christopher Street, Marsha "Pay-It-No-Mind" Johnson was a presence and outspoken champion of the LGBTQ+ community for years. Though it is often said that she started the Stonewall Riots, by her own admission she didn't get to the bar until 2 a.m.—after the riots had started. That said, she was a loud voice and rallying cry during the riots. With her friend Sylvia Rivera, she started STAR, the Street Transvestite Action Revolutionaries. In 1972, Johnson and Rivera established the STAR House to help street kids, many of whom, like Johnson, worked as sex workers to get on their feet and find places to live. By most accounts and friends, Johnson had a hard life, often homeless

Marsha P. Johnson

and surviving on very little, but she got by on the kindness of a multitude of friends in the Village. However, her hardships never imputed on her activism. Johnson always looked for ways to help her community, becoming involved in ACT UP in the 1980s and their fight against AIDS. She eventually moved into the apartment of fellow activist Randy Wicker in 1980, and stayed there off and on until her death. Johnson was found in the Hudson River in 1992, and though her death was originally seen as a suicide, evidence later came to the fore that made some believe Johnson was murdered. A film about her death, *The Death and Life of Marsha P. Johnson*, was released in 2017. In 2019, New York State announced it would honor both Johnson and Rivera with monuments near the Stonewall Bar on Christopher Street.

Bill T. Jones (1952–)

Jones is a director and choreographer who has been making work that pushes the limits of dance and physical storytelling for more than thirty years. Jones met his lover and collaborator, Arnie Zane, while at Binghamton University in 1971. The two began working together almost immediately, relying heavily on improvisation to find their particular dance voice. Jones was a dancer of style and great movement who wanted to bring words and story into his dance pieces. Zane was a photographer who gave the work its keen visual sense and use of light. The two collaborated until Zane's death in 1988. In 1994, Jones created *Still/Here*, a controversial dance piece dealing with Jones's own story of becoming HIV-positive. He began choreographing for other companies and eventually brought his talents to the Broadway stage with hits like *Fela!* and *Spring Awakening*. He has been awarded almost every major award in dance and theatre, including the MacArthur Fellowship, Tony Awards, and the Kennedy Center Honor.

Cleve Jones (1954–)

A longtime activist for LGBTQ+ rights who got his start with Harvey Milk, Jones moved to San Francisco in the 1970s, looking for a place in the world. He found it in the Castro. Milk saw in young Cleve a determination and drive that he knew would be important to the fight for gay liberation. While still a student, Jones worked on Milk's campaign and also fought the infamous Briggs Initiative, a bill that would make it illegal for LGBTQ+ people to work in schools. A fire was lit within the young Jones, who knew that activism would be a lifelong pursuit. After the death of Harvey Milk, Jones continued to fight for the rights of the LGBTQ+ community. With the outbreak of the AIDS crisis in the 1980s, Jones focused his work on the survival of gay people. In

1983, he co-founded the San Francisco AIDS Foundation. It was when doing this work for a community in deep mourning that Jones first came up with the idea for the AIDS Memorial Quilt. He made the first panel in 1987. Slowly but surely, panels began to pour in from around San Francisco and the country as people mourned the thousands of friends and lovers lost to the plague. The quilt now stands as the largest piece of community folk art in the world, with panels commemorating over eighty-five thousand victims of AIDS. The quilt was laid out on the National Mall in 1996. The Names Project, which handles the quilt, was nominated for the Nobel Peace Prize in 1989. Jones continued his fight for LGBTQ+ rights, fighting against California's Prop 8 and working with the UNITE HERE labor movement. Jones wrote about his life in activism in the book *When We Rise: My Life in the Movement*, which was adapted for television by Dustin Lance Black in 2017.

Grace Jones (1948–) ICON

A recording artist and actress of incredible power, Grace Jones is a force of nature. How many sixty-years-olds can sing before millions, all the while hula-hooping without missing a beat? With her iconic short haircut and haunting stare, Grace Jones has been pushing art and audiences for decades. Jones became a darling of disco that transitioned to the synth dance hits of the 1980s with songs like "Pull Up to the Bumper," "La Vie En Rose," and "Slave to the Rhythm." A fashion icon, she has been the star and muse of many contemporary designers, like Yves Saint Laurent and Kenzo. Her work with artist Keith Haring is indicative of a career that has reached out and embraced creativity and vitality since the beginning. Jones has appeared in a number of films including *Conan the Destroyer*, the Bond classic *A View to a Kill*, and *Boomerang*. In 2015, Jones released her memoir, *I'll Never Write My Memoirs*, followed up in 2017 by the documentary *Grace Jones: Bloodlight and Bami* in 2017.

Owen Jones (1984–)

Gay voices are very often the voice of dissent when it comes to politics, and Owen Jones is one of the most exciting and witty voices of dissent out there today. Jones started writing about left-wing politics, especially having to deal with class, in 2011 in his first book, *Chavs: The Demolition of the Working Class*. The book was an instant hit and set Jones on his way to become a favorite voice for progressive causes in the United Kingdom. Jones continues to write books as well as a weekly column for *The Guardian*, championing progressive causes. In 2019, after posting on Twitter about his birthday celebrations, he and his friends were assaulted by a group of right-wing extremists. Though Jones was relatively unhurt, it became a news story about the disintegrating political debate in the United Kingdom and around the world.

Saeed Jones

Saeed Jones (1985–)
Jones is a writer, host, poet, and former executive editor of culture at BuzzFeed. His 2014 collection of poems, *Prelude to Bruise*, was heralded as a masterpiece, winning critical praise and recognition from PEN/Joyce Osterweil and Lambda Literary. Jones has written the memoir *How We Fight for Our Lives*.

Leslie Jordan (1955–)
It took a year-long quarantine and a series of Instagram videos to prove to the country at large that Leslie Jordan is a national treasure. He has been delighting audiences with his wit, whimsy, and charming honesty for decades. And he's just getting started. He is perhaps best known for his role in Del Shores's *Sordid Lives* as "Brother Boy" Ingram, or as Karen Walker's arch-nemesis Beverley Leslie

on *Will & Grace*. Known as a consummate scene stealer, Jordan moved from his home in Tennessee to Hollywood in 1982 and quickly found work in television, playing a multitude of roles, all with a signature Jordan touch. He's done everything from *Pee-Wee's Playhouse* to *Lois & Clark*, but it wasn't until *Will & Grace* that Jordan began to be properly recognized for the comedic genius that he is. He received an Emmy Award for his role as Beverley Leslie in 2006. But it's not just television where Jordan excels—besides being in the original stage production of *Sordid Lives*, he's also written a series of autobiographical solo plays that he's toured around the country. His recent memoir, *How Y'all Doing*, was released in 2021 to critical and commercial success.

Christine Jorgensen (1926-1989)
The grand dame of American transsexuals, Christine Jorgensen started it all. Jorgensen transitioned as an

Christine Jorgenson

adult in the early 1950s. She traveled to Sweden to have her gender confirmation surgery, and when Jorgensen returned to America she began a press tour to talk about her operation and the lives of transsexual people. Her arrival back in the States was front-page news on the *New York Daily News*, but despite the tawdry way that she was sometimes treated in the press, Jorgensen always handled herself like the lady she was. Jorgensen began a career as a nightclub entertainer and writer, releasing her memoir, *Christine Jorgensen: A Personal Autobiography*, which was a national bestseller and eventually made into a film in 1970.

Julian and Sandy

A sketch of two "fancy men" on the 1965 BBC radio program *Round the Horne*, Julian and Sandy became a favorite with audiences as voiced by Hugh Paddick and Kenneth Williams. Dripping in Polari (see page 219), Julian and Sandy were flamboyant and fabulous, and in a time that did not regularly accept homosexuals, they were beloved. The joke with Julian and Sandy was that we all knew what and who they were, but it was never directly said. Their double and triple entendre kept audiences in stitches.

Miranda July (1974–)

It's hard to find a category for Miranda July. She's a filmmaker, writer, performance artist and actress, musician, and visual artist. She crosses genre and medium as easily and effortlessly as some people cross the street, and she brings her own unique sense of intensity and intrigue with her along the way. Her first film, *Joanie 4 Jackie*, was about taking her riot grrrl sensibility into the film world, and there she found a great deal of success. She followed it up with *Me and You and Everyone We Know* in 2004 and *The Future* in 2011. But filmmaking is just one aspect of July's work. She released her first EP, *Margie Ruskie Stops Time*, in 1996. A combination of spoken word and music, it launched July into yet another arena. Storytelling is central to July's work, so it came as no surprise when, in 2007, she release her first collection of short stories, *No One Belongs Here More Than You*. July released her first novel, *The First Bad Man*, in 2015. She continues to make a variety of work, keeping the riot grrrl spirit of DIY, personal truth, and expression alive and well into the twenty-first century.

K

is for . . .

Frida Kahlo and
Frank Kameny

Frida Kahlo (1907–1954)

You know her face, but there's a lot more to Frida Kahlo then a unibrow. One of the most recognizable faces in the modern world, Frida Kahlo was a painter who used herself as the subject through which to express her work. She began drawing and painting at an early age, but a bus accident in 1925 almost killed the young artist and left her unable to walk for three months. Her injuries from this accident would plague her for the rest of her life. In 1928, she met the famous painter Diego Rivera. Though he was twenty years older than her and a notorious womanizer, Kahlo fell for the painter and married him in 1929. Both Rivera and Kahlo had numerous affairs, Kahlo most notably with actress and dancer Josephine Baker, ranchera singer Chavela Vargas, and Russian revolutionary Leon Trotsky. Kahlo traveled around the world with Rivera, who was during their life together the much-more famous artist, and continued to create her own work as long as her health would allow. Kahlo's health continued to decline and by the mid-1940s it had left her mostly bedridden, depleting her output as an artist. In the early 1950s she had a series of operations to help with her chronic back pain that only left her more incapacitated. In 1953, she had her right leg amputated, leaving her almost permanently bedridden and depressed. She finally died in 1954. In the years since her death, her life and work have achieved legendary status and she has become the most recognizable face of Mexico.

Frank Kameny (1925–2011)

The great granddad of the gay rights movement, Frank Kameny was fighting for the rights of LGBTQ+ people when they were still considered mentally ill and criminal. Kameny was an astronomer hired by the US government in the 1957. But as the McCarthy era rampaged on and the purging of homosexuals became a cause in Washington, Kameny was dismissed from his post after it was learned that he had been arrested for solicitation in a San Francisco restroom. He was barred from working for any government agency in 1958. Kameny took his case to the courts, citing that he had been wrongly fired and should be fully reinstated or compensated for his work. He lost twice, and when he took his case to the Supreme Court, they refused to hear it. An activist was born. In 1961, Kameny co-founded the Washington chapter of the Mattachine Society and picketed the White House, the Pentagon, and the Civil Service Commission in one of the earliest open protests by homosexuals in this country. In the 1960s, he worked to overturn sodomy laws, and in 1972, along with longtime friend and colleague Barbara Gittings, convinced the American Psychiatric Association (APA) to have an open debate about homosexuality. Following the debate, the APA dropped homosexuality from its list of mental disorders. Also in the 1970s, Kameny was appointed to Washington's Human Rights Commission as its first openly gay member. Though Kameny's health deteriorated, he continued to be an outspoken and fiery voice for the rights of the LGBTQ+ community until his death in 2011.

David Kato (1964–2011)

A strong and outspoken voice for LGBTQ+ people in Africa and around the world, Kato is often called "Uganda's first openly gay man," and with good reason. He was the first to openly fight the prejudice against LGBTQ+ people in his country, and for this cause it is believed he gave his life. Kato was a teacher for many years, and when he saw the plight of homosexuals in his country, he decided to do something about it. He came out publicly in 1998 and was arrested and held in custody for over a week. Uganda has strict laws about homosexuality, often fueled by American evangelicals. Kato became involved with the underground LGBTQ+ rights group SMUG, Sexual Minorities Uganda, in 2004. When the Uganda Anti-Homosexuality Act, or "Kill the Gays" as it came to be known, was first introduced, Kato fought hard against its passing and thus became a target. In 2010, the Ugandan newspaper *Rolling Stone*, published the identities of one hundred "known homosexuals" and called for their execution. Kato, along with two other defendants, sued the newspaper and eventually won. However, in January of 2011, Kato was attacked at his home and bludgeoned in the head. He died from his injuries. The murder was blamed on a sex worker as part of botched robbery, but there are still lingering doubts about its true cause.

Moisés Kaufman (1963–)

A Venezuelan playwright and director whose work has brought LGBTQ+ stories to the forefront in brilliant and heartbreaking ways, Moisés Kaufman founded the Tectonic Theater Project with Jeffrey LaHoste in 1991. The company wanted to concentrate on the making of plays and having company members involved in their consecration, as well as performing in them. The first play that set the company apart was Kaufman's *Gross Indecency: The Three Trials of Oscar Wilde.* Using court documents and writings from the period and by Wilde himself, Kaufman constructed the details of Wilde's downfall with brilliant grace and form. In 1998, when Matthew Shepard was found brutally murdered, Kaufman and company members went to Laramie, Wyoming, to talk to the community and make a piece about its response to the tragedy. That piece became *The Laramie Project.* Kaufman went on to direct *I Am My Own Wife,* a biographical piece about Charlotte von Mahlsdorf, a transwoman and founder of the "Museum of Everyday Things." The play moved to Broadway and Kaufman received his first Tony nomination for Best Direction. Considered one of theatre's most exciting and daring directors, Kaufman just recently directed a major revival of Harvey Fierstein's *Torch Song Trilogy* starring Michael Urie.

John Kelly (1959–)

A performance artist, singer, writer, actor, and acrobat whose work is hard to describe without one word—*brilliant*—Kelly began making work at the Pyramid Club in the 1980s, with drag creations like Dagmar Onassis, the abandoned love child of Maria Callas and Ari Onassis, but quickly moved on to larger-scale projects. He has always mined the fields of LGBTQ+ history to create his works. He has crafted pieces about the works of Egon Schiele and the drag acrobat Barbette, always staying true to his insightful vision of queer life and its history. Kelly is also well-known for his glorious tributes to singer-songwriter Joni Mitchell, performing as Joni in many of her original keys. He continues to make breathtakingly beautiful work, most recently in *Time No Line,* a personal piece he performs with his own portraits of those we've lost to AIDS.

Karl-Maria Kertbeny (1824–1882)

Kertbeny coined the terms *homosexual* and *heterosexual.* Though he has pissed off etymologists for over a century by mixing Latin and Greek, he at least gave the world a medical-sounding term to identify people living outside the two-gendered-attraction paradigm. Kertbeny was originally a translator, but he wrote about homosexuality a great deal. He fought for the rights of homosexuals while trying to get people to understand them.

Kertbeny fought against the Prussian sodomy law, Paragraph 143, and felt that the term *sodomite* was instantly prejudicial—that to see homosexuality as a mere variation in sexual behavior rather than a sin would allow people to feel more compassion and understanding for the group. He believed that homosexuality was fixed from birth and unchangeable and sought to bring awareness and understanding to the homosexual cause. Though he brought the term *homosexual* into existence in 1868, it did not become more widely used until Richard von Krafft-Ebing's *Psychopathia Sexualis* in 1886, four years after Kertbeny's death.

Kesha (1987–)

A singer, songwriter, and rapper who first came to prominence by guesting on Flo Rida's 2009 single *Right Round*. The song became such a big hit that people immediately began clamoring for music from Kesha. Her first album, 2010's *Animal*, threw her into the spotlight, with singles like "Blah Blah Blah," "Your Love Is My Drug," and "Take It Off" all doing well on the charts. She was born into a songwriting family in Los Angeles, and while her mother struggled to keep the family together, Kesha's interest in music was fostered from an early age. Kesha signed her first songwriting contract with Dr. Luke when she was eighteen, and the two were locked in a cruel and at times violent relationship from the beginning. After the release of her first two albums, Kesha sued Dr. Luke for sexual assault in 2014. The courts ruled against her in two appeals, and Kesha was left to wait out her contract with Sony before releasing new music. In 2017, Kesha released her single, "Praying," which went platinum twice in the first weeks of its release, and the album that followed, *Rainbow*, did spectacularly.

Key West

This island off the coast of Florida has been an LGBTQ+ oasis for nearly sixty years and still holds a lot of history and magic for the LGBTQ+ community. It was a favorite spot for Tennessee Williams and Elizabeth Bishop, as well as noted homophobe Ernest Hemingway, so I guess you can't have everything. This small island community prides itself on its acceptance and diversity and hosts many LGBTQ+ events to this day.

The Killing of Sister George

A 1968 dark comedy about a lesbian love triangle directed by Robert Aldrich of *What Ever Happened to Baby Jane?* fame, the film stars Beryl Reid, Susannah York, and Coral Browne, and it is at best a camp thriller with some incredible lines and turns by three actresses let loose to chew any scenery they could get their hands on. Originally written as a play by Frank Marcus as a serious take on the lives of lesbians, the movie remains more of a sardonic romp through the lives of sinister lesbians.

Billie Jean King (1943–)

A tennis goddess who fought misogyny on and off the court, Jean is perhaps most remembered for her famous Battle of the Sexes against Bobby Riggs in 1973, King has done more than just the one game. Over her illustrious career, King won thirty-nine Grand Slam titles, in singles and doubles, but it has been her work for the rights of women in sports and queer women that has long been her calling card. In 1973, she founded the Women's Tennis Association, which sought to promote women's tennis and see that women athletes were paid along the same lines as men. King also founded the Women's Sports Foundation in 1974 to promote female athletics and athletes. It was to highlight this work that she participated in the famous Battle of the Sexes in 1973. The televised event was an exhibition game in the truest sense of the word, with Riggs hamming it up for the cameras. King played it cool and collected and beat Riggs. The game was watched by an estimated 90 million people worldwide. After the game, King continued to play, but her advocacy for the rights of women in sports became the focus of her career. She was inducted into the Tennis Hall of Fame in 1987 and awarded the Presidential Medal of Freedom in 2009 for her work in tennis and for female athletes.

King Princess (1998–)

A uniquely queer voice in pop is emerging in the persona of King Princess. This young, queer woman out of Brooklyn has her own sound and an ability to write to the modern queer experience with a lot of brilliance and just as much fun. Some her songs are written with clear queer undertones, like "1950," a tribute to Patricia Highsmith's *The Price of Salt*. She's called her most recent "Hit the Back" a "bottom anthem." Her first full-length album, *Cheap Queen*, was released in 2019, with Mark Ronson producing.

The Kinsey Reports

The brainchild of Dr. Alfred Kinsey, a zoologist and entomologist, these two studies, *Sexual Behavior in the Human Male*, published in 1948, and *Sexual Behavior in the Human Female*, published in 1953, have become the cornerstone of understanding human sexuality. Kinsey's approach was unprecedented and to this date unsurpassed. He felt he was collecting data without judgment. The root of his study was not to find out what was wrong with people, but to find out what people were doing and why. Kinsey and his researchers did hours upon hours of studies and interviews with people from all walks of life and sexualities to find out about their practices and their lives. The first book made the astonishing claim that 10% of the adult-male population were homosexual. It also introduced the idea of sexuality being on a scale. Thus, the Kinsey scale was born as a measurement from 0 to 6: 0 being exclusively heterosexual and 6 being exclusively homosexual. The study also proved to be a great depository for sexual ephemera and stories. Kinsey opened the Kinsey Institute in 1947 in association with the University of Indiana. The report still stands as one of the broadest and most groundbreaking studies into human sexuality and is often cited as a turning point in how Americans view sex.

The Kinsey Sicks

The Kinsey Sicks

A wild and wonderful singing group of four drags queens that takes on politics and gay life in delightful parodies and original songs, the Kinsey Sicks have been around since the early 1990s and are still going strong. The group was started as a lark, with friends dressing up for a Bette Midler concert as the Andrews Sisters, but quickly formed an act. That act has taken them everywhere from Las Vegas to off-Broadway. They've recorded several albums, and while the lineup has changed a bit over the years, the core message and merriment of the group remains the same.

Lincoln Kirstein (1907–1996)

Known for many things, but primarily for co-founding the New York City Ballet, Lincoln Kirstein was the money and the brains behind the operation, which left his friend and collaborator, the great George Balanchine, free to create some of the world's greatest ballets. Kirstein was a great connoisseur of art, and it was his keen eye and patronage that made him sought out among artistic circles for most of the twentieth century. Kirstein grew up in a wealthy Jewish family and went to Harvard, but it was seeing Balanchine's *Apollo* with the Ballets Russes that shook Kirstein to his core and made him swear then and there to bring Balanchine to America. Through Kirstein's shrewd fundraising and enthusiasm for the project, he founded the New York City Ballet in 1948. He served as the company's general director for the next forty-three years, bringing a golden age of ballet and Balanchine to New York and the world.

Kiss of the Spider Woman

This novel by Manuel Puig was released in 1976 in Argentina and since the very beginning has been loved by a world audience. Written among the turbulent political scene in the 1970s, it tells the story of two cellmates in prison: one the brooding revolutionary Valentin Arregui, and the other an effeminate gay window dresser Luis Molina, who often escapes into his memories of his favorite movies. The two form a strange and at times loving relationship with a host of complications. The book was turned into a stage play in 1983, and then a successful film in 1985 with William Hurt and Raul Julia. The film was later adapted into a musical by songwriters Kander and Ebb in 1993 with Chita Rivera in the role of the famous Spider Woman.

Frankie Knuckles (1955–2014)

An award-winning record producer, remixer, and DJ called the "Godfather of House Music," Knuckles became famous nationally through his work at the famous Chicago dance club Warehouse, where he kept the gay clientele dancing to all hours of the night. Starting there in 1977, he soon developed a style and musical vocabulary all his own. Knuckles began incorporating a drum machine into his work, sampling from a myriad of sources and remixing songs to make them more danceable. As the house movement started to grow, he became one of the most sought-after DJs in the country. Knuckles won a Grammy for Remixer of the Year in 1997 and was inducted into the Dance Music Hall of Fame in 2005.

Larry Kramer

Larry Kramer (1935–2020)

Often the loudest in the room, and with good reason, Larry Kramer's voice is passionate, strong, and often filled with a beautiful sense of justice and care. Kramer is a writer, playwright, and advocate for LGBTQ+ rights. Kramer is most remembered for founding ACT UP in 1987. AIDS gave birth to Kramer the activist, but his keen eye toward humanity had been there since the beginning. He started his career as a screenwriter. His adaptation of D. H. Lawrence's *Women in Love* was brought to the screen in 1969. The film was a huge success and earned Kramer an Oscar nomination for Best Adapted Screenplay. Kramer continued to write and found that he wanted to cover gay themes. He wrote his satirical novel *Faggots* in 1978. The book took a critical eye to promiscuity and bar culture that dominated gay life in the disco era. With the advent of AIDS, Kramer and a group of friends founded the Gay Men's Health Crisis (GMHC). From the very beginning, Kramer was a controversial firebrand, standing up for the community to a country at large that just didn't want to listen. Kramer left the GMHC in 1983, as tensions within the group grew too difficult. Kramer wrote about the experience in his play *The Normal Heart.* The play opened at the Public Theater in 1985 to rave reviews and thunderous applause from an audience finally being seen. It was turned into a film by HBO and Ryan Murphy in 2014. Kramer continued to write, with a follow-up to *The Normal Heart, The Destiny of Me*, in 1992; a published lecture, *The Tragedy of Today's Gays*, in 2004; and a gay history of the United States, *The American People, Volume 1*, published in 2015. Kramer continued to be a fierce and fiery advocate for the LGBTQ+ community, even as age and the disease he fought so long slowed him down a bit. A documentary about his life, *Larry Kramer in Love and Anger*, premiered on HBO in 2015. Many have said, and I concur, that many people owe their lives to Larry Kramer, and for that, and for so much more, he deserves our deepest respect and gratitude.

Lisa Kron (1961–)

Kron is a playwright, humorist, and actress who has always stayed true to her queer self throughout her long and varied career, and we're all the richer for it. Kron co-founded the Five Lesbian Brothers with Maureen Angelos, Dominique Dibbell, Peg Healey, and Babs Davy. The theatre company was a huge success in New York, giving a lesbian twist and feminist take on the world around them. Kron was always a standout in the group, and she went on to write some of her best work. She performed in her plays *2.5 Minute Ride* and *Well.* Both pieces are highly autobiographical, taking insightful looks at the author's life that often contradict her own perception of herself. *Well* premiered at the Public Theater with Kron in 2004, with Jayne Houdyshell as her mother. It became a massive hit and moved to Broadway in 2006, but it failed to find a broader audience. Kron's next big success came with 2013's *Fun Home.* Adapted from Alison Bechdel's graphic novel of the same name, the musical written with Jeanine Tesori opened at the Public and then moved to Broadway in 2015, where it earned Kron two Tony Awards for Best Book of a Musical and Best Original Score.

Kiyoshi Kuromiya (1943-2000)

Kiyoshi Kuromiya was born in a Japanese internment camp in Wyoming in 1943. Though he was far too young to feel the full impact of this injustice, its memory linerged and forced Kuromiya into a lifelong pursuit of social justice. During the civil rights movement of the 1960s, Kuromiya was an aide to Dr. Martin Luther King, and then became an outspoken voice in the anti–Vietnam War movement. He was a founding member of the Gay Liberation Front, and with the emergence of the AIDS crisis in the 1980s, Kuromiya was an outspoken member of ACT UP. He founded the Critical Path Project, which was the first newsletter to talk about care for people living with AIDS.

Tony Kushner (1956–)

Kushner is the author of the seminal *Angels in America*, his play in two parts. *Part One: Millennium Approaches* and *Part Two: Perestroika*, deals with the AIDS crisis and the Reaganomic world in which it developed. For *Angels*, Kushner received the 1993 Pulitzer Prize and the Tony Award for Best Play. It continues to wow audiences with its very human and political discourse, and so does Kushner. He's continued to write plays and films that take harsh-but-human looks at how politics play their ways into our personal lives. Since *Angels*, Kushner has debuted plays like *A Bright Room Called Day*, and *The Intelligent Homosexual's Guide to Capitalism and Socialism with a Key to the Scriptures*, and a translation of Brecht's *Mother Courage and Her Children* starring Meryl Streep. Kushner wrote the book and lyrics to the musical *Caroline, or Change* in 2003, with a score by Jeanine Tesori and starring Tonya Pinkins and Anika Noni Rose. It debuted at the Public and moved to Broadway, winning a Tony Award for Rose. Kushner has also written for the screen, adapting *Angels* for HBO's 2003 film version and co-writing with Eric Roth *Munich*, directed by Steven Spielberg. His screenplay for Spielberg's *Lincoln* was nominated for multiple awards. Kushner is continuing his association with Spielberg on the upcoming remake of *West Side Story*. Kushner is an outspoken supporter of human rights, and he was awarded the National Medal of Arts by President Obama in 2013 for his activism and writing.

L

is for . . .

The L Word

The gay show that both you and your dad like, this lesbian drama debuted on Showtime in 2004 and immediately drew a wide queer audience, as well as our dads. It followed the lives of a group of lesbians living and loving in Los Angeles. Starring Jennifer Beals, Pam Grier, Laurel Holloman, Leisha Hailey, Katherine Moennig, Mia Kirshner, and Erin Daniels, taking on a lot of issues facing modern gay women, with a healthy slice of drama. The show ran for six seasons and added to its sizable cast with notable additions like Rachel Shelley and Oscar-winner Marlee Matlin. A reboot of the original series, *The L Word: Generation Q,* debuted in 2019, with much of the original cast as well as new trans-identifying characters.

La Cage aux Folles

This story of a gay couple who goes to great lengths, and drag, to help their son find love has been a beloved tale of family in all its many iterations for more than forty years. Originally a 1973 play by Jean Poiret, it was adapted to the screen in 1978 by Édouard Molinaro, starring Ugo Tognazzi and Michel Serrault in the lead roles. The film was wildly successful and spawned a sequel, but that was just the beginning. Jerry Herman and Harvey Fierstein turned the movie into a musical in 1983. An American film version, made in 1996 under the name *The Birdcage*, starred Nathan Lane and Robin Williams and became a classic all its own.

Patti LaBelle (1944–) **ICON**

There are divas, and then there are supernovas that can't be held by such a simplistic word like that. Patti LaBelle is one such performer. With sickening vocals that defy human skill and, at times, sense, Miss Patti, as she is affectionately known to fans, is in a league all her own. Getting her start with Patti LaBelle and the Bluebelles, then transitioning to the now-iconic Labelle with Nona Hendryx and Sarah Dash, LaBelle gave us the original "Lady Marmalade" and a host of fabulous looks. After leaving Labelle, Miss Patti went out on her own with a series of hits and incredible, gravity-defying hairstyles. With iconic performances of singing out of her shoes and rolling on the floor just to get the gorgeous notes out of her, LaBelle has become an icon and advocate to the LGBTQ+ community.

Bruce LaBruce (1964–)

The bad boy of gay cinema who keeps the sexy in film, this Canadian filmmaker, writer, and artist brings a playful and the grotesque sense of humor and sexuality to all his projects. LaBruce started making his original artwork and writing in the zine *J.D.s*, which he founded in 1985 with G. B. Jones. It was a huge success and is credited with opening the floodgates for the queer-zine revolution that followed in its wake. LaBruce began experimenting with short films in 1987. He made his first feature-length film, *No Skin Off My Ass*, in 1991. The film combined sexually graphic scenes within a larger narrative, and starred both LaBruce and Jones. His 2008 film, *Otto; or, Up with Dead People*, debuted at Sundance. It broke out with its theme of a gay zombie looking for love, though LaBruce has yet to cross over into totally mainstream film. His 2013 film, *Gerontophilia*, had less sex than is typical of a LaBruce film, but still explored the intergenerational relationship between a young man and an octogenarian.

David LaChapelle (1963–)

LaChapelle is a photographer and film director whose stunning visuals and risk-taking approach to glamour and its excess have set him apart in the realm of visual art. His work has been featured in many of the world's top magazines, bridging the gap between commercial and high art. He's photographed spreads for *Rolling Stone*, *Vanity Fair*, and *Vogue*, and launched campaigns for Diesel and many other fashion brands. LaChapelle got his start at seventeen when he met Andy Warhol, who hired him to photograph for *Interview* magazine. LaChapelle quickly set himself apart, relying heavily on Catholic imagery of saints and redemption. He does it all with a sense of camp and color that gives his work a sheen of humor and opulence. His first book of photography was released in 1996, and he's since released several books with Taschen. He is a favorite for many celebrities—he's even taken the Kardashian Christmas card—and has found a friend, collaborator, and muse in model Amanda Lepore. LaChappelle has also moved into directing, with music videos for Gwen Stefani, Amy Winehouse, and Christina Aguilera, just to name a few.

Lady Gaga (1986–) **ICON**

Gaga is the gay icon for the millennial era who has turned heads since the very beginning. Her commitment to her gay audience and her connection with her "Little Monsters" have made this pop princess stand head and shoulders above the rest for over a decade. Lady Gaga hit the scene in 2008 with a slew of hits, like "Poker Face" and "Just Dance." Her driving dance beats and stylish outlandishness led her right to the forefront of pop, but that wasn't nearly enough. With her anthem "Born This Way" in 2011, she took a stand for her LGBTQ+ fans and ushered herself into the diva category with ease. Gaga continues to reach new heights with albums like *Artpop* in 2013, the more introspective *Joanne* in 2016, and a collaboration with the legendary Tony Bennett. Acting has been the most recent addition to her arsenal with a Golden Globe–winning turn on *American Horror Story: Hotel* and the box office hit *A Star Is Born* with Bradley Cooper. Gaga is here to stay and slay, and a throng of LGBTQ+ fans everywhere are living for it.

Karl Lagerfeld (1933–2019)

The large, dark glasses. The white hair tied into a ponytail. The studded leather gloves and the paper fan. Karl Lagerfeld's look became almost as well known as the clothes he designed. As the creative director of Chanel, as well as Fendi and his own label, Lagerfeld stands as a giant in the fashion world for the second half of the twentieth century and two decades into the new millennium. He was born in Hamburg, Germany, and got his first big break in 1967, when he was hired by Fendi. As he would later do with Chanel, Lagerfeld was brought in to revitalize the brand and bring it into the modern age. With the success at Fendi, Chanel sought him out in 1983. After the death of the famous designer Coco Chanel, the label struggled to find its

way, and Lagerfeld felt like the perfect fit. He took the dying Chanel and turned it into one of the leading fashion houses in Paris. Lagerfeld was fashion royalty, but that was not without controversy. He often made comments that were labeled fat-phobic, misogynistic, and at times even racist. Despite all his faults, Lagerfeld made fashion and was fashion for longer than almost any of his contemporaries.

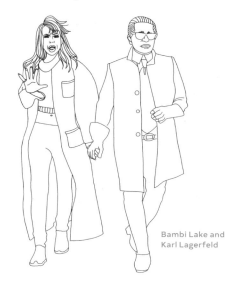

Bambi Lake and Karl Lagerfeld

Bambi Lake (1950 -2020)

This San Francisco artist's antics, performances, and poetry have made her an icon. Bambi Lake was a member of the legendary Cockettes, but after the group disbanded, Lake made her way to the Angels of Light with Cockettes founder Hibiscus. Lake began to separate herself from the rest of the group with her no-nonsense approach to performing. Her work as a singer-songwriter, with songs like "The Golden Age of Hustlers," made Lake a must-see commodity on San Francisco's artistic scene. While so many may have their own Bambi Lake story in the Bay Area, Lake's poetry and writings have long held her in great esteem for those in the know. Lake wrote her memoir, *The Unsinkable Bambi Lake*, in 1996. The book, which is as hilarious as it is poignant, includes many of Lake's songs and lyrics. It is a book that demands an audience, much like the authoress did herself.

Adam Lambert (1982–)

The man who brought the smokey eye and the high-range vocals back to pop music, Lambert is an American singer and performer who got his start on *American Idol* in 2009. While he was only the runner-up that season, Adam Lambert has gone on to sell 3 million records worldwide. Lambert was not out on the show, but after the season wrapped, he came out in an interview with *Rolling Stone*. His first album, *For Your Entertainment*, did very well and opened his Glam Nation Tour in 2010. In 2012, the mega band Queen wanted to go out on tour again, but finding someone who could sing the jaw-dropping vocals of Freddie Mercury with any sense of accuracy was a tough role to fill. Since joining Queen, Lambert has toured with the band five separate times to sold-out arenas around the world. Lambert's newest album, *Velvet*, was released in 2020.

Ryan Landry

Keeping the tradition of camp and drag theatre alive in Provincetown for more than twenty years, Ryan Landry and his Gold Dust Orphans theatre company are a raucous and ridiculous group of merrymakers. Landry got his start in drag and performance art, learning a lot from the work of Charles Ludlam, but he eventually wanted to put his own stamp on ridiculous theater. He founded the Gold Dust Orphans in 1995 with friends Scott Martino, Afrodite, and Billy Hough. Landry has also written over eighty plays, each taking on the classical tradition as well as the classic tropes of Hollywood. He is a staple of Provincetown to this day, continuing his work with new plays every year and collaborations with artists like Varla Jean Merman.

Nathan Lane (1956–)

With more hits than many can count, Nathan Lane can do it all. He's played everything from comedy to tragedy, and in each he brings his own unique sense of truth and humor that illuminates his characters. He's a three-time Tony winner, with multiple Drama Desk and Outer Critics Circle awards. Lane made his Broadway debut in a 1982 revival of Noël Coward's *Present Laughter* starring George C. Scott.

It was after this that he began a long association with playwright Terrence McNally. Their first collaboration was in McNally's play *The Lisbon Traviata* in 1987. Lane would go on to star in McNally's *Lips Together, Teeth Apart* in 1991, and in the huge hit *Love! Valour! Compassion!* in 1995. In 1992, Lane made a splash in a Broadway revival of *Guys and Dolls* playing Nathan Detroit opposite Faith Prince and followed it up with a star turn in *A Funny Thing Happened on the Way to the Forum* in 1996, winning his first Tony. But his biggest Broadway hit came in 2001 playing Max Bialystock in Mel Brooks's *The Producers*, opposite Matthew Broderick. Lane continues to push himself to new and uncharted territories, taking on Beckett, David Mamet, and most recently *Angels in America* playing Roy Cohn. On top of this extensive theatre resume, Lane has also had success in film and television. He voiced Timon the meerkat in Disney's classic *The Lion King* and stars opposite Robin Williams in *The Birdcage*. He's also been a staple on television, nominated for multiple Emmys for his recurring role of Pepper on *Modern Family*.

k. d. lang (1961–)

Even as she crosses genres and styles, k. d. lang continues to bring her soulful magic to each and every song she sings. Lang started her career in the 1980s, melding country, a heavy influence of her hero Patsy Cline, and the punk and alternative scenes into a style all her own. It was 1989 when Roy Orbison heard her and asked her to sing a duet of his hit "Crying." The song won them both a Grammy and propelled lang into a whole new arena of music. Her 1992 album, *Ingénue*, did very well, with songs like "Constant Craving" and "Miss Chatelaine." From the very beginning, lang played with gender roles, always wearing a suit and a butch haircut, yet singing sweetly. She came out in 1992 and has always been an open and outspoken advocate for the LGBTQ+ community. She continued to produce a wealth of great music, contributing songs to Gus van Sant's cult classic *Even Cowgirls Get the Blues*, 2004's *Hymns of the 49th Parallel*, celebrating songwriters from her native Canada, and an album of now-classic duets with Tony Bennett. Lang continued to push her music boundaries in her 2016 collaboration with Neko Case and Laura Veirs, *case/lang/veirs*.

Chi Chi LaRue (1959–)

Drag queen and porn director supreme, Chi Chi LaRue, born Larry David Paciotti, has been a staple of the gay-porn scene for decades and a loud-and-proud voice for gays and the sex they have for just as long. LaRue got started in gay porn in the 1980s, working for the legendary Falcon Studios. When his close friend, actor Joey Stefano, tragically died in 1994 of a drug overdose, LaRue was asked about the role of drugs in the sex industry. Though LaRue is always honest and candid, he's defended the industry, which he sees as necessary and fun. LaRue has repeatedly stood up for the sexual health of his performers, refusing to work with Vivid Video in 2006 when they were not insisting on condom use in their movies. LaRue has been public about his own struggles with drugs, alcohol, and weight, going public about his addiction issues in 2015 and asking his community for support. A big personality and hilarious laugh, LaRue is a mainstay of the LGBTQ+ community. Even as trends change, LaRue is here to stay.

Cyndi Lauper (1953–) ICON
This girl still wants to have fun, and after forty years in the music industry, no one wants to stop her. Lauper is a singer, songwriter, and activist whose songs like "Girls Just Want to Have Fun," "True Colors," and "Time After Time" have made her one of the most beloved artists in the world. Since her debut in 1983, Lauper has continued to push her boundaries as an artist. She's recorded in different genres of music, which only seem to highlight her otherworldly vocal power and her great understanding of the power of music. In 2013, Lauper took on a new adventure, writing the score to the Broadway musical *Kinky Boots* and winning Tony Awards for Best Musical and Best Score. Lauper has always been an advocate for the LGBTQ+ community, first with her True Colors Fund in 2008, followed by her Give a Damn campaign in 2010, seeking to support homeless LGBTQ+ youth.

Arthur Laurents (1917–2011)
Laurents started writing radio dramas in the late 1930s, but turned his attention toward Broadway after returning from the Second World War. He also wrote for film, most famously adapting the screenplay for Alfred Hitchcock's *Rope*. A subtle and sly retelling of the Leopold and Loeb story, Laurents layered the work with a slight gay subtext that still sizzles on the screen. It was in Hollywood that Laurents was hit with the brutality of the Hollywood blacklist for his socialist leanings. Unable to find work, he returned to Broadway and eventually found *West Side Story*. The infamous collaboration of "four gay Jews" writing a musical about Puerto Ricans and street kids fighting it out turned out to be a tremendous hit, through no small effort from Laurents. After *West Side Story*, he went on to work with Stephen Sondheim again for the mega-hit *Gypsy*, starring Ethel Merman. In the years that followed, Laurents held on to the vision of these two pieces and often directed them in subsequent revivals. He returned to film, writing *The Way We Were* based on his experience of the blacklist. He also wrote *The Turning*

Point with Anne Bancroft and Shirley MacLaine. Laurent's heart always belonged to the theatre though, and he continued to direct *West Side Story* and put his stamp on all the major *Gypsy* revivals with Angela Lansbury, Tyne Daly, Bernadette Peters, and Patti LuPone.

Eva Le Gallienne (1899–1991)

An actress, director, writer, producer, and translator who pushed the art form of theatre toward the values of art and accessibility for all, Le Gallienne became a Broadway star at the age of twenty-one, having a huge hit in Ferenc Molnár's *Liliom*, which was later turned into the musical *Carousel*. In 1926, she opened the Civic Repertory Theatre in Manhattan on Fourteenth Street and Sixth Avenue. For almost ten years, Le Gallienne directed, starred in, and produced a series of plays revolving in repertoire, all while running a school for young actors. She learned Russian because she was unhappy with the translations of Chekhov, and translated the plays of Ibsen, which became the standard for many years. A kerosene explosion at her home left Le Gallienne severely burned. She survived and went back to the Civic Rep.

Eva Le Gallienne

When it closed under the pressures of the Great Depression, Le Gallienne continued pushing the benefits of repertory and playing in the great works of Ibsen and Chekhov. She wrote a few children's books, a translation of Hans Christian Andersen's work, and a personal biography of her hero Eleonora Duse. Le Gallienne performed well into her eighties, having stunning turns in a revival of *The Royal Family* in 1975 and the 1980 film *Resurrection* opposite Ellen Burstyn.

Le Gateau Chocolat (1983–)

The chocolate cake that everyone wants to take a bite out of, Le Gateau Chocolat is a British drag performer who has broken boundaries for drag, taking it from the sidelines and fringes of art to the legitimate stage where it belongs. Le Gateau made his debut in 2011 at the Adelaide Fringe Festival and made an impressive showing. A tall, strapping Black man with a full beard and wig was bound to make a splash, but that was just the beginning. Le Gateau has been a cabaret star in London for many years, winning multiple awards for his solo shows in 2011 and 2013, has been featured in *The Threepenny Opera* at the National Theatre, and took on the role of Feste in *Twelfth Night* at the Globe Theatre.

Le1F (1989–)

A producer and rapper who has in many ways opened doors for more queer musicians in hip-hop, Le1f was born Khalif Diouf in Manhattan, where he studied dance. His debut mixtape, 2012's *Dark York*, was wildly played in dance clubs and his "Fuckin' the DJ," in collaboration with Mykki Blanco, was a summer hit. In 2014, Le1f was signed to Terrible Records, who got the young rapper a spot performing on *Late Show with David Letterman*. Leif released his first full-length album, *Riot Boi*, in 2015 to great acclaim.

Leather

Some would say it's a lifestyle, some would call it drag, but whatever or however you come to leather, many people will be glad you did. Leather has had a large appeal in the gay community. With strong ties to S&M, leather has taken on a mythos all its own. The dark leather jackets, the cuffs, the chaps, it all sends off an image of someone who means business, or at least is very warm. It's hot in many senses. There are whole competitions and conventions set up around the fetish of leather, with the International Mr. Leather founded in 1979 and held yearly in Chicago. The competition made history in 2019 for crowning its first trans male of color.

Annie Leibovitz (1949–)

She's the lady who makes the stars look more luminescent. Annie Leibovitz is a major American photographer who has given the world insight and inspiration on famous faces for more than forty years. She got her first job as a staff photographer at *Rolling Stone* in 1970 and helped define the look of the magazine throughout the decade. At *Rolling Stone*, she photographed so many of the twentieth century's musical icons, from the Rolling Stones to John Lennon on the day he died. After leaving the magazine in 1983, she moved on to a long tenure at *Vanity Fair*, where she took some of the most iconic photographs of the period. Demi Moore's famous cover, naked and pregnant, was all Leibovitz. She has received numerous awards and accolades for her work, and has achieved legendary status in the realm of photography. But this legend is still hard at work—Leibovitz remains on the cutting edge of celebrity photography.

Tamara de Lempicka (1898–1980)

The painter behind the bedroom-eyed beauties of the 1920s, Tamara de Lempicka was a world-famous artist whose sleek paintings of art-deco women with heavy-lidded eyes defined the style of an era. Polish-born Lepicka lived in Paris between the two world wars, and her dazzling social life and scandalous libido made her a much-talked-about heroine of her age.

Leo Lerman (1914–1994)

His diaries are a fun and fascinating look at both the celebrity world of the twentieth century and a gay life before and after Stonewall. A dishy, clever editor and writer who cultivated the best of New York and the world into a group of intimate friends and party guests, Lerman wrote for many years as a contributor to *Harper's Bazaar* and *Playbill*, eventually landing at *Vogue*, where he reigned on high for many years. He was an intimate friend of Marlene Dietrich, Maria Callas, and a party host to many of the twentieth century's biggest luminaries. He wrote about his friendships and parties in a multivolume diary, of which a tenth was published in 2007, under the title *The Grand Surprise*. Lerman was openly gay and lived for almost forty years with his partner, the artist Gray Foy.

Amanda Lepore (1967–)

You know her lips, and you probably know her boobs, but that's just the beginning of the work of art that is Amanda Lepore: a Club Kid, singer, and muse who is instantly recognizable and, once seen, never forgotten. A pioneer for trans visibility, Lepore has been at the forefront of fashion and the fashionable for more than thirty years. Her time as a Club Kid with the likes of Michael Alig and James St. James gave her the opportunity to mix with and meet the world of fashion and photography. She became a long-standing muse for photographer and artist Dave LaChapelle, who has used her exaggerated features to create some of his most beautiful images.

Amanda Lepore

Lepore continues to be a mainstay of the club scene, and has also branched out, releasing an album in 2011 and a memoir of her life, *Doll Parts*, in 2017.

Leslie-Lohman Museum

While LGBTQ+ art can be found in museums all over the world, there is only one museum that is dedicated to LGBTQ+ art, and that's the Leslie-Lohman Museum of Art in New York City. It was founded by J. Frederick Lohman and Charles W. Leslie in 1987, who had been collecting and selling queer art for years. The museum now hosts their permanent collections as well as the ever-emerging works of new artists. The Leslie-Lohman Museum continues to be a hub for artists of all mediums and hosts many events to support the creation and the creators of LGBTQ+ art.

David Levithan (1972–)

Gay kids need books too, and David Levithan is seeing that they have them, writing young adult fiction and championing LGBTQ+ stories for young readers. His first major success, 2003's *Boy Meets Boy*, was a sweet love story that set the kid-lit world on fire and established Levithan as an author to watch. And watch they did, as more bestsellers flew from Levithan's pen. He's ventured into sci-fi and fantasy, and released his first book targeted toward adults, *The Lover's Dictionary*, in 2011. Levithan is also an editor at Scholastic and has ushered in a new era of inclusive storytelling there.

Dan Levy (1983–)

We should all send him a huge thank-you note for bringing Catherina O'Hara to TV, but for now, I'll put him in this book. Levy writes the award-winning series *Schitt's Creek*, which he co-created with his father, the famous comedic actor Eugene Levy. Dan gained experience as a host on MTV in Canada, but found that he was looking for a project that would stretch his talent and give him a chance to work with his sister, Sarah, and his father. Thus, the idea for *Schitt's Creek* was born. A riches-to-rags story of the Roses—starring Dan, Sarah, and Eugene, with Catherine O'Hara—features one of the best relationships on TV, and it's a gay one. The show was an instant hit with audiences. Dan has been much lauded and awarded over six seasons for his work in telling an LGBTQ+ story with dignity and affection.

J. C. Leyendecker (1875–1951)

Before Norman Rockwell dominated the *Saturday Evening Post*, J. C. Leyendecker was a favorite cover artist for the magazine. Known for his lush and often humorous illustrations, he defined masculine beauty for most of the 1920s. He was the original illustrator of the Arrow Collar Man, the name given to the various male models who appeared in advertisements for shirts and detachable shirt collars. Sophisticated and delicately beautiful, the men in his illustrations were often seen as exemplars of male beauty for the period. Though Leyendecker fell out of fashion as tastes changed during the Great Depression, his work is often referred to and sought after to this day.

Liberace (1919–1987)

When looking back at the career of Liberace, you have to wonder. No one knew? A man with a candelabra and capes, Liberace was a mainstay of American entertainment for over thirty years. He trained as a classical pianist

Dan Levy and Liberace

but found that the stuffiness of the concert hall was not for him. Liberace was meant to entertain. He began playing popular music and quickly developed a huge fan base. He had his own television show starting in 1952, and he became one of the most popular entertainers of the early days of television. Known for his love of sequins and sparkles, Liberace became a staple of Las Vegas, where he lived and performed for many years. Though he never came out, his personal life was often speculated about. After his death of complications from AIDS in 1987, the whole truth of his life in the closet came out. Most recently, Liberace's life was the subject the HBO movie, *Behind the Candelabra*, starring Michael Douglas.

Lil Nas X (1999–)

The biggest rap hit of 2019 was a country mash-up brought to you by a young, Black, gay man. Yes, we live in fascinating times. Lil Nas X had a huge hit with the song "Old Town Road," which topped the Billboard charts for a whopping nineteen weeks. It was at this time that Nas decided to come out as gay, to the shock and awe of the nation. For many years, he didn't know if he could actually come out, but when his song went to number one, it seemed like a great time to test the waters. When Nas came out, "Old Town Road" had already reached number one, and was seemingly unaffected by the news. While "Old Town Road" may have

brought him to national attention, it was his 2021 song, "Call Me By Your Name," that made a Lil Nas X an international queer superstar. Mixing a queer narrative into a religious framework, Nas is taking no prisoners. As he slides down the a pole to hell and gives the devil a lapdance, Nas is continuing to express his queerness, in ways that shock and delight. We can't wait for more.

Liniker (1995–)

A trans singer and activist who has been taking Brazil by storm with their seductive voice and solid musicianship since 2014, Liniker quickly set themself apart with their soulful interpretations and dazzling sense of self. Liniker has been public about their transition and hopes to use the platform of music to build acceptance and love in Brazil for the trans community. In 2015, Liniker formed their band, Liniker and the Caramelows. They have released two albums and toured the world many times over, taking their music and authenticity wherever they go.

Lips

If you're looking for a fun night out on the town, with laughs, drinks, and lots of drag, look no further than Lips—the drag restaurant where the queens are the waiters as well as the entertainment. Lips has become a legendary spot to find up-and-coming talent on the drag scene, as well as a great night on the town. Serving the community for the last twenty-five years, with locations in New York, Chicago, Atlanta, Fort Lauderdale, and San Diego, Lips is a place to go and enjoy all that drag can be.

Lipstick Lesbian

High femmes or lipstick lesbians are a recent category added to the lesbian lexicon. A lady who likes being a lady (in that she enjoys the fashions and accessory options traditionally associated with femininity), but also enjoys the company of other ladies (in that she likes to do it with them). These "girlie" lesbians have always been a part of the LGBTQ+ landscape, but the term really took hold in the late 1990s and especially with the advent of Showtime's *The L Word*, which was just chock full of 'em.

Anne Lister (1791–1840)

Sometimes called the "first modern lesbian," Lister was a wealthy landowner and intellectual who kept a diary of her life. Written mostly in code, she detailed her relationships with several women and her longing for a steady partner that she could settle into a "married" life with. She was an infamous figurine in her native Halifax, but it wasn't until more than a century later that the true workings of Lister's life and loves were truly known. Since being published in 2010, her diaries have gained much attention and offered insight into a very shadowy lesbian past. Her diaries are the basis for

the HBO show *Gentleman Jack*, written by Sally Wainwright and starring Suranne Jones as Lister.

Little Richard (1932–2020)

Little Richard nee Richard Wayne Penniman was the originator and archetitect of rock and roll. If you didn't know that before, he was happy to remind you. Richard got his start singing in church and was soon discovered by Sister Rosetta Tharpe, another originator of rock music and also rumored to be gay. Richard took gospel rhythms and blew them out with strong beats and suggestive lyrics, but like many Black artists of the 1950s, Richard and his music were overlooked or at times even ripped off by white musicains. It was Richard's talent that was undeniable, with hits like "Tutti Frutti" and "Long Tall Sally," Richard earned his place in rock and roll history. His flambuoyance on stage, with outlandish outfits, makeup, and sexually charged performance style have made him a queer icon for generations. Often boisterous about his role in the music, Richard defended himself with, "I'm not conceited, I'm just convinced."

Lizzo (1988–) ICON

She's got the juice and gay fans are clamoring for more! The pop and R&B, flute-playing, body-loving, ball of positivity that blew up the music scene in 2019, Lizzo is not only a friend to the LGBTQ+ community, she's also an asset. While the rest of the world is just

of African American literature and social writing. Even Martin Luther King Jr. identified him as a pioneer for the civil rights movement. Called the dean of the Harlem Renaissance, Alain Locke encouraged and showcased younger writers of color, promoting the art and intellectual integrity brimming over in the Black community. His *The New Negro* was a collection of writing by Locke himself and a host of other Black writers, and set out to tell the contemporary story of Black lives in the 1930s.

Logo TV

When it debuted in 2005, LGBTQ+ cable channel Logo TV was one of the first of its kind. Founded by Matt Farber and run by Brian Graden, the channel showed a lot of promise in the early days, with original programming and reality television. It was the original home of *RuPaul's Drag Race* and host of other original gay programming, but gradually started to shift its focus away from the LGBTQ+ community as other networks began to diversify their own lineups. As of 2012, Logo TV fully shifted toward more of a general lifestyle and entertainment network, but still has a strong pull for LGBTQ+ viewers.

Longtime Companion

Released in 1989, Norman René's film was the first wide-release motion picture to deal with the subject of AIDS, and it did it beautifully. It gets its

waking up to the wonder that is Lizzo, gay fans have been well aware of this fantastic diva since she first released music in 2013. Her unapologetic look at her curvaceous body and her wondrous sense of self have endeared her to the gay community, and it's a love that works both ways. With early albums like *Coconut Oil* and *Big Grrrl Small World* in 2015, Lizzo was earning a loyal following of gays who shared her dynamic sense of individuality. With 2019's *Cuz I Love You*, and hits like "Truth Hurts," Lizzo has become an international phenomenon, but as is so often the case, the gays knew about her the whole time.

Alain Locke (1885–1954)

A philosopher and writer, he is an often-overlooked giant in the history name from the way in which many surviving partners were described in obituaries in papers like the *New York Times*. Starring Campbell Scott, Bruce Davidson, Patrick Cassidy, Dermot Mulroney, and Mary-Louise Parker, the film follows a group of friends as they deal with the encroaching doom of the crisis while a vast majority of the world turns a blind eye. The film was universally praised and won several awards on the film-festival circuit. It's a gay movie that feels gay in that it's always a mix of sadness and joy and complications amid a crisis. Watch this movie for the last scene alone, which will make even the bitterest among us shed a tear.

Looking

I knew we were in trouble when Jonathan Groff said, " . . . in the butt." We're gay; *in the butt* is implied. The controversial HBO show is about a group of gay friends in San Francisco navigating the modern gay world. The show, which debuted in 2014, was written by Michael Lannan, directed by Andrew Haigh, and starred Jonathan Groff, Russell Tovey, Murray Bartlett, Frankie Alvarez, and Lauren Weedman. It was marred by a lot of criticism from the gay community for being a bit heavy-handed and, at the same time, out of touch, and was canceled after two seasons. A film to finish off the story was released in 2016.

Federico García Lorca (1898–1936)

Lorca is one of Spain's most revered and legendary poets and playwrights. His works for the stage, such as *The House of Bernarda Alba, Blood Wedding*, and *Yerma*, have become classics, translated into multiple languages and performed in theatres all over the world. His poetic works, like the *Gypsy Ballads* and *Poet in New York*, are shining examples of his prowess and some of the greatest examples of the surrealist poetry movement. Lorca was a controversial figure during his lifetime. A supporter of the right of the people, he was critical of the fascist movement growing in Spain prior to the Spanish Civil War. For his views, he was one of the first victims of the war. Lorca was assassinated in 1936 and buried in an unmarked grave.

Audre Lorde (1934–1992)

Lorde is one of the most respected and read feminist poets and writers in the modern age. Her theory of "no hierarchy of oppressions" is now

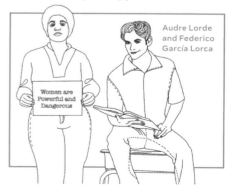

Audre Lorde and Federico García Lorca

Women are Powerful and Dangerous

seen as one of the best-explained and thought-out theories of intersectionality, and is often cited in modern activism. Lorde was touching on the role of suffering in oppression, harkening back to the idea that your freedom is contingent on mine, and that in fighting for freedom, we must reach out to all, instead of taking piecemeal scraps of freedom for some. Lorde's poetry often deals with her political leanings, calling attention to the struggles of women of color, including those in the LGBTQ+ community specifically. Her novel *Zami: A New Spelling of My Name* is said to be one of the best pieces of lesbian fiction in the last forty years. A teacher and educator, Lorde and her insights have influenced generations of artists and activists. Even though she died from cancer at the relatively young age of fifty-eight, Lorde's reach into the modern age is as deep and as real as her poetry at its best.

Lance Loud (1951–2001)

Let's face it, LGBTQ+ people make reality TV work, and have done so even in the beginning. Take, for example, Lance Loud. Unlike most teenagers in the 1970s, Loud had to come out to his parents on television. He was part of the famous Loud family, the subject of the groundbreaking television show *An American Family*. Shown in 1973, it is often considered the first reality television show in America. Lance was the oldest son of the Louds, who had moved to New York to meet Andy Warhol. When his mother, Pat, came to visit him at the Chelsea Hotel, he took her around New York, and even to Jackie Curtis's show *Vain Victory* at La MaMa. Lance was a standout on the show for his funny witticisms and natural charisma. After *An American Family*, Loud went on to form a popular punk band, the Mumps. He also became a regular columnist for many magazines. Loud contracted AIDS, and his final days in hospice are detailed in *Lance Loud! A Death in an American Family* for PBS.

Greg Louganis (1960–)

A hero with the speedo to prove it, four-time gold-medalist diver and LGBTQ+ activist Greg Louganis has been called "the greatest diver in history," and with good reason—besides his numerous awards, he stood up to bigotry and suspicion at the height of the AIDS crisis. While competing in the 1988 Olympics, Louganis had an accident and bumped his head on a lower diving board. Louganis was concussed and bled into the pool. At the time of the accident, he was newly HIV-positive, though he did not disclose it at the time. When he did go public with his HIV status, there was an uproar about Louganis endangering other divers, though the CDC confirmed that any blood in the water would have dissipated and the chlorine would have killed the HIV. Louganis took the opportunity to demystify HIV and to use his celebrity to fight for the rights of HIV-positive people, a cause that he supports to this day.

Édouard Louis (1992–)

Louis is a French writer making a huge splash on the international literary scene. His first novel, *The End of Eddy*, was released in 2014 to almost universal praise for its hard depiction of life in lower-middle-class France and its heartbreaking honesty about the lives of gay youth. His second book, *History of Violence*, was released in 2016 and detailed Louis's rape and attempted murder. The book has continued to highlight Louis as a writer of brilliant and breathtaking honesty. Louis continues to be an outspoken champion for gay rights in France and in 2018 published his third book, *Who Killed My Father*, about his relationship with his own father and the growing right-wing extremism in Europe.

Demi Lovato (1992–)

Demi Lovato has earned a huge following with their amazing vocals, but it's their personal journey that has often gotten the headlines. A child actor with credits like *Barney & Friends* and Disney's *Camp Rock*, Lovato started their pop career in 2008 with the album, *Don't Forget*. A slew of hits followed, as did oppurtunites like hosting *The X Factor*. But beneath the glittering success, a troubled past bubbled to the surface. Lovato struggled with addiction. Getting sober and coming out as queer and nonbinary have given Lovato an ease and a solidity of self that even they find refreshing after so much struggle.

Love, Simon

Well, you know you've made it when you get a rom-com. Based on the popular YA novel *Simon vs. the Homo Sapiens Agenda* by Becky Albertalli, *Love, Simon* was directed by Greg Berlanti and was the first wide-screen release of a gay-themed romantic movie for a youth audience. The film is a heartwarming look at love and coming out, and while maybe a little sacarine for some bitter old queens (i.e. me), it's a heartwarming look at how far we as a community have come in terms of representation. A TV spin-off, *Love, Victor*, debuted on Hulu in 2020 after being dropped from the Disney+ platform for not being "family-friendly" enough. The show is now in its second season on Hulu.

Charles Ludlam (1943–1987)

The genius of the ridiculous who brought the crass, the crude, and the hilarious to a brilliant and hilarious pitch, Charles Ludlam was an actor, director, and playwright who took the idea of camp to new and dizzying heights. Ludlam performed in and out of drag, but it was his writing and attention to the weird becoming the wonderful that set him apart and made him and his company of actors, the Ridiculous Theatrical Company,

an internationally recognized treasure. Ludlam used iconography from movies and theatre to create new works that were off-kilter and disruptively hilarious. Ludlam also proved that drag could be taken seriously, as he produced both laughs and tears in his adaptation of *Camille*. He was prolific and wrote roles for his company of actors that included Black-Eyed Susan, Lola Pashalinski, Bill Vehr, and Everett Quinton. Quinton and Ludlam became lovers, and with Quinton by his side, Ludlam went on to create some of his most endearing works, like *Galas*, based on the life of Maria Callas, and *The Mystery of Irma Vep*, in which he and Quinton played eight characters of different genders, with as many quick changes as there are jokes. Ludlam died of complications from AIDS in 1987. His legend and work have only grown in stature through the help of Quinton, who still carries a flame for the Ridiculous and its proper place on stage.

Patti LuPone (1949–) ICON

Broadway likes its stars big, and she certainly fits the bill. Patti Lupone is a Broadway diva of the old school who reminds us all what a broad is like and an incredible artist with a vocal and acting prowess that puts her at the top of her profession. LuPone's offstage antics and stories have often delighted audiences as much as her performances. LuPone first came to national attention creating the role of Eva Perón on Broadway in Andrew Lloyd Webber's *Evita*, for which she won a Tony Award for Best Actress. A slew of captivating roles followed: Reno Sweeney in *Anything Goes* in 1987, a doomed turn in *Sunset Boulevard* in 1993, and then finally the role of a lifetime, taking on the mantle of Mama Rose in *Gypsy* in 2008, which earned her a second Tony for Best Actress.

Jane Lynch (1960–)

A comedic actress who was first spotted in her turns in Christopher Guest's *Best in Show* and *A Mighty Wind*, Lynch took this attention and landed the role of Coach Sue Sylvester on Fox's hit show *Glee*. The country fell in love with the always-funny—and on *Glee*, at least, always a little frightening—Lynch. Though she's always been working, in the years since *Glee*, Lynch has taken more of a starring role front and center. She's joined the Disney family in both *Wreck-It Ralph* movies, and since 2013, she's been the host of NBC's *Hollywood Game Night*. She's also an accomplished singer who travels the country with her comedy variety show, *See Jane Sing*.

Paul Lynde (1926–1982)

The king of the center square who delighted audiences with his double entendres on television for years, Paul Lynde is most remembered for *Hollywood Squares*, on which he starred from 1968 to 1981. He had the rare ability of taking his comedy right up to the line, but never really crossing it, at least not on primetime. He owned the saucy one-liner that left audiences pretty certain about where he preferred to keep company, but happy to laugh along with him. A trained Broadway actor, he won a Tony for his role as the exasperated father, Harry MacAfee, in *Bye Bye Birdie*, and also was a regular on the sitcom *Bewitched*, playing Samantha's sassy Uncle Arthur. Lynde defined himself in a period when that definition was still seen as something shameful, and made America laugh with him.

George Platt Lynes (1907–1955)

A fashion and dance photographer, Lynes was highly respected during his lifetime, but his nudes and private gay work, released after his death, have made him into somewhat of an early gay icon in the world of photography. Lynes shot for all the big magazines, like *Harper's Bazaar* and *Vogue*, and was the favorite photographer of the early days of the New York City Ballet. His private work, now known for its stark lines and, at times, surrealist leanings, has placed him in an artistic realm he could never have imagined.

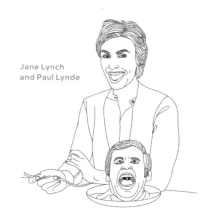

Jane Lynch and Paul Lynde

Alfred Kinsey often relied on him to document case studies, and the Kinsey Institute acquired many of his images.

Lypsinka (1955–)

The next time you see a drag show and a queen goes into a recorded monologue from the *Real Housewives of Beverly Hills*, know that someone invented that and did it better. That person is the legendary Lypsinka. A true pioneer and drag artist, Lypsinka, a.k.a. John Epperson, has taken the art form of drag and given it voice. Known around the world for her stunning and hilarious spoken-word lip-syncs to the voices of Hollywood's icons, Lypsinka has created performance art that has delighted and enraptured audiences for more than thirty years. Besides always looking like a goddess who's just stepped out of one of the films that she's emulating, Lypsinka is and always has been an actor. Working with legends Charles Busch and Ethyl

Eichelberger at the Pyramid Club, Lypsinka stood out with her madcap dialogue mash-ups. Her telephone act is a thing of legend and is still a hilarious thing to see. But beneath the makeup is a true artist. An actor who has appeared off-Broadway and on film, Epperson played a disgruntled accompanist in the film *Black Swan*. Lypsinka's one-person shows, in and out of drag, are wonderful to see, showcasing not only her sparkling wit and incredible legs, but also her expert piano playing.

Lypsinka

M

is for...

Moms Mabley (1894–1975)

A toothless lady in a house-dress who talked about sleeping with young men—and I'm not talking about you on a Saturday night—Moms Mabley was a comedy legend who was hugely popular with Black audiences along the "Chitlin' Circuit" well before white audiences caught up. She was famous for her outrageous and sexual comedy, showing an open preference for "younger men," though in truth most of her offstage relationships were with women. She also released a touching version of "Abraham, Martin and John," which was a relative hit on the charts in 1969. She was a huge influence and hero to Whoopi Goldberg, who produced a documentary about her, *Whoopi Goldberg Presents Moms Mabley*, in 2013.

Taylor Mac (1973–)

Mac is a playwright and performer bringing Radical Faeries realness to the masses whose preferred pronoun is

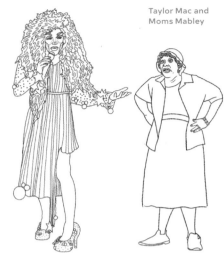

Taylor Mac and Moms Mabley

judy. With outlandish and glitter-filled costumes designed for judy by friend and collaborator Machine Dazzle, Mac cuts a wonderful, sparkly figure on the contemporary theatre scene. Judy's *A 24-Decade History of Popular Music*, a twenty-four-hour performance piece going through American history and song, set Mac apart and shortlisted judy for the Pulitzer Prize in 2017. Mac continues to make work that dares to engage and incorporate an audience in the magic made in the room. Mac's first Broadway endeavor, *Gary: A Sequel to Titus Andronicus*, debuted in 2019 with Nathan Lane and Kristine Nielsen and was nominated for the Tony Award for Best Play.

Machine Dazzle (1972–)

Where you see unused tinsel and some broken dolls, designer Machine Dazzle sees the beginning of magic. Meet the weird and wonderful designer of some of the most outlandish fashions on the scene today, and a costuming genius like no other. Using found fabrics and uncommon designs, Dazzle has crafted costumes for Justin Vivian Bond and Julie Atlas Muz, and has been in close collaboration with artist and muse Taylor Mac. For *A 24-Decade History of Popular Music*, Dazzle designed a new outfit for each of Mac's twenty-four-hour sections, and of course one for themself. Their work has been seen all over the world, including a recent solo exhibition event at the Guggenheim in New York.

Bob Mackie (1939–)

No man has ever made more legends look more sparkly for more years than Bob Mackie. The king of the sequins, this designer dazzles audiences with his showstopping gowns on some of Hollywood's most fantastic women, including Diana Ross, Mitzi Gaynor, and Liza Minnelli. Mackie is most remembered for his work with Carol Burnett—he designed the infamous curtain dress for her classic *Gone with the Wind* parody. He's also been a favorite of Cher's, and designed the costumes for the musical about her life, *The Cher Show*, for which he won a Tony Award in 2019.

Cameron Mackintosh (1946–)

If you love a mega-musical, you have one man to thank. Cameron Mackintosh is the producer of such long-running hits as *The Phantom of the Opera*, *Cats*, *Miss Saigon*, and *Les Misérables*. Basically, if there was a hit musical in the '80s and '90s out of England, most likely Mackintosh had his hand in it. To celebrate his many accomplishments and numerous hits, the show *Hey, Mr. Producer!* was mounted in 1998.

Rachel Maddow (1973–)

The most trusted name in news today is a smart short-haired lesbian in a black suit. That's progress for you. An admitted news and politics nerd who puts her enthusiasm and insight into understanding an increasingly confusing world, Rachel Maddow has become the voice of liberal reason since her show debuted in 2008. Maddow is one of the most trusted faces in news, winning multiple Emmys for her in-depth reporting.

Madonna (1958–) ICON

The Queen of Pop, Madonna has been so many things to so many people for so many years, it's hard to define her. The word that comes to mind is *superstar.* From the lace and punk pop of her early days to her emergence as the Material Girl, Madonna has always showed a passion for reinvention. It has given her longevity and mass appeal. She is never afraid to push herself and the envelope toward some new discovery or new controversy. Madonna has always been able to get the world to pay attention, from her controversial "Like a Prayer" video, to the infamous *Sex* book of 1992, to her 2019's video for "God Control," off her album *Madame X*, where Madonna uses graphic images to take on gun control and remind us all of the tragedy at the Pulse nightclub in 2016. Besides her work as a searing social critic, Madonna has also wanted to delight, with pop and dance music that has given her hits like "Ray of Light" and "Hung Up." As one of the world's bestselling musical artists, her tours are still huge events in every city they touch down in. They showcase Madonna's love for theatricality and her long commitment to give her audience one hell of show. Madonna has also tried her hand at acting, with mixed results. Her turns in films like *Desperately Seeking Susan*, *Dick Tracy*, and *Evita* have had both success and critical failure. Though at times she may stumble, Madonna maintains the attitude of defiance and fierceness that has attracted the LGBTQ+ community to her from the very beginning. And for this love, she has paid the community back tenfold. She was an advocate for the struggles during the AIDS crisis, bringing the ballroom scene to the mainstream culture with 1990's "Vogue" and her iconic Marie Antoinette performance on the MTV awards. In her continuing support of LGBTQ+ rights and the rights of women, Madonna has in many ways defined what a gay icon looks like for a new generation. And something tells me there's still more in store.

Making Love

This 1982 big-studio attempt at making a gay-themed drama was a favorite with some, and a little too dry for others, but remains one of the earliest examples of Hollywood's attempt to take gay relationships seriously. Michael Ontkean plays Zach, married to the lovely Claire, played by Kate Jackson of *Charlie's Angels* fame. The two have a loving marriage, but Zack needs something more. "More" comes along in the guise of Bart, played by Harry Hamlin. The film details Zach's coming to terms with his love for Bart, and of course, making love. It was directed by Arthur Hiller, written by Barry Sandler, and based on a story by A. Scott Berg. While the film may seem a little too earnest and lush today, it's still a great tale of coming to terms with the truth in the beatings of one's own heart.

Barry Manilow (1943–)

He writes the songs! Manilow was one of the biggest-selling artists of the 1970s, with songs like "Mandy," "I Write the Songs," "Can't Smile Without You," and "Copacabana." He is a powerhouse performer who, besides making moms around the country swoon for decades, also has produced albums for artists like Bette Midler, Nancy Wilson, and Sarah

Vaughan. Manilow got his start as Bette Midler's accompanist in the old bathhouse days, but didn't come out publicly until 2017.

Chelsea Manning (1987-)

Chelsea Manning is an American hero, activist, and whistleblower who exposed the gross mishandlings of the wars in Iraq and Afghanistan. While working as an intelligence analyst in the army, Manning saw the army's mishandling of the conflict and released documents to Wikileaks to expose to the American public the horrors that were being committed in their name. For this Manning was sent to jail under the Espionage Act. While in prison, Manning began her transition. President Obama commuted her sentence, and Manning was released in 2017. Manning began a series of speaking engagements and even ran for Congress. Manning was arrested again in 2019 and jailed for one year for her connection to Wikileaks founder, Julian Assange.

Alec Mapa (1965–)

One of the most recognizable and sought-after actors out there, Alec Mapa has done it all. Starting his career on Broadway in *M. Butterfly*, he moved seamlessly to film and television, most recognizably in roles as Suzuki St. Pierre on *Ugly Betty* and Vern on *Desperate Housewives*. Mapa also writes his own work, like his one-man show *Alec Mapa: Baby Daddy*,

which details his experience adopting his son. It was filmed for Showtime in 2015. Mapa is an outspoken advocate for the rights of LGBTQ+ families.

Robert Mapplethorpe (1946–1989)

His work covers everything from self-portraits with a whip up his ass, to gorgeous flowers, and the light-loving Patti Smith. Robert Mapplethorpe is an iconic photographer of the late twentieth century whose images of gay sex shocked a generation and brought a new queer sensibility and sensuality front and center to the art world. His work is often cited for its graphic depictions of gay sexuality, and also for his use of light, of which most agree he was a true master. His picture series of flowers and celebrities of his time are some of the most recognizable images of the period. He famously took the picture of Patti Smith that would be the cover of her 1975 album, *Horses*. Mapplethorpe and Smith were lovers and friends, and her book *Just Kids* details their life together. A documentary about him, *Mapplethorpe: Look at the Pictures*, debuted on HBO in 2016.

Deb Margolin

Margolin is a playwright and performer who continues to push the boundaries of theatre and subject matter, bringing the hidden pains and beauties of human life to the fore in exciting and brilliant ways. She was one of the founders of the Split Britches Theatre Company with Peggy Shaw and Lois Weaver. After leaving the company, Margolin has continued to be a fount of solo work and plays, and was awarded an Obie for continued excellence in 1999.

Rob Marshall (1960–)

When it comes to big-budget movie musicals, this director seems to have the monopoly. Marshall started out as a dancer on Broadway, later moving into choreography with shows like *Kiss of the Spider Woman* in 1993 and *Damn Yankees* in 1994. He moved to the screen with 2002's *Chicago*, which won the Oscar for Best Picture. He has since moved on to 2009's *Nine*, 2014's *Into the Woods*, and 2018's *Mary Poppins Returns*. He is set to direct the live version of Disney's classic *The Little Mermaid*.

Del Martin and Phyllis Lyon

Del Martin (1921–2008) and Phyllis Lyon (1924–2020)

Lovers and partners for more than fifty years, these two pioneers of the LGBTQ+ movement met in the early 1950s in San Francisco and soon found a commonality in their drive toward social justice and the rights of women. Both Martin and Lyon were involved in the Daughters of Bilitis and acted as editors and contributors to the organization's magazine, *The Ladder*. They were active organizers in San Francisco, fighting both the church and the state for the rights of LGBTQ+ people. They were the founders of the Alice B. Toklas Democratic Club, a group seeking to find support for LGBTQ+ causes within the Democratic party. The Lyon-Martin Health Services, founded in 1979, which worked hard to provide health care for lesbian women in the Bay Area, named themselves after the pair. Fierce supporters of marriage equality, the couple were married by Mayor Gavin Newsom in 2004—before it became the law of the land—and remarried in 2008 as one of the first couples in San Francisco to partake, just two months before Martin's death.

Ricky Martin (1971–)

If you were like me, "Livin' La Vida Loca" was an awaking of sorts, and Ricky Martin has been "awakening" me ever since. One of the bestselling Latin-music artists of all time, Martin first hit the American music scene with 1999's "Livin' La Vida Loca." While the song was a huge smash in the States, Martin had already been selling millions of records around the world.

He was a member of the Latin American boy band Menudo, and went solo in the early 1990s. Since "La Vida Loca," Martin has continued to record music in both Spanish and English, and has crossed over into acting in 2018's *The Assassination of Gianni Versace*.

Dina Martina

The hairy-backed malaprop-slinging drag queen of your dreams, Dina Martina debuted in Seattle in 1989 and

Dina Martina and Johnny Mathis

continues to be one of the funniest and most original drag performers in the world today. With her incredible use of word play and mispronunciation, Dina brings audiences across the country to their knees with laughter. Her stunning song renditions in a garbled and grating voice are endlessly hilarious, and her video work, supplanting her own head into classic film, gives her an edge and artistic voice that sets her in a class all her own.

Ross Mathews (1979–)

Whenever I feel low, I think of Ross Matthews encouraging drag queens on *RuPaul's Drag Race* and push on. Ross believes in all of us. This chipper and cheerful host and comedian has been making audiences laugh since his early days as Ross the Intern on the *Tonight Show with Jay Leno*. Since then Ross has been busy as a regular guest and writer on *Chelsea Lately* with Chelsea Handler, then as a contestant and host of *Big Brother*. Ross is also a regular, and perhaps the most supportive of the judges, on *RuPaul's Drag Race*.

Johnny Mathis (1935–)

For many, Christmas wouldn't sound like Christmas without his soft, lilting voice singing "It's beginning to look a lot like . . ." One of the most successful singers of all time, Mathis got his start in the '50s, singing touching ballads like "Chances Are" and "It's Not for Me to Say." He sold millions of records around the globe, breaking records and racial barriers with his cool and sentimental sound. A class act and an out gay man, he taught us all the power of a slow dance with the one you love.

Armistead Maupin (1944–)

This great chronicler of San Francisco and the kooky people who live there is the author of the famous *Tales of the City* books. The stories began as a column in the *San Francisco Chronicle* newspaper and eventually grew into nine separate novels. Maupin is also the author of *Maybe the Moon* in 1992 and *The Night Listener* in 2000, which was later turned into a movie of the same name starring Robin Williams. Maupin co-wrote the screenplay. Most recently, Maupin released a memoir, *Logical Family*, in 2017. A documentary about him, *The Untold Tales of Armistead Maupin*, was released in 2018.

Tarell Alvin McCraney (1980–)

McCraney is a playwright and screenwriter of enormous skill and feeling who is MacArthur Fellow and Oscar winner. His plays include *Wig Out!*; *Choir Boy*, recently seen on Broadway in 2019; and *Head of Passes*. His *Brother/Sister* plays premiered at the Public Theater and at the Young Vic, for which he won an Olivier. His short piece, *In Moonlight Black Boys Look Blue*, was the basis for the 2016 film *Moonlight*. McCraney also worked on the screenplay. *Moonlight* won Best Picture in 2017. McCraney also wrote *High Flying Bird*, which premiered on Netflix in 2019 and was directed by Steven Soderbergh.

Roddy McDowall (1928–1998)

In Hollywood, everyone needs a gay friend, and for many of Hollywood's best and brightest leading ladies, that friend was Roddy McDowall. He was a longtime confidante to Elizabeth Taylor, whom he'd known since childhood when they were both actors at MGM. From child actor to Cornelius in the original *Planet of the Apes*, McDowall was truly a member of Hollywood royalty. McDowall starred in many notable films, like 1965's *The Greatest Story Ever Told*, 1972's *The Poseidon Adventure*, and even *A Bug's Life* in 1998. While he may be mostly remembered for his role of Cornelius in *Planet of the Apes*, McDowall was a versatile actor who was beloved by both audiences and the Hollywood community alike.

Jonny McGovern (1976–)

There have been many iterations of Jonny McGovern, from his stint on Logo's *The Big Gay Sketch Show* to his years recording music as the Gay Pimp, and now as the host of Stream TV's *Hey Qween!* Through it all, McGovern has stayed true to his hilarious and lascivious comedy. *Hey Qween!*, co-hosted with friend Lady Red Couture, is one of the most-watched interview shows on the Internet, and the after-show, *Look at Huh!*, is a great place to find all the great tea and shade from your favorite drag queens from *RuPaul's Drag Race*. While Lady Red passed away in 2020, a heartbroken McGovern continues *Hey Qween!* in her memory.

Claude McKay (1889–1948)

McKay was one of the most original and interesting writers of the Harlem

Renaissance. In recent years, McKay's work has gone through a renaissance all its own. His final novel, *Amiable with Big Teeth*, was published in 2009, and it has caused McKay and his work to be reevaluated in the eyes of literary circles everywhere. The Jamaican-born McKay was a registered Communist in the 1930s, and his left-leaning works still stand as some of the most brilliant and freewheeling pieces of the period. Besides being a masterful poet and novelist, McKay was a guiding influence on authors like Richard Wright and James Baldwin.

Ian McKellen (1939–)

Always remember, both Gandalf and Magneto are super gay. Ian McKellen's also been considered one of the greatest actors of his generation, wowing audiences on stage and screen for over fifty years. From star turns in roles like *Richard II*, *Richard III*, and *Macbeth*, to blockbuster films like *Lord of the Rings* and *X-Men*, McKellan has won a throng of fans and admirers worldwide. McKellan has been a strong and vocal champion for LGBTQ+ rights around the globe. His coming out in 1988 spurned a huge time of activism for McKellan. He co-founded Stonewall, an LGBTQ+ lobbying group in the Uinted Kingdom and fought hard for the overturning of Section 28, which prohibited local authorities from promoting homosexuality. Now, even in his eighties, McKellan is still helping advocate for LGBTQ+ community, doing work to assist gay seniors.

DeRay Mckesson (1985–)

Mckesson is the activist and writer with the iconic vest making change and a difference in contemporary politics and culture. Mckesson first came to national prominence as an outspoken champion for the Black Lives Matter movement, commenting on the goals and the atrocities suffered by Black and Brown people at the hands of the police in this country every day. He has been an active voice and organizer for the protests in Ferguson, Missouri, and Baltimore, Maryland. In 2018, he released a memoir, *On the Other Side of Freedom: The Case for Hope*, to critical raves.

Kate McKinnon (1984–)

She's Rudy Giuliani; she's Elizabeth Warren; she's Hillary Clinton; she's Kate McKinnon. McKinnon got her start on Logo's *The Big Gay Sketch Show* in 2007, and she was a standout even there. But her truly big break came in 2012, when she became the second openly gay cast member on *Saturday Night Live*. Since then she has dominated *SNL*, so it didn't take long for Hollywood to want her. She's starred in *Ghostbusters* in 2016, *Rough Night* in 2017, and *The Spy Who Dumped Me* in 2018, opposite Mila Kunis. McKinnon is often called one of the funniest women in comedy today, and only more hilarity can be expected in her future.

Terrence McNally (1938–2020)

McNally was a pioneering playwright for gay story lines who was one of the most lauded writing talents of his generation. Terrence McNally's work is far-reaching and varied, from his now-classic *Frankie and Johnny in the Clair de Lune* to his tour-de-force *Master Class*, based on his muse and obsession, Maria Callas, to his groundbreaking response to the AIDS crisis, *Love! Valour! Compassion!* McNally created a body of work with more twists and turns than any of his contemporaries. Besides writing his own plays, he was also a much-lauded book writer for musicals like *Kiss of the Spider Woman*, *Ragtime*, and *The Full Monty*, just to name a few. A documentary on his life and work, *Every Act of Life*, was released in 2018.

Alexander McQueen (1969–2010)

One of the most revered and innovative fashion minds of his generation, Alexander McQueen stood head and shoulders above the rest as a designer and couturier. McQueen was hoisted into superstardom in 1996, when he was chosen as head designer for Givenchy. But it was his own label of the same name that he started in 1992 that ultimately became more important to McQueen. When he left Givenchy in 2001, he was one of the most sought-after designers in the world. Known for his experimental use of color and shape, McQueen was never afraid to take risks with his clothes or the theatrical nature of his runway shows. After his death by suicide in 2010, a collection of his work was presented by the Metropolitan Museum of Art as a testament to the man and the artist.

Taylor Mead (1924–2013)

Mead was an actor, poet, and writer who was a personality in a field of personalities. His wit and outrageousness always stood out. He became an underground celebrity after starring in Ron Rice's film *The Flower Thief* in 1960. This caught the attention of Andy Warhol, who started to put Mead in many of his films, including *Couch* and *Taylor Mead's Ass* in 1964 and *The Nude Restaurant* in 1967. Mead was a staple for underground film throughout his life, but his writing was often what kept him in the public eye. He wrote blistering, sexual, and often-funny poetry that he frequently read at the Bowery Poetry Project, almost until his death.

Mean Girls

Get in the car, whore, we're going back to the jungle that is high school. Written by Tina Fey and directed by Mark Waters in 2004, *Mean Girls* is the hilariously quotable camp film about the queen bees of high school and how to defeat them. It starred Lindsay Lohan as the new girl Cady, torn between her real friends, Janis played by Lizzy Caplan and Damian played by Daniel Franzese, and the plastics, Regina

George played by Rachel McAdams, Karen played by Amanda Seyfried, and Gretchen played by Lacey Chabert. The film was an instant hit, and its shine has not been lost in the years since its release. With so many famous lines, and now a musical that debuted on Broadway in 2018, *Mean Girls* is here to stay. And that's *very* fetch.

Freddie Mercury (1946–1991)

His was a voice that comes once in a lifetime. With a huge four-octave range that extended from low base notes to stunning heights of thrilling clarity and power, Mercury was the lead singer of the mega group Queen. With hits like "Don't Stop Me Now," "Somebody to Love," "We Are the Champions," and the wild and wonderful "Bohemian Rhapsody," *Queen* became one of the bestselling groups of all time. Flambouyant Mercury was known for his outrageous performances on and off stage. Rami Malek played Mercury in 2018's film *Bohemian Rhapsody*, which was a worldwide hit and won Malek an Oscar for Best Actor.

Ethel Merman (1908–1984) `ICON`

In today's world, you may see yourself as a Beyoncé or a Gaga. If this were the 1940s, the choices would be Merman or Garland. Ethel Merman was a brassy-voiced broad who won the hearts of Broadway for over forty years and delighted audiences with her incredible diction and stunning way of belting it out to the back of the house. She'd originally trained to be a secretary, but Broadway called with *Girl Crazy* in 1930, where Merman and her amazing voice debuted the song "I Got Rhythm." Success followed success with shows like Cole Porter's *Anything Goes* in 1934 and *Red, Hot and Blue* opposite Bob Hope in 1936. She was the original Annie in *Annie Get Your Gun* in 1946 and the original Mama Rose in *Gypsy* in 1959. For her loud, booming belt and her idiosyncratic way of singing, Merman became a favorite of critics and audiences alike, and she is still cited as a queen of the American musical theatre.

Varla Jean Merman

The opera-singing, muscle-bonded, baby-doll-voiced drag queen of your dreams, Varla Jean Merman, as played by Jeffrey Roberson, has been delighting gay audiences around the world for decades. Originally billed as the love child of Ernest Borgnine and Ethel Merman (yes, they were married, look it up), Merman can do it all. A mainstay in Provincetown, Merman is often seen collaborating with friend and theatre legend Ryan Landry, but this is the just one aspect of Merman's outreach. She's starred in films like 2003's *Girls Will Be Girls*, as well as more mainstream faire, like *All My Children* where she played drag queen Rosemary Chicken. Internationally heralded and loved, Merman continues to tour, delighting audiences with her impressive vocals, scandalous humor, and Kewpie doll smile that endears her to every audience she encounters.

James Merrill (1926–1995)

A poet of more formal and lyric work early in his career, Merrill was moved to experimental and exploratory works in his later years, utilizing a Ouija board and tarot cards to free himself in the writing of messages from the other realms. Despite his dabbling into the occult, Merrill was a very respected poet during his lifetime, winning the Pulitzer Prize in 1977 for his collection *Divine Comedies*. Merrill also wrote novels; plays; and a memoir, *A Different Person*, in 1993.

George Michael (1963–2016)

The golden-voiced singer of the '80s pop group Wham!, George Michael achieved a stardom built on sex appeal and personal expression that blew the world away. He had huge hits with songs like "Careless Whisper," "Faith," and "Freedom! '90," but it was the push and pull of stardom that marked much of Michael's career. Rumors swirled around him before he finally came out in 1998, after which the controversy didn't stop. Twice arrested for public sex, Michael shrugged it off with a wink and nod that proved this bad boy of pop still had a little bad to go around. He was a strong advocate for the LGBTQ+ community and a long-time supporter of HIV/AIDS charities.

Michelangelo (1475–1564)

Whenever religious people get on their high horse about LGBTQ+ people, I always remind them that they wouldn't even know what God looks like if it wasn't for one of us. His artwork is seen everywhere from his beautiful frescos on the ceiling of the Sistine Chapel to his iconic David. Michelangelo Buonarroti is a titan in the field of art. A skilled sculptor and painter, he was considered a master during his lifetime and little has changed in the centuries since his death. Besides his abilities as an artist, he was also an impressive poet, and it is perhaps here where his true longing for love becomes most clear.

Middlesex

Jeffrey Eugenides's Pulitzer Prize–winning novel about a young intersex child and the family into which they are born was published in 2002. The novel's protagonist, Callie, comes to terms with their intersex identity in some of the most beautiful and haunting prose in the modern American literary canon. Though Eugenides is not intersex himself, the book has been embraced by the queer community for its chillingly honest portrayal of gender nonconformity.

Bette Midler (1945–) `ICON`

The queen of the bathhouse, Bette Midler is a legendary singer, performer, and actress who has delighted the world and always kept a close eye and ear on

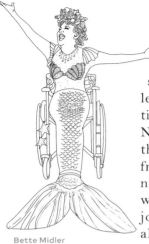

her gay fan base. Midler got her start singing in the legendary Continental Baths in New York City in the 1970s. Bette from the beginning was a broad who loved a good joke. She was also an incredible actress. With her star turn in 1979's *The Rose*, Midler showed the world the versatility and emotional truth of which she was capable. She's gone on to produce decades of amazing work, from albums like *The Divine Miss M* and *Divine Madness* to fun and funny movies like *Ruthless People* and *Big Business* with Lily Tomlin. But it was 1988's *Beaches* that gave Midler another chance to tug at our heartstrings and make us laugh. Her recording of "Wind Beneath My Wings" was a huge hit, winning Midler two Grammys that year, for Song of the Year and Album of the Year. Since *Beaches*, Midler's done residencies in Vegas, recorded tribute albums to her inspirations Rosemary Clooney and Peggy Lee, and starred in the cult classics *Hocus Pocus* and *The First Wives Club*. In 2017, Midler returned to Broadway in the role of Dolly Levi, first made famous by Carol Channing. The reviews were universally rapturous and she won the Tony for Best Actress.

Mika (1983–)

With his flamboyant style, stunning vocals, and expert piano playing, Mika first hit the music scene in 2007. At the time, people were already buzzing about what new heights this musical genius would take us to. His debut album, *Life in Cartoon Motion*, became one of the most talked-about albums of the year, with the single "Grace Kelly" becoming a feel-good hit for the summer of 2007. Mika has since released five more albums, including 2019's *My Name Is Michael Holbrook*.

Harvey Milk (1930–1978)

An icon of the gay rights movement and an inspiration to not only the LGBTQ+ community today but to all marginalized people, Harvey Milk sat on the San Francisco Board of Supervisors for only eleven months before he was brutally murdered by Dan White in November of 1978. Before his election, Milk had been a leader in the gay community around the Castro. Opening and operating his own camera shop on Castro Street put him front and center to deal with the concerns of his community. Milk

campaigned hard against the Briggs Initiative in 1978, and saw the discriminatory bill defeated. Even during his lifetime, Milk was an inspirational figure, setting both Cleve Jones and Anne Kronenberg on lifetime paths toward activism. As evidenced by the 2008 Oscar-winning biopic *Milk*, his message of compassion and hope rings as true today as it did almost forty years ago. As Milk always reminded us, "You gotta give 'em hope."

Tim Miller (1958–)

Miller is one of the NEA Four, a group of artists denied funding by John Frohnmayer in 1990 and who then sued the NEA, successfully winning their case for wrongful dismissal. He is a performance artist and storyteller whose work deals head-on with gay identity and personal growth and is often cited for its humor and unflinching honesty when it comes to gay sexuality and love. He also wrote extensively about the trials of the immigration system for gay people in his piece *Glory Box* in 1999 and *Us* in 2003. Miller still creates new works in Los Angeles, with a close association with the Highways performance space in Santa Monica.

Kate Millett (1934–2017)

Millett was a feminist writer and activist who set herself apart as one of the most influential and important voices in second-wave feminism. Her insights into the ever-changing plights of women and the struggle for mental health were but a few of the causes that she wrote about during her long and storied career, but were perhaps two of her biggest touchstones. Millet first came to public attention with her book *Sexual Politics* in 1970, which was based on her dissertation. She often took the personal and analyzed it from the realm of the political, taking on the mother-daughter dynamic in her book *Mother Millet*, released in 2001.

Nicki Minaj (1982–) `ICON`

This lady with the pinkest hair and the sickest beats brings her unique take on rap to the top of the charts. Minaj is the rapper of a thousand voices, using different personalities to express herself, from the boyish roughness of Roman to Martha Zolanski, who is Roman's mother with a British accent. Minaj got her start on a series of mixtapes in the 2000s, and broke out on her own in 2010 with *Pink Friday*. Since her first record, Minaj has been on a steady climb toward superstardom, with multiple Grammy nominations and a series of hits like "Pills N Potions" and "Anaconda," released in 2014. An artist unafraid of controversy on and off the stage, Minaj has become a beacon to her queer following, for spinning rhymes and spilling tea.

Sal Mineo (1939–1976)

This actor became famous for his role of Plato in *Rebel Without a Cause* opposite James Dean. Mineo was known for his sensitive characters while still in his twenties. He had major hits with movies like *The Gene Krupa Story* and *Exodus*, for which he was nominated for a Best Supporting Actor Oscar. In his thirties, he sought out new opportunities, trying to break the typecasting he experienced as a young man. He directed and acted on the stage, and it seemed that in his late thirties he was finally about to return to his earlier stardom, when he was found stabbed to death behind his apartment in West Hollywood.

Liza Minnelli

WITH A "Z"

Liza Minnelli (1946–) ICON

When your mother is Judy Garland, your father is Vincente Minnelli, and your godmother is Kay Thompson, you don't have much of a choice when it comes to becoming a gay icon. Luckily for all of us, Liza not only showed up for the mantel, but has put her own particular and delightful spin on the role for the last fifty years. While some could argue that she came up in her mother's shadow, even from the beginning one could see that she had a magic and a star power all her own. She performed with her mother in those early days on television and in the legendary concert at the London Palladium. It was Broadway that first set Minnelli apart. She won her first Tony award at just nineteen years old in the musical *Flora the Red Menace*. The show was not a runaway success, but it formed a bond between Minnelli and the songwriting team of Kander and Ebb that would lead both parties to the greater, starry heights. Their music led her to the film version of *Cabaret* in 1972, where her iconic portrayal of Sally Bowles won her the Oscar. What followed were a long string of legendary concerts and shows. Her television special *Liza with a Z* in 1972, *The Act* on Broadway in 1977, and her 1992 concert at Radio City Music Hall are just a few of the fiery and heartbreaking performances that have endeared Minnelli to her eager audience. Though Minnelli has also suffered with addiction, life is, at least publicly, always a cabaret for Liza. She's been a hallmark for the gay community, palling around with 1970s fashion designer Halston, and even marrying Peter Allen. Liza has been an outspoken supporter of LGBTQ+ rights since the beginning. She's had continued success with the *Arthur* films of the 1980s, Scorsese's *New York, New York*, which birthed the famous song of the same name, and even a recurring role on *Arrested Development*.

Kylie Minogue (1968–) `ICON`
An Australian pop princess who has given the gay community more dance music than probably any other singer of her generation, Minogue started her career with a pop-hit remake of the 1960s song "The Loco-Motion," but found her true self in the world of dance music. In the 1990s, Kylie began to find her groove with albums like *Rhythm of Love* and *Let's Get to It*, each producing danceable hits that reached clubs all over the world. Minogue continues to delight audiences with her positivity-infused dance music and her dedication to her fans, both of which only continue to grow.

Rumi Missabu (1947–)
An original member of the infamous Cockettes who keeps the tradition of free and ecstatic theatre alive and well in an ever-changing world, Rumi Missabu had a starring role in *Elevator Girls in Bondage*. She didn't join the subversive group on the fated trip to New York, but continued to perform with them on their return to San Francisco, and then went on to Hibiscus's Angels of Light. Missabu continues to tour and create new works for ecstatic theatre with stories steeped in history, fabulous costumes, and frivolity. A documentary about Missabu's life and work, *Ruminations*, was released in 2018.

Gabriela Mistral (1889–1957)
A Chilean poet and winner of the Nobel Prize for Literature, Gabriela Mistral is one of the most beloved poets of South America, rivaled only by fellow Chilean Pablo Neruda. Her work is deeply rooted in the soil and life of South America, and often uses the landscape and its history as a context in which she can express her deepest feelings of love and loss. Mistral was awarded the Nobel Prize in 1945, and though she was often seen as a bit of a spinster poet of love, her archives released long after her death showed a loving and glorious lesbian woman who knew much of love firsthand.

John Cameron Mitchell (1963–)
Mitchell is the actor and auteur who wrote and created *Hedwig and the Angry Inch*. He wrote the iconic piece with composer Stephen Trask, and starred not only in the original off-Broadway production in 1998, but also the film version in 2001, which he also directed. Mitchell continued his directing career with 2006's *Shortbus*, a sexually graphic and heartfelt movie about love and lust in New York. Mitchell has continued with 2010's *Rabbit Hole* and 2018's *How to Talk to Girls at Parties*, both with Nicole Kidman. In 2015, Mitchell had another turn as Hedwig, replacing Neil Patrick Harris in the revival and

receiving a special Tony Award for his work. Mitchell is the host of the Mattachine Party, a legendary party in New York, which features music DJed by Amber Martin and Angela Di Carlo. Mitchell's musical podcast, *Anthem: Homunculus*, debuted in 2019 and stars Cynthia Erivo and Glenn Close.

David Mixner (1946–)

An activist and author who works for the rights of LGBTQ+ people, Mixner got his start working in politics during the turbulent days of the 1960s. He was an outspoken critic of the war in Vietnam, and actually tried to bring a Moratorium to End the War in Vietnam in 1969. Mixner worked with the Democratic Party during the Clinton presidency and tried to fight against the "Don't Ask, Don't Tell" policy. Mixner continues his advocacy for LGBTQ+ causes as well as staying part of the conversation with his political blog.

Bob Mizer (1922–1992)

The granddaddy of homoerotic photography, Bob Mizer was a photographer and publisher of male erotica from the mid-twentieth century onward. He created the male pin-up, and his fans loved him for it. In a time when his kind of work was considered degrading, and, in most cases, illegal, Mizer created thousands of beefcake-style images that can still be seen today. His work, while at times seen as simply pornography, has also had an influence on fine art, with both Robert Mapplethorpe and David Hockney citing Mizer as an influence. A documentary on his life and work, *Beefcake*, was released in 1999.

Isaac Mizrahi (1961–)

Mizrahi is a designer whose personality has been called as colorful as his designs. At the height of his fame in the 1990s, his shows and his work with legendary supermodels like Naomi Campbell, Cindy Crawford, and Linda Evangelista made him one of the most talked-about designers in fashion. The 1995 documentary *Unzipped* showed him hard at work on his new show, with all the fun, sweat, and tears that went into it. Since the 1990s, Mizrahi has been all over the map of the fashion world. His first label folded in 1998, so he moved more into the spheres of television, and he also designs more commercial lines for Target. He's also gone on stage in a series of cabaret shows.

Janet Mock (1983–)

Mock is an openly trans writer, director, and activist whose winning personality and beautifully phrased arguments for the rights of trans women of color have made her a huge voice for LGBTQ+ people everywhere. Her stunning memoir *Redefining Realness* became a *New York Times* Best Seller and vaulted her in front of the camera. She became a regular on Oprah's *Super Soul Sunday*, and uses her platform to continually lift trans people of color up with her encouragement and her truth. This commitment has transferred to her other work—not only has Mock written a second memoir, 2017's *Surpassing Certainty*, she's also become a writer and director of the FX show *Pose*. In 2019, Mock became the first openly trans person to sign a major deal with Netflix.

Slava Mogutin (1974–)

Mogutin ia a Siberian-born artist and writer whose stunning views of gay sexuality made him a target of state condemnation in his native Russia but have made him a bright star in the international LGBTQ+ art scene. For his activism and his outspoken views on the treatment of LGBTQ+ people in Russia, Mogutin was forced to leave his homeland in the 1990s. Granted amnesty in the United States, Mogutin continued to push the envelope for gay visibility. His written works include poetry, essays, and journalism for which he won the Andrei Belyi Prize for Literature in 2000. But it's his photography that has catapulted him to art stardom. His pictures are respected and sought after the world over, and Mogutin continues to create images of intimacy and carnality in the LGBTQ+ landscape.

Janelle Monáe (1985–)

A pop singer, songwriter, and actress showing the world how to dance with open authenticity and a solid beat,

Janelle Monáe first hit the music scene in 2003, releasing endlessly danceable music coupled with strong story concepts. Her 2007 EP, *Metropolis: The Chase Suite*, started gaining Monáe traction in the industry not only as a strong writer and performer, but as a new voice telling stories through pop. Her albums with Bad Boy Records, starting in 2011 with *The ArchAndroid* to the most recent *Dirty Computer*, released in 2018, have turned her into one of the most respected songwriters of the modern era. Monáe has also crossed over into film with roles in *Moonlight* and *Hidden Figures*.

Janet Mock and
Paul Monette

Paul Monette (1945–1995)

Monette struggled to find his voice in Hollywood, yet when he turned to books, his beautiful prose sent him a success he'd never imagined. The writer's first major work, 1988's

Borrowed Time, is a memoir about the world of AIDS in which Monette and a whole generation of men found themselves. His second major work, *Becoming a Man*, which won the National Book Award, was a harrowing and often humorous tale of Monette's coming out and meeting his first partner. Monette died of complications from AIDS in 1995.

Moonlight

This beautiful film that debuted in 2016, written and directed by Barry Jenkins, is based on a story written by Tarell Alvin McCraney and tells of a young Florida man in three stages of his life. First as a young boy (i. Little), then as a teen (ii. Chiron), and an adult (iii. Black), it follows Chiron's journey of connection. His first is to a drug-dealer father figure, who's trying to help the young boy as his mother slides into the pit of addiction, then with a fellow student in high school. The two have a sexual relationship, and while Chiron grows up to become a very different person from the young, sensitive man of the earlier sections, he still misses the connection with his high-school partner, whom he finds again. Critics loved the stunning debut by Jenkins and awarded both he and McCraney the Oscar for Best Screenplay. The movie also won Best Picture, becoming the first movie featuring LGBTQ+ people of color to win the award.

Indya Moore (1994-)

Indya Moore is giving the world "Face-Face-Face," but with it comes a very thoughtful advocate for the trans community. Most famous for their star turn as Angel Evangelista in FX's *Pose*, Moore came to acting after years in the modeling industry. While modeling has taken a back seat to acting, Moore still continues a love affair with the catwalk and the camera loves them. Moore became one of the first transgender models to appear on the cover of *Elle* in 2019. Moore uses their considerable outreach to speak for change and justice for the trans community, and has been out on the streets fighting with Black Lives Matter.

Juanita MORE!

A legendary queen from the Bay Area, this entertainer, activist, and restaurateur uses the power of drag to get her point across. A staple of the gay community in San Francisco for more than twenty years, More has done everything from creating art in her performances and outdoor murals to opening a restaurant. Mother has to feed the children, but More isn't just about food—she offers insight and help to the LGBTQ+ community of San Francisco and for many years has been an outspoken champion and activist for the rights of that community. In 2020, More was elected Empress of Imperial Council of San Francisco, a position once held by Jose Sarria.

Mark Morris (1956–)

A colossal figure in American dance, Morris and his company have been redefining the way in which dance is viewed and enjoyed by audiences around the world. His work plays largely on his sense of fun and play, his solid and breathtaking understanding of what dance can do, and also what the human body can express all on its own. He has worked with classically trained dancers like Mikhail Baryshnikov and musicians like Yo-Yo Ma. He's also broadened the feel and the style of contemporary dance, using music from pop to hip-hop and blending them in a style all his own.

Cookie Mueller (1949–1989)

One of John Waters's original Dreamland players, Cookie Mueller was an actress, artist, and writer. She can be seen in many early Waters films like *Multiple Maniacs*, *Pink Flamingos*, and playing Conhetta in *Female Trouble*. But it's been her writings that have become a subject of interest for many of her fans. Mueller wrote a series of small books, as well as a series of art criticism and a health column called Ask Dr. Mueller. She was also a muse of famed photographer Nan Goldin. Mueller died of complications from AIDS in 1989, and a book about her life and work, *Edgewise*, was compiled by Chloé Griffin and published in 2014.

Nico Muhly (1981–)

A classical composer and arranger who has become a rock star on the classical circuit, if that isn't mixing too many metaphors or genres, Muhly was a bit of prodigy, studying with mentor Philip Glass right out of Juilliard and beginning to write for the opera stage and film at the age of twenty-two. He began to release albums of his compositions with 2006's *Speaks Volumes*. He's also collaborated with a host of contemporary pop artists from Björk to Glen Hansard. In 2013, his opera *Two Boys* was performed at the Metropolitan Opera in New York, and he was later commissioned by the Met to write a new opera. His opera *Marnie*, based on the Alfred Hitchcock film of the same name, debuted in 2017.

Ryan Murphy (1965–)

He makes you scream, he makes you sing, he makes you think about the pain of Joan Crawford. There's lots to be thankful for when it comes to Ryan Murphy, one of the biggest directors and producers in television. His eye toward camp and the heightened emotion that can only be done with horror or music have made him a legend. While he'd worked for a while before, Murphy's first hit was *Nip/Tuck*, a sexy and smart drama about the plastic-surgery industry. From there, he created *Glee* in 2009. The show became a major hit for Murphy, with its feel-good musical numbers and openly gay story lines. After *Glee*, Murphy again went into uncharted territory with *American Horror Story*, an anthology with ever-changing story lines and a revolving company of players. The show has taken its viewers to a school for witches in New Orleans, a roadside freak show, a demonic hotel filled with vampires, and the end of the world. The company of actors has changed from season to season but maintained some regulars like Jessica Lange, Denis O'Hare, and Sarah Paulson. Murphy continues to be a prolific producer and writer, with series like *American Crime Story*, *Feud*, *Scream Queens*, and *Pose*, but the most refreshing part is that he never shies away from telling LGBTQ+ stories in rich and authentic ways.

My Beautiful Laundrette

In this 1985 film, Daniel Day-Lewis and Gordon Warnecke play two young men on opposite sides of the racial divide of English and Pakistani relations in the age of Margaret Thatcher. Directed by Stephen Frears and written by Hanif Kureishi, has been a favorite with audiences and critics alike since its debut. The comical yet heartfelt tale of the two young men finding each other and falling in love, despite the odds of family and their own troubled pasts, still maintains its honesty and laughs after all these years.

My So-Called Life

The short-lived network classic that first gave us Claire Danes and obsessed so many with the charms of Jordan Catillano was one of the earliest and best depictions of gay angst in the 1990s. It debuted in 1994 and was immediately a critical hit. The story centered around young Angela Chase as she struggles to find herself in the toils and tribulations of high school. It also took on bigger stories with the character of Rickie, played by Wilson Cruz. Rickie wore makeup, hung out in the girl's bathroom, and came out in a manner all his own. It was a brave move toward visibility that was just breaking into the mainstream in the 1990s.

Eileen Myles (1949–)

Myles is a poet and author who has been blasting a hole in the patriarchy for more than forty years. Their work has been praised across the board for decades and some of their writings have become classics in the LGBTQ+ canon. Their book *Chelsea Girls*, published in 1994, is renowned for its honesty and frankness about lesbian lives. Myles ran for president in the 1992 election, and Zoe Leonard's poem "I want a president" was based on their candidacy. Myles's work now inspires a whole new generation of writers and poets, and they continue their amazing output, most recently with *Afterglow*, a memoir based on the life of their dog.

Myra Breckinridge

A satirical novel by Gore Vidal about a trans woman trying to make it in Hollywood. *Myra Breckinridge* still causes quite a stir for many of its readers, but poses more questions about our own sensibilities around gender. Far ahead of its time, the book was an international best seller and was adapted into a truly terrible movie starring Raquel Welch as Myra.

Myra Breckinridge

N is for...

Martina Navratilova (1956–)

Sometimes you can age people by the first important lesbian they remember. For early millennials, Martina Navratilova is their lesbian. One of the world's most successful tennis players in history and a winner of eighteen Grand Slam singles titles as well as thirty-one doubles titles, Navratilova has easily earned her place in the tennis history books. But it was her coming out in 1981 that brought her to the forefront of the fight for LGBTQ+ rights. She embraced the community and has become an outspoken advocate for LGBTQ+ rights ever since. An oftentimes hard and aggressive player, she's used this same sort of forthrightness in her approach to advocacy.

Alla Nazimova (1879–1945)

A Russian-born actress of intense emotional depth, Nazimova taught America how to adore the works of Chekhov and Ibsen. She had become a stage star in her native Russia by 1903, but with the promise of grander successes still awaiting her in the new world, she moved to New York in 1905. From her Broadway debut in 1906 until the end of her career, she was a major star. She appeared in the plays of Ibsen and Chekhov, and while they had already been seen on American stages, she infused them with the passion that made them hallmarks. The playwright Tennessee Williams said that it was seeing Nazimova in Chekhov that truly changed his life. She began making films in 1916, and was soon writing and directing her own work. Her infamous film version of Wilde's *Salomé* in 1923 was a failure with the box office and critics alike, but still stands out for its sheer visual decadence. It's also said that the cast was made up of entirely queer people as a secret homage to Wilde.

Meshell Ndegeocello (1968–)

A hard-rocking singer-songwriter whose work as a musician and social activist have made her a favorite for decades, Ndegeocello has had hits with "Wild Nights," a Van Morrison song she covers with John Mellencamp, and the Bill Withers cover, "Who Is He and What Is He to You" in 1996. But it's Ndegeocello's self-written work that often speaks to the subjects and truths that mean the most to her heart. Her socially conscious lyrics and jamming beats have made her a favorite among musicians and fans alike.

She's performed with everyone from Madonna and Chaka Khan to the Rolling Stones. Ndegeocello has long been an out and proud bisexual and a fierce advocate for the rights of LGBTQ+ people.

Hari Nef (1992–)

Nef is an actor, model, and writer hitting the runway and Hollywood hard at the moment, and everyone should take note. After graduating from Columbia, Nef began writing for many online outlets, including *Vice* and *Dazed*, but ultimately wanted to pursue her real passion—acting. After playing Maura's great aunt Gittel on *Transparent*, Nef moved into film, gaining roles in *Mapplethorpe* and *Assassination Nation* in 2018.

Maggie Nelson (1973–)

One of the most lauded writers of her generation, Maggie Nelson mixes a vibrant poetic sense with a keen eye toward storytelling in works that move and provoke. Her 2015 book, *The Argonauts*, was a critical and commercial hit that made Nelson a much-sought-after writer and won her the National Book Critics Circle Award. She has written deeply and beautifully about the murder of her aunt in *Jane*, and a 2007 memoir of the trial, *The Red Parts*. Nelson continues to release work that defies convention and touches an audience that hangs on her every beautifully chosen word.

Alex Newell (1992–)

When you're a gender-nonconforming Black child with a voice that was made to ring out in the rafters, what is the path for you to take? Alex Newell is currently laying it down. Getting his start on Ryan Murphy's *Glee* in 2014, Newell made his Broadway debut in the 2018 revival of *Once on this Island*. Since then Newell has joined the cast of NBC's *Zoey's Extraordinary Playlist*, and continues to release banging pop music with hits like 2016's "Kill the Lights," and 2019's "As I Am" with Bryan Adams.

Daniel Nicoletta (1954–)

Nicoletta got a job at Harvey Milk's camera shop in the Castro in the 1970s, and the meeting of the young man and the camera was a match made in heaven. He began simply documenting his friends living their best gay lives in the heady atmosphere of the '70s, but soon people could see that he had a lot more to offer than snapshots. Besides being a major chronicler of Harvey Milk's life, Nicoletta also captured the ever-evolving world of gay culture as it moved from the decadence of the '70s to the much more harrowing '80s. His work became emblematic of the city in which he lived, and has reached people around the world, showing everyone the brilliance that is queer people in their element. Nicoletta also moved into film and was one of the founders of the San Francisco International LGBT

Film Festival in 1977. The festival still operates under the name Frameline Film Festival.

Vaslav Nijinsky (1890–1950)

Perhaps the world's first male ballet superstar, Vaslav Nijinsky captured the hearts and imagination of the world at the turn of the twentieth century. Known for his almost supernatural jumping abilities, he was the star of Diaghilev's Ballets Russes. The two were also lovers who lived openly and honestly in a period of time when that was still illegal. Nijinsky at the Ballets Russes starred in and created a body of work that, to this day, still commands enormous reverence in the ballet world. Nijinsky choreographed his *L'après-midi d'une faune* in 1912 and created a worldwide scandal by finishing the piece with a highly sexual gesture. He went on to choreograph the infamously difficult ballet *The Rite of Spring* by Igor Stravinsky. Nijinsky broke it off with Diaghilev in 1913 and married Romola de Pulszky, but in the years after began to suffer from mental problems. He was later diagnosed with schizophrenia, and from 1919 onward he spent the majority of his life in psychiatric care. His diaries, kept during his years after leaving the Ballets Russes, were published by his wife and have since become classics.

Willi Ninja and Vaslav Nijinsky

Anaïs Nin (1903–1977)

A writer of novels, erotica, and most famously her own diaries, which have become classics for their sexual candor and their insight into the lives of women, Nin is remembered for her erotic work, which while surely titillating, broke barriers for its purely feminist view of sex. Her characters are interested in their own pleasure and satisfaction and in many ways, belying the prejudices of the period, are open and equal partners with their male counterparts. Her *Delta of Venus* is seen today as a masterpiece of the genre. In the releasing of her diaries, Nin put her private life on full display, making her as notorious as some of her work. She had many affairs with the literati of her day, but a long-term affair with writer Henry Miller is especially famous, as Nin chronicled it in her journal *Henry and June*.

Willi Ninja (1961–2006)

He taught the world how to vogue, and things have never been the same since. The world first met Willi Ninja in the film *Paris Is Burning* in 1990, but by that point he'd already been making a stir in New York's ball scene for years. Ninja was the king, or the queen as it were, of voguing. This physically grueling and acrobatic dancing, where posing and body shaping is paramount, was an art form that Ninja mastered. With the advent of *Paris Is Burning* and Madonna's song "Vogue," Ninja wanted to take his style of dance everywhere. He appeared in many videos, including two from Janet Jackson's *Rhythm Nation 1814* album, and even released a single of his own. He continued to be a proponent and teacher of voguing for the rest of his life, and the world looks so much better for it.

Cynthia Nixon (1966–)

Perhaps most known for her role as Miranda on the show *Sex and the City*, this celebrated stage and screen actress was also the first openly gay woman to run for the governor of New York. She's a two-time Tony Award–winning actress who's won for *Rabbit Hole* in 2006 and 2016's revival of *The Little Foxes*, opposite Laura Linney. Linney and Nixon would alternate roles of the sophisticated and sinister Regina and the much-maligned Birdie. In 2018, Nixon challenged incumbent Andrew Cuomo for his job as governor. While her campaign was unsuccessful, Nixon continues her long history of being an advocate for social change and LGBTQ+ equality in all forms.

Noah's Arc

A groundbreaking series about a group of gay men of color navigating love and life in the modern world, *Noah's Arc* ran for only two seasons, but that was enough for it to become a cult favorite and a touchstone for the LGBTQ+ community of color looking for representation. *Arc* followed the loves of Noah, played by Darryl Stephens, and his friends, Alex played by Rodney Chester, Ricky played by Christian Vincent, and Chance played by Doug Spearman. It also followed Noah's relationship with Wade, played by Jensen Atwood, who comes out to him. The show was a hallmark of the early days of Logo TV and continues to draw a large audience on streaming services.

Klaus Nomi (1944–1983)

When you're a German countertenor with a sci-fi aesthetic and real need to sing pop music, there doesn't seem to be a clear path for you to take. If you're Klaus Nomi, you make one. A classically trained countertenor who took his art form to the stages of downtown New York and perfected the role of a strange and entrancing alien with a voice from another world, Nomi was born in Germany, and immigrated to

Klaus Nomi

the United States in 1972. He began performing in New York City, exciting downtown artists with his vocal acrobatics and stunning stage presence. He formed friendships with many of the greatest artists of the period, including a long-standing collaboration with Joey Arias. His recordings of songs like "Lightning Strikes" and videos of live performances like "Total Eclipse" are much-coveted remnants of the brilliant artist. His work caught the attention of David Bowie, who asked both Nomi and Arias to perform on *Saturday Night Live* with him in 1979. Nomi continued to release music and perform around the world until his death of complications from AIDS in 1983.

Connie Norman (1949–1996)

This AIDS activist and trans trailblazer fought the good fight for the LGBTQ+ community at the height of the plague with the humor and passion that made her a legend. A writer and television personality of the time, Norman brought LGBTQ+ issues to the fore all across Los Angeles with her caustic wit and ability to fight any argument and fight it hard. Norman was endlessly honest about her past, which was filled with drug use and sex work, and saw that honestly as the best way to address the plights of her community. Norman died of complications from AIDS in 1996, but her legacy lives on in the many people she touched. A documentary about her

Connie Norman

life, *AIDS Diva: The Legend of Connie Norman*, was released in 2018.

Tracey "Africa" Norman (1952–)

Tracey "Africa" Norman is a groundbreaking trans model, who was first shot for Italian *Vogue* by famed photographer Irving Penn. In the early 1970s, Norman was outed as trans at a photoshoot and her career in America slowed to a halt. Norman then moved to Europe and was signed to an exclusive contract modeling for the famed house of Balenciaga. In 2015, *New York Magazine* did a biographical article on Norman, telling her story of breaking into fashion as a trans model, when most of this country didn't know that trans people even existed. Norman has been active in the ballroom scene in New York for years, and parts of her story were used as inspiration for the first season of FX's *Pose*.

Harold Norse (1916–2009)

A poet and writer who seemed to always be in the right place at the right time, with the right people, Norse knew most of the great writers of his day and was a particular favorite of the Beat Generation. Though often considered a Beat, Norse had been writing well-respected poetry before he met Beat writers like Allen Ginsberg, Gregory Corso, and Williams S. Burroughs. But their work and encouragement helped Norse move his own work into varied and unchartered waters. His poetry is still respected and anthologized, and his *Memoirs of a Bastard Angel*, published in 1989, is a vital and often-funny look into the literary world of the twentieth century.

Ann Northrop (1948–)

This pioneering activist and journalist has been on the frontlines of the LGBTQ+ movement for more than thirty years. Northrop started her long career writing in television and print journalism, concentrating on the issues of women during the fierce and fiery days of the early feminism movement. In 1981, she joined the team at *Good Morning America*, then shifted to *CBS Morning News*. But when she saw the LGBTQ+ community in the throes of the AIDS crisis, Northrop left her job to join the fight. She was the only openly

Ann
Northrop

gay person to speak at the Democratic National Convention in 1992, and has continued to use her voice and vast talents to take on the challenges faced by the LGBTQ+ community. Today, Northrup hosts *Gay USA* with co-anchor Andy Humm.

Graham Norton (1963–)

The most charming man on British television, Graham Norton is one of Britain's most beloved and awarded talk-show hosts in history. Norton, with his affable wit and sinister side glance, has hosted his own show on the BBC since 2007. He's interviewed countless celebrities and notables, who love his charm and free and easy style that bring all the guests together for a little roundtable chat with drinks. It's wonderful, and the key component is Norton, who always keeps the party moving with his sparkling commentary. While Norton has worked in many other iterations, including hosting the *Eurovision Song Contest*, it has always been his show that has won him fans and devotees from around the world.

Ramon Novarro (1899–1968)

A huge star in the silent movie era who was seen as a second Rudolph Valentino, Novarro starred in many great movies of the silent period, but perhaps his most famous role came in the original version of *Ben-Hur* in 1925. After sound came into motion pictures, he unfortunately could not make the transition. He effectively retired from film in 1935. Novarro became a notorious case when, in 1968, he was horribly murdered by two hustlers in Hollywood.

Ivor Novello (1893–1951)

A Welsh singer, songwriter, and actor, with a wit to rival Noël Coward and a sentimental, sophisticated style that made him a star, Novello found success on the British stage as a matinee idol, but it was his songs and writing that made him one of the most sought-after performers of the age. He wrote many hits of the day, including his most famous song, "Keep the Home Fires Burning," which became a sentimental ballad of the First World War. The Ivor Novello Awards for songwriting are named in his honor, and considered one of the highest awards a songwriter can achieve in England.

Richard Bruce Nugent (1906–1987)

For many who study the Harlem Renaissance, there appear to have been a lot of gay people involved, which is probably what made it so great. On closer look it seems that while many of the artists of this period were living gay lives, very few were out. That is not the case with painter and writer Richard Bruce Nugent. Nugent wrote poetry and fiction for many of the newly founded Black publications of the period, and became a collaborative visual artist for many of his famous writer friends like Claude McKay and Ralph Ellison. Strangely, though he was out, Nugent married his friend Grace Marr in 1952 and remained with her until her death in 1969. Nugent's work came back into focus in the 1970s, as younger gay men of color were looking for their art-making ancestors. Nugent became a mentor to many artists in the 1980s, right up until his death.

Rudolf Nureyev (1938–1993)

With his stunning stage presence and emotional dancing, Nureyev was an imposing and important figure in the world of ballet. He was a star in his native Russia, but famously defected to the West in 1961, where he became an international sensation. He carried on a long affair with fellow dancer Erik Bruhn for a number of years, but it was his onstage partnership with ballet legend Margot Fonteyn that turned the eyes of the world on Nureyev. Together, they performed all the major roles in the ballet repertoire, and created a few new ones. Nureyev continued to dance and direct after his partnership with Fonteyn, and became director of the Paris Opera Ballet in 1983. Nureyev died of complications from AIDS in 1993.

Laura Nyro (1947–1997)

One of the most unmistakable voices of the latter half of the twentieth century, this enigmatic songwriter expanded the chordal vocabulary of pop music with songs like "Stoned Soul Picnic,"

"Wedding Bell Blues," and "Stoney End." At the time, Nyro's song were more well-known than she was. They were major hits for the 5th Dimension, Barbra Streisand, and Bette Midler. Nyro's solo work is impressive and influential. She was a deeply emotional artist who endlessly sings on the break of her voice, bringing her music to new heights. Her album from the great Motown era, *Gonna Take a Miracle*, was an instant classic, with Nyro on lead vocals and the group Labelle backing her up. She died from cancer at the young age of forty-nine, and was inducted into the Rock & Roll Hall of Fame in 2012.

O

is for . . .

Tyler Oakley (1989–)

Far from the days of cinnamon-eating contests and tasting Tide Pods, Tyler Oakley is making the Internet think and feel, mostly with his clothes. Perhaps the first breakout star of the YouTube generation, Oakley is a young man with a following and affability that have endeared him to a generation that's grown up on the Internet. Oakley began making personal vlogs in 2007, and his energetic and warm personality soon made him a YouTube success story. With over 7 million followers, he has amassed an audience that hangs on his every word and laughs at all of his quirky jokes. But YouTube was just the beginning for Oakley. He's taken his stardom to television, competing on reality television in *The Amazing Race* and debuting a new show on Ellen DeGeneres's Internet network called *The Tyler Oakley Show*. He also wrote a collection of essays called *Binge* in 2015.

Frank Ocean (1987–)

The sweet soulful music you put on to put down, Frank Ocean is the master of the modern sexy slow jam. The singer, songwriter, and artist drew the praise of music critics and fans alike with his debut solo album, *Channel Orange*, in 2012. Though Ocean had been producing music prior to its release, the album announced the coming of a new and brilliant artist with a wealth of emotion and musical integrity. It earned Ocean a huge fan base and a Grammy Award for Best Urban Contemporary Album. With songs like "Thinkin Bout You" and "Sweet Life," Ocean became well-known and loved for his innovative use of sampling, mixing, and his beautiful voice. His album *Blonde* was released in 2016 after many delays, but again proved that Ocean is an artist of ever-growing skill and brilliance.

Ryan O'Connell (1986–)

A writer and performer whose 2015 memoir, *I'm Special*, was the source material for the wildly successful *Special* on Netflix in 2019, Ryan O'Connell began his career writing articles for the Internet, but quickly moved into writing for television with MTV's *Awkward*. He continued to write personal essays for sites like *Vice*, then made the move to the revival of *Will & Grace*. When his own sitcom *Special* debuted, it was heralded as a triumph for showcasing the stories of LGBTQ+ people with disabilities.

Rosie O'Donnell (1962–)

Once hailed as the queen of nice, this comedic and opinionated voice has been in the culture since she first won the competition show *Star Search* in 1984. Perhaps most remembered for her daytime talk show, *The Rosie O'Donnell Show*, which ran from 1996 to 2002, O'Donnell introduced a whole generation to her love for Broadway and the fun of throwing a Koosh ball. After the show ended, O'Donnell was briefly a host of ABC's *The View*, famously clashing with conservative host Elisabeth Hasselbeck live on air. O'Donnell is a deep supporter of liberal causes and LGBTQ+ rights, and for this she has taken some heat over the years. Look no further than her spat with Donald Trump that continues to this day. O'Donnell also found success on the big screen in films like *Sleepless in Seattle*, *A League of Their Own* and

Rosie O'Donnell and Frank O'Hara

The Flintstones, and in acting roles on television in *The Fosters* and *SMILF*. O'Donnell and her then partner, Kelli Carpenter, also ran a series of "Rosie" cruises especially geared for gay families.

Paul O'Grady (1955–)

O'Grady is the creator of the drag persona Lily Savage and host of *The Paul O'Grady Show*. As Lily Savage, the foul-mouthed lady from Liverpool with her roots showing, O'Grady became a much-beloved guest on British television, and a particular favorite of legendary interviewer Michael Parkinson. Lily hosted the game show *Blankety Blank* from 1997 to 2002. When O'Grady finally decided to step out of Lily's stilettos, things started to take on a different light. He hosted a few iterations of *The Paul O'Grady Show* from 2004 to 2015 and was a huge hit with audiences. He has since continued to work in television, presenting shows that deal with his advocacy for animals.

Frank O'Hara (1926–1966)

A poet and art critic who brought a new wild casualness and humor into American poetry, and still maintains a wide and devoted readership, O'Hara was deeply intrenched in the New York School of Poetry with other gay writers like friends John Ashbery and James Schuyler. He was also heavily involved within the abstract expressionism art movement. O'Hara curated shows for New York's Museum of

Modern Art, and wrote extensively about the art scene and the people who made it in that time. But it's O'Hara's poetry that continues to entice readers. His *Lunch Poems*, published in 1964 by City Lights, has become a classic.

Denis O'Hare (1962–)

There's nobody who plays a "baddy" like this actor and writer, but that's just a tenth of his range. Denis O'Hare is a respected Broadway actor who came to the public's attention for roles in shows like *Take Me Out* and Sondheim's *Assassins*, which established O'Hare as an actor of range and talent. Roles on television like that of Russell Edgington in HBO's *True Blood* saw to it that he would soon be performing on a much more natural front. A favorite of Ryan Murphy's, O'Hare has appeared in *American Horror Story* since 2011, in notable roles like the manservant Spalding in *Coven* and Liz Taylor in *Hotel*. O'Hare continues to do great work on stage and film and use his platform to be outspoken for LBGTQ rights and the rights of their families.

Edgar Oliver (1956–)

He has a voice like no other, haunting and mysterious but endlessly warm; to hear Edgar Oliver is to fall into a world of dreams. He's a writer, actor, poet, and storyteller, with a fascinating voice and even more alluring way of spinning the truth. Oliver's work has often been featured on *The Moth*, and has driven countless people to his many works for stage. He has written a number of plays, with notable works being *The Poetry Killer, The Drowning Pages*, and most recently *Victor*, which ran at the Axis Theatre in New York to excellent reviews. A writer of great beautiful, simplicity, and emotion, Oliver has also released two volumes of poetry.

Isaac Oliver (1983–)

Oliver is a writer and comedian making strides and making us all laugh as he does it. His 2015 memoir, *Intimacy Idiot*, was an instant hit in LGBTQ+ lit and established Oliver as a fresh new voice with a deeply sardonic honesty about sex in the app age. He went on to write regularly for the *New York Times*, and has now written on HBO's *High Maintenance* and Netflix's *Glow*.

Mary Oliver (1935–2019)

The work of Mary Oliver, one of the most beloved and respected poets of the latter half of the twentieth century, is deeply personal and yet wholly accessible, which has made her one of the bestselling poets of her time. The natural world and her appreciation for it appear often in her poetry, as does the wonder of this "precious human life." Oliver wrote many collections of poetry, and her 1984 collection, *American Primitive*, won the Pulitzer Prize. She won the National Book Award for Poetry for her *New and Selected Poems* in 1992.

Catherine Opie (1961–)

A photographer who has been investigating queer life in her work for over three decades, Opie creates a sort of communion with her subjects, allowing them to drop their guard. Instead of becoming an object, they collaborate with Opie in how they wish to be viewed. Opie has always worked with queer subjects and has had close and brilliant relationships in art with the trans community. Her shows, like *Being and Having* in 1991, have created stirs, as well as awe and understanding for their portrayals of LGBTQ+ people. Opie, who lives and works in Los Angeles, has worked closely with the Hammer Museum and the Museum of Contemporary Art, and her work has been seen and sought after in galleries around the world.

Oranges Are Not the Only Fruit

Jeanette Winterson's 1985 novel details the life of a young girl, Jeannette, growing up with her evangelical parents. When she discovers she's attracted to girls, her mother and friends try to exorcise the demons within her. You wouldn't think exorcism could provide for a playful and fun romp, but *Oranges* doesn't disappoint. The book won the Whitbread Award and was later turned into a miniseries for the BBC.

Orlando

This comic novel about the immortal, gender-shifting Orlando, written in 1928 by Virginia Woolf, is a classic study on the role of gender and the freedom of the queer spirit. It's said to be based on Woolf's impressions of her lover Vita Sackville-West. Orlando travels through eras and sexes with relative ease, but never loses Woolf's keen eye to satire. The book has been adapted several times, most notably by Sally Potter in 1992, in a film of the same name starring Tilda Swinton in the titular role.

Orry-Kelly

Orry-Kelly (1897–1964)

He dressed some of the most famous women in Hollywood's Golden Age, making these golden goddesses look even better than they could have imagined. The Australian-born designer immigrated to the United States in the late 1920s with the original vision of being an actor. He soon met the young Cary Grant, and according to Kelly, the two became lovers. Kelly began making costumes, and by 1932, he moved to Hollywood to be the chief costume designer at the Warner Bros.

Studio. He was a particular favorite of Bette Davis and Katharine Hepburn. Kelly was responsible for some of the most fashionable looks in Hollywood, from the sleek beauty of *Casablanca* to the outrageousness of *Auntie Mame*. For his work on film, Kelly won three Oscars for Best Costume Design.

Joe Orton (1933–1967)

This cheeky and irreverent playwright of London's swinging '60s crafted dark comedies to shake up social mores and conventions. Orton's life was as spectacular as his writing. An openly gay man, he went to prison with his best friend and sometimes lover, Kenneth Halliwell, for hilariously defacing library books. After their release from prison, Orton and Halliwell began to write a novel, but it was Orton whose talent emerged. With his first full-length play, *Entertaining Mr Sloane* in 1964, Orton was crowned a star. He went on to write plays like *Loot* in 1965, and *What the Butler Saw*, which was first performed after Orton's death. Orton's professional and personal successes put stress on his relationship with the emotionally unstable Halliwell who, in a rage of jealousy, beat Orton to death before killing himself. Orton's diaries, showcasing his enormous wit and sexual appetite, were published after his death. A film of Orton's life, *Prick Up Your Ears*, based on the biography of the same name by John Lahr, was released in

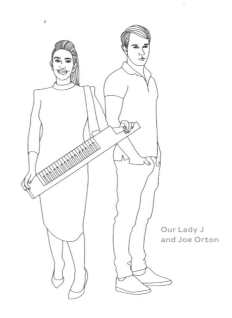

Our Lady J
and Joe Orton

1987 with Gary Oldman as Orton and Alfred Molina as Halliwell.

Our Lady J (1978–)

Musician, writer, and performer who has created a career in a multitude of forms. Originally trained as a classical pianist, Our Lady J began playing shows downtown, bringing her world view to the works of Dolly Parton in her show, *The Gospel of Dolly*. But it turned out there's more to this trailblazer than star performance. She joined the writing staff of Amazon's *Transparent* and wrote for the show for three seasons, also appearing on camera in the 1930s flashbacks of season 3. Writing suited the multi-talented artist, so when the show *Pose* was looking for writers that could lend a sense of authenticity to the world, Our Lady J happily joined the team.

Out

Founded in 1992 as an entertainment and culture alternative to the news and politics of *The Advocate*, this magazine has been a staple of LGBTQ+ media for almost three decades. Editor Michael Goff launched it, but through the years the magazine has been through a host of different editors and taken a lot of different directions in an attempt to best service the community, while staying true to its mission. In 2018, Raquel Willis was named the new executive editor, making her the first trans woman to ever hold the position.

P is for . . .

Elliot Page (1987–)

Page became a huge star for his role in 2007's indie hit *Juno*, where he played a wisecracking pregnant teen. Page was lauded for his performance and nominated for several awards, but the film was just the beginning of Page's success. Since then he's starred in a multitude of films, from Kitty Pryde in the *X-Men* franchise to the mega-hit *Inception*. Page has always been committed to telling different stories and has continued to have a foot firmly planted in the world of independent film. Page came out in 2014 and has since been an outspoken advocate for the rights LGBTQ+ people. In 2021, Page announced he was transistioning and the world got to meet a very happy young man named Elliot, who we all love.

Camille Paglia (1947–)

Paglia is a controversial feminist thinker whose work has examined and reevaluated pop culture and the society that makes it for decades. Her book, *Sexual Personae*, published in 1990, was a stunning work that put Paglia on the map, and her abrasive and punchy nature made her a great guest on television. She garnered a lot of attention for openly taking on other feminists like Susan Sontag and Germaine Greer. While Paglia's views are often entertaining and interesting, her takes on subjects from Madonna to Taylor Swift's "girl squads" have rubbed people the wrong way. Paglia is, as ever, unapologetic and continues to comment on the world around her with historical perspective and a rollicking wit.

Amanda Palmer (1976–)

Palmer is a powerful singer-songwriter who uses social media for social change. She first hit the music scene with her duo, the Dresden Dolls, formed with drummer Brian Viglione. The group garnered attention for its playful-yet-intense music that rollicked as much as it rocked. A combination of cabaret and punk, the Dresden Dolls drew a huge following for Palmer, and when she eventually went out on her own in 2008, she continued to attract large numbers of adoring fans. Since then Palmer has continued to create music and wrote her memoir, 2014's *The Art of Asking*, in which she detailed her use of social media to continue her life as a touring musician. She set up a Patreon to connect directly with her audience, and became an outspoken advocate for this way of supporting artists. Palmer is married to writer Neil Gaiman.

Pariah

This 2011 film was a breakout hit at the Sundance Film Festival, and with good reason. The searing drama focuses in on young Alike, a young woman coming to terms with her homosexuality, and beautifully played by Adepero Oduye. The film follows Alike's journey of coming out and the trials of dealing with a religious family. Directed and written by Dee Rees, it is a thrilling and beautifully shot story of a young woman of color finding her own butchness and gaining a world of friends and lovers, albeit at the terrible cost of the family and only world she's ever known.

Paris Is Burning

Paris Is Burning

Basically, everything you think you're inventing or so cleverly coming up with was already done, said, and styled in this movie. This 1990 documentary has become a classic of the form and a much-beloved gay revelation about the lives and loves of people in the '80s gay ballroom scene. With stars like Dorian Corey and Pepper LaBeija gracing its screen, the movie was an instant cult hit and soon moved into the wider culture, drawing fans from critics and audiences alike. It's a brilliant, honest portrayal of the ballroom scene as directed by Jennie Livingston. It's instantly quotable—basically anything that's said on *Drag Race* now was most likely first heard in *Paris Is Burning*. A stunning, funny, and at times deeply touching film about the triumph of fantasy and freedom against impossible odds, this film is a classic.

Al Parker (1952–1992)

This stud of the "clone" era (see page 58) is a gay-porn legend. When the gay uniform was facial hair and plaid shirts, Al Parker emerged as the best of the lot. With his steely good looks, thick moustache, and sizable endowment, Parker was immediately a favorite with gay fans around the world. He appeared in many early gay films from Colt Studios and Falcon Studios. But he eventually wanted more creative control, and struck out on his own with his Surge Studios. His was one of the first porn studios to show condoms on film in the early days of the AIDS crisis. Parker died of complications from AIDS in 1992.

Jim Parsons (1973–)

Openly gay actor Parsons played the delightfully awkward Sheldon Cooper on *The Big Bang Theory* for all twelve seasons, for which he won four Emmys. Besides being a lead on one of the most-watched sitcoms in the United States, Parsons has continued to hone his craft as a stage actor, appearing on Broadway in plays like *The Normal Heart, An Act of God*, and recently in *The Boys in the Band*. Parsons also produced Ryan O'Connell's show *Special* for Netflix.

Dolly Parton (1946–) `ICON`

One of the most beloved figures in country music, and an undeniable icon for the LGBTQ+ community, Dolly Parton has been delighting audiences for more than fifty years. The "Backwoods Barbie" is loved for her distinctive look—the boobs, the hair, the makeup—but more than any of the trappings, she is a tremendous artist who has written some of the greatest country songs of the second half of the twentieth century. Parton got her start singing with Porter Wagoner and started a solo career in the 1960s that took the country by storm. She achieved wide acclaim with a series of crossover hits but never lost sight of who she was. While her music continues to change and evolve, it is always uniquely Dolly. Parton also made the crossover into acting with films like *9 to 5, Steel Magnolias*, and *Straight Talk*. As well as a musical legend, Parton is also the theme park owner of Dollywood in Pigeon Forge, Tennessee. With all her awards and accolades over the years, Parton remains committed to charitable work. Her program, Dolly Parton's Imagination Library, donates millions of books yearly to schools and kids in need. In the height of the Coronavirus pandemic, Parton contributed $1 million to the development of the Moderna vaccine.

Dolly Parton

Pier Paolo Pasolini (1922–1975)

A poet, essayist, novelist, and film director who was an admired intellectual and artist force in post–Second World War Italy, Pasolini became an international figure with films like *The Gospel According to St. Matthew* and the controversial *Salò, or the 120 Days of Sodom*. His poetry was the first thing that brought him to the attention of the Italian public, but it was his social criticism that soon launched him into much broader fields. His films were often adaptations of classic Europeans works like *The Decameron* and *The Canterbury Tales*, but his early film *Mamma Roma*, with Anna Magnani, was based on his experiences during the Second World War. *Salò* was based on the work by the Marquis de Sade, but much of the imagery came from the cruelty of the war. Pasolini was killed in 1975.

Many thought the mafia had killed the famed director, and even though a seventeen-year-old hustler named Giuseppe Pelosi confessed to the murder, the exact details of his death have remained a mystery.

Robert Patrick (1937–)

For many years, Patrick enjoyed the title of being the most produced playwright in New York. He got his start at the legendary Caffe Cino in the 1960s. The Cino became a home for Patrick as it did for other writers, but his works like *The Haunted Host* and his other gay plays quickly stood out. He soon formed a bond with Ellen Stewart at La MaMa, where he presented many of his plays. His greatest hit came in 1975 with his play *Kennedy's Children*, which played on Broadway. Patrick's work has always been openly and honestly gay, and has approached gay themes with a clarity and brilliance that only he could bring.

Peaches (1966–)

She's the musician and performance artist who creates the dirty songs you love to sing out loud (I sing "Dick in the Air" at least once a week) and whose sexually explicit lyrics have made her a favorite of the LGBTQ+ community. Though she began her career as a folk musician, Peaches wanted to try something daring and new. After moving to Berlin, she released her first album as Peaches, *The Teaches of Peaches*, in 2000. Her punkish and in-your-face style made her a crowd favorite and she began touring with Marilyn Manson and Queens of the Stone Age. Peaches has since released four more albums, and her music is often featured in the soundtracks of movies and television.

Peaches Christ (1974–)

If you've never seen a live Peaches Christ movie parody, you're missing out on some of the best camp theatre in the world. San Francisco's queen of the screams, Peaches Christ has been creating and starring in live stage shows since the 1990s. A film buff since the beginning, Christ has been showing camp and gay classics at her Midnight Mass since 1998. The show was a must-see in her native San Francisco, attracting all sorts of guests from

Peaches Christ and Orville Peck

Elvira to Mink Stole. In recent years, Peaches Christ has taken to live-staged drag parodies of classic gay favorites. With stage versions of films like *Death Becomes Her* and *Mean Girls*, Christ has shown herself to be an insightful writer and smart producer, inviting some of the stars from *RuPaul's Drag Race* to perform in her shows.

Orville Peck

Who is that masked man? Well if you're asking about the Lone Ranger–mask-wearing pop star out of Canada, you're probably referring to Orville Peck. Peck is an enigma on the pop scene, a mask-wearing, age-defying artist who identifies as queer but as little else. His 2019 album *Pony* was a critical hit and soon had the masked artist on all the top lists of the year and even more red carpets. Though some rumors have hinted at Peck's true identity, he hopes maintaining his anonymity will allow fans to concentrate on his message and music.

Andreja Pejic (1991-)

The face that launched the androgyny moment of the mid 2010s was discovered working at a McDonald's in Yugoslavia. Andreja Pejic is an international transgender model who has graced the covers of countless magazines and runways around the world. Pejic came out as transgender in 2013, and continued to work in fashion becoming the first transgender model to be profiled by Vogue in 2015.

Perfume Genius (1981–)

Perfume Genius, a.k.a. Mike Hadreas, is an electronic indie pop star whose honest lyrics about queer life have made him a favorite among audiences and fans. He recorded his first album, 2010's *Learning*, mostly in his home in Seattle. His second album, *Put Your Back N 2 It*, made sensations with its promotional video featuring porn star Arpad Miklos. Since the very beginning and throughout his career, Hadreas has played with gender roles and gay sexuality. With tracks like "Queen," off his 2014 album *Too Bright*, Hadreas brings a haunting and exciting queer presence to pop music.

Anthony Perkins (1932–1992)

Most remembered for his stunning portrayal of murderer Norman Bates in the original *Psycho*, Perkins was nothing like his sadistic counterpart. A serious actor who cared deeply about his craft, he came to Hollywood after success on Broadway in the play *Tea and Sympathy*. He landed his first major role in *Friendly Persuasion* in 1956, for which he was nominated for an Oscar. While 1960's *Psycho* would later eclipse much of his work, it should be remembered that Perkins starred in many great films, and was considered a Hollywood heartthrob for many years. He dated fellow Hollywood heartthrob Tab Hunter. Perkins would continue to work in Hollywood and on stage, but the role of Bates always haunted him and forced him into a number of sequels later in life. Perkins married Berry Berenson in 1973, with whom he had two children. He died of complications from AIDS in 1992.

Miss Coco Peru (1965–)

Things bother Coco, and she's not afraid to tell you so. This drag legend is a favorite with audiences across the country and has been a staple of the drag and comedy community since 1991. With her trademark red flip wig, and a dry wit tinged with her Bronx accent, Peru has appeared in many of her own live shows. She's won a number of MAC Awards for cabaret and has been nominated for GLAAD media awards, winning one in 2004. But it's been her film and television work that has brought Coco to a national audience, with scene-stealing roles in *To Wong Foo, Thanks for Everything! Julie Newmar*; *Trick*; and most recently in the revival seasons of *Will & Grace*. Peru is also one of the stars of the drag classic *Girls Will Be Girls* with Jack Plotnick and Varla Jean Merman.

Pet Shop Boys

The synth-pop duo of Neil Tennant and Chris Lowe, the Pet Shop Boys have been making electronic music since the 1980s, with hits like 1986's "West End Girls," 1987's "It's a Sin," 1988's "Heart," and 2008's "Always on My Mind." The duo is famous for their pulsing beats and their fierce and sexy lyrics. Though the duo has at times been skittish about directly coming out—Tennant came out in 1994 and Lowe has never confirmed or denied the rumors of his homosexuality— they have produced a body of work loved by the LGBTQ+ community. They were awarded a lifetime-achievement award from the Ivor Novello Awards in 2000.

Kim Petras (1992–)

Pet Shop Boys and Kim Petras

A German-born pop princess who is taking music by storm with a steady stream of bops and solid vocals that call everyone to dance, Petras was born in Cologne, Germany, and started her transition at a young age, which in some ways became a news story in its own right. Her music career started with the release of her first EP in 2011, but her real success came in 2018 with her independent releases like "Feeling of Falling" and "Heart to Break." She started to gain traction in mainstream media and used this attention to release her Halloween EP, *Turn Off the Light, Vol. 1* in 2018. A full-length version with new songs was released in 2019.

Philadelphia

This 1993 drama starring Tom Hanks and Denzel Washington was a big-budget response to the AIDS crisis that won critical praise and Tom Hanks his first Oscar. Hanks plays a young lawyer who is wrongfully fired when it's discovered that he is suffering from AIDS. Washington plays a young and slightly homophobic lawyer whose own awakening about the humanity of gay people helps him in his fight for justice. A beautiful film, it is most remembered for its impactful scene of Hanks explaining the aria "La mamma morta," sung by Maria Callas, to Washington. A bravura acting moment for Hanks, the scene is iconic and sets this tender and heartfelt movie apart as a classic.

Piano Bars

What is it about singing show tunes that makes gays so excited? Well, whatever it is, let's make sure there's more of it. Piano bars have long been a staple for queer folk in many American cities and continue today to be a great meeting place for the show queen in all of us. Though many have closed over the last few years, they are still popping up in places like New York, with The Duplex and Marie's Crisis. These bastions, where the songs and drinks go all night, give gay and straight patrons a chance to "Sing out, Louise!" to their heart's content.

Tommy Pico (1983–)

Pico is a Native American poet and podcaster whose work is thrilling for its rawness and willingness to say the unspoken in the twentieth century. His first collection of poems, *IRL* published 2016, established him as a young voice to watch and won him the 2017 Brooklyn Public Library Prize. He followed it with *Nature Poem*, winning further acclaim and the 2018 Whiting Award for Poetry. Besides his poetry, which is deeply personal, often sexually graphic, and belies a natural wit that sparkles throughout, Pico is one of the hosts of the *Food 4 Thot* podcast. Pico is a hilariously raw and open and gives insight into his life as a young queer native person making it in the modern world.

The Picture of Dorian Gray

Oscar Wilde's only novel, this gothic tale deals with the wonders of beauty and the pitfalls of the superficial. *The Picture of Dorian Gray* was originally published in *Lippincott's Monthly Magazine* in 1890, but was deeply censored for the delicate sensibilities of Victorian society. It tells the story of the beautiful yet evil Dorian Gray, who keeps his outward appearance pristine while a portrait of him, hidden away from view, rots for all his numerous sins. The book was startling in its day and was even used as evidence against Wilde in his criminal trial for gross indecency.

Charles Pierce

Charles Pierce (1926–1999)

The female impersonator who brought down the house with his wild takes on Hollywood's golden era of leading ladies, Charles Pierce was ahead of his time. His satire was both wicked and flattering to the legends he impersonated—this he knew because he was friendly with many of them. A staple of the drag scene for years, Pierce also played in mainstream venues to packed houses and a host a Hollywood friends. As an actor, he made many guest appearances on sitcoms and talk shows. At his memorial, his best friend Bea Arthur memorialized his favorite joke about a gravy ladle and a "special roommate." The joke went over so well that Arthur retold it in her one-woman show, *Just Between Friends*.

Pierre et Gilles

A couple in front of and behind the camera, Pierre Commoy and Gilles Blanchard have been creating decadently delicious photographs for more than forty years. Their work is highly stylized, with touches of kitsch and risqué humor, as it reinvents religious and cultural iconography from around the world. Famous for their imaginative portraits of celebrities, Pierre et Gilles, as they are known in the art world, have created a body of work that celebrates the fabulous and the forbidden.

Pink Triangle

In the concentration camps of Nazi Germany, prisoners were marked with patches to designate their "transgression against the Reich." The pink triangle was used to designate homosexual prisoners. For many years, the symbol was seen as a chilling reminder of the extermination of homosexuals during the Nazi regime. During the AIDS crisis, however, the triangle made a comeback. ACT UP brought it back as a reminder of one government's response to gay people and a powerful tool to fight against another government's response to the death of thousands. The pink triangle today may have lost some of its shock value, but for those who know its history, it is still a chilling reminder that "Silence = Death."

Ben Platt (1993–)
A wholesome-looking powerhouse singer who wowed audiences with his stunning portrayal of the title character in Broadway's *Dear Evan Hansen*, Platt has been working as an actor since childhood, but it was his star turn in *Hansen* that turned him into a hot commodity on Broadway and in Hollywood. He won the Best Actor Tony Award for the role in 2017. He released a solo album, *Sing to Me Instead*, in 2019 and made the leap to television with guest spots on *Will & Grace*, and then as a lead in Ryan Murphy's *The Politician* in 2019. In 2021, Platt reprised his role of Evan in the *Dear Evan Hanson* movie alongside actress Julianne Moore.

Podcasts
Gays love to talk—just ask us. No wonder we've begun dominating the field of podcasts. In a world where almost everyone you know has something to say, the field of the podcast may seem like a wild and unruly jungle. But with gay podcasts, there are a few that really stand above the rest. Of course there's RuPaul's *What's the Tee?*, and a host of others, like *Homophilia* with Matt McConkey and Dave Holmes; *Food 4 Thot* with Tommy Pico, Dennis Norris, Fran Tirado, and Joe Osmundson; and *Las Culturistas* with Matt Rogers and Bowen Yang. If I didn't include yours, I'm sorry. There are hundreds.

Polari
A street language of codes and clues to gay life in London, Polari is a mixture of Italian, Romani, and street slang that some scholars date back to the sixteenth century. Until the 1960s, it was commonly spoken among the lower ends of London society, when many Polari words, like *cackle* (gossip), *camp* (effeminate), *bevvy* (drink), and *screech* (speak) made their way into mainstream language.

Billy Porter (1969–)
While some show up to a red carpet to be seen, Billy Porter shows up to SLAY! Whether it's his grand entrance as an Egyptian god at the 2019 Met Gala or his acceptance speech for his groundbreaking Emmy win for his work on *Pose*, Porter is here to make the scene. He got his start on Broadway, playing the Teen Angel in the 1994 revival of *Grease*, and released a hit song, "Love Is on the Way," for the *First Wives Club* soundtrack. Porter solidified himself in the Broadway pantheon with his star turn in *Kinky Boots* in 2013, for which he won the Tony Award for Best Actor. Porter played the role of Pray Tell in FX's *Pose*. He won an Emmy Award in 2019, making him the first

openly gay Black male to ever win for Best Actor.

Cole Porter (1891–1964)

In all of the Great American Songbook, rarely is there as much wit flowing from a single pen as there is in the works of Cole Porter. The legendary songwriter delighted audiences with classics like "I've Got You Under My Skin," "You're the Top," "In the Still of the Night," and "Night and Day," just to name a smattering in his huge song catalog. For decades, he was America's most sophisticated and sought-after composer, churning out hits on Broadway and in film. He had huge hits with shows like *Anything Goes* with Ethel Merman in 1934 and the often-revived *Kiss Me, Kate* in 1948. Porter was as sophisticated as his music, living in

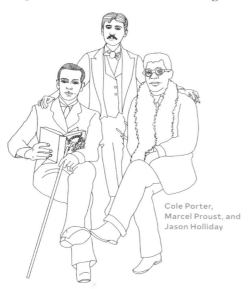

Cole Porter, Marcel Proust, and Jason Holliday

Paris during the 1920s, where he met Linda Thomas. While Porter was a homosexual, the two hit it off and got married. Though they both had other lovers, they were deeply attached to each other. A horseback riding accident in 1937 that almost killed Porter left him in crippling pain for the rest of his life, eventually leading to his having his right leg amputated. But his sophisticated music and stunning lyrics continue to live and harken back to a time of charm and champagne.

Portrait of Jason

Oh, let's get drunk and gossip and philosophize and tell stories and make each other cry. You know—fun stuff! Such is the premise of 1967's *Portrait of Jason*, a documentary by Shirley Clarke starring Jason Holliday. The film is mostly Jason telling stories of his life to the probing questions of Clarke, who remains unseen. Jason runs the gambit of emotions, from joyous to sorrowful, as the drinks and film continue to flow. Though some have accused Clarke and the film of exploiting Jason into an almost manic breakdown on film, there's a stunning look into the pre-Stonewall world of gay people making up their own existences as they went along their merry and perilous way.

Pose

Work! *Pose* debuted on FX in 2018 and got everyone in a voguing mood. Set in the New York ballroom scene of the late '80s and early '90s, this groundbreaking series follows the life of the burgeoning House of Evangelista. Created by Ryan Murphy, Brad Falchuk, and Steven Canals, it introduced the larger world to the world of ballroom and the acting talents of trans actors like Mj Rodriguez, Indya Moore, and Dominique Jackson. Broadway actor and singer Billy Porter joined the cast as Pray Tell, the no-nonsense announcer for the scene. The role won Porter an Emmy Award. *Pose*'s second season garnered even more praise and guaranteed its renewal for a third season. Pose drew to a close after its third season in 2021.

Prince (1958–2016) `ICON`

An icon in American music who transcended genre, but also transcended gender to see himself truly as a symbol, Prince went so far as to change his name to the "Love Symbol" in 1993—partly motivated by a dispute with his record company, but largely out of exploration of sexuality and gender that pervades almost all Prince's work. When he released his first album in 1978, his funky style and virtuosic guitar playing quickly set him apart from the musical landscape of the time. But it was 1984's album *Purple Rain* and film of the same name that made Prince an icon. He also fostered the careers of other up-and-coming artists like Vanity 6 and Sheena Easton, and wrote countless songs for artists as varied as Cyndi Lauper, Sinead O'Connor, Chaka Khan, the Bangles, and Alicia Keys. Prince's sexually explicit lyrics and stage presence pushed the envelope for sexual expression in music, but also opened the world up to all sorts of desire being represented in art.

Marcel Proust (1871–1922)

Proust is one of the most respected and enigmatic writers in Western culture. His seven-volume novel, *À la recherche du temps perdu* (In Search of Lost Time), is a profound study of life and love. Called the greatest book ever written, it is told from the perspective of a slightly disguised Proust and written as a memory brought on by the tasting of a madeleine dipped in tea. He wrote most of the novel from his bed as he was ill throughout his adulthood; the last two volumes were published after his death. The novel's reputation has only grown in stature since it debuted, and it has even been said that reading it in its entirety can improve brain function.

Provincetown

LGBTQ+ people love "P-town," and "P-town" loves them right back. This Cape Cod town has been the haven for artists and intellectuals for more than a century, hosting American writers from Eugene O'Neill and Tennessee Williams to Michael Cunningham. Provincetown is a simple beachside town with a strong gay community that lights up its streets and theatre spaces with a host of performers and spectacle over the summer season. From the infamous party known as Bear Week to the productions of impresario Ryan Landry and as many drag shows as one can see in a lifetime, Provincetown has been a sought-after destination for the LGBTQ+ community for decades.

Brontez Purnell (1983–)

Whether Brontez Purnell is writing about barebacking or heartbreak, he always creates a stir. As a writer, performer, musician, and dancer, this queer Black artist out of the San Francisco Bay Area has pursued many avenues in his long career. Purnell started making zines at a young age and has continued a massive amount of output to the modern day. Whether it's choreographing work for his dance company or making music with his band, the Younger Lovers, Purnell is always making work that challenges, delights, and makes an audience hungry for more. He has found success with his first novel, 2014's *The Cruising Diaries*, and *Since I Lay My Burden Down*, published in 2017, and was awarded the Whiting Prize for Fiction.

Pussy Riot

This take-no-prisoners punk group of activists, artists, and musicians in brightly colored balaclavas have been shaking shit up and standing up to authority and authoritarians for over a decade. In 2011, Pussy Riot

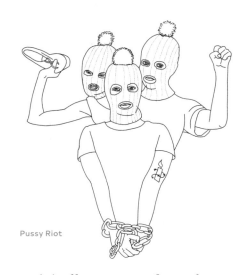

Pussy Riot

was originally a group of anywhere between eleven and fifteen masked women playing music and making thoughtful protest art and demonstrations against the Putin regime. The group came to major prominence in 2012, while staging a performance in the Cathedral of Christ the Savior in Moscow. Three of the group's members, Nadezhda Tolokonnikova, Maria Alyokhina, and Yekaterina Samutsevich were arrested for the protest, which prompted international outrage and brought the group a new platform as well overwhelming support. After serving twenty-one months in jail, Tolokonnikova and Aloykhina were released and have continued to be outspoken critics of authoritarian rule wherever they find it. They have criticized the Trump presidency and have lent their brand of merry mayhem to causes like Black Lives Matter and women's reproductive health.

Pyramid Club

If you wanted to get down, get funky, or get educated in the 1980s and early '90s in New York, there was one place you had to go: the Pyramid Club. Located at 101 Avenue A, the Pyramid was a dance club that hosted live performances from the best and brightest of the new drag scene in the 1980s. On any given night you could see the likes of Ethyl Eichelberger, Lypsinka, Peggy Shaw, or even RuPaul honing their acts at the iconic club. While the club did host major musical talents like Madonna, the Red Hot Chili Peppers, and Nirvana, it is more remembered as the breeding ground for some of the most important and groundbreaking queer art of the period.

Q

is for . . .

George Quaintance (1902–1957)

Where Tom of Finland went for smiling muscular gays on the prowl, Quaintance went for dreamy-eyed muscular gays. While both illustrators took on the beauty and perfection of the male body, Quaintance's drawings and paintings, mostly done in brilliant color, are more sensual and soft. Most of his males look dreamily cast, as if they are being seen through the bottom of a glass or in a dream. His pictures are also less sexually graphic, though they subvert in the way these masculine prototypes are portrayed with distinctly feminine features. His work was published a great deal in his lifetime, and at the time of his death, he'd become hugely popular for his drawings of strapping matadors.

The Queen

The last scene of this fantastic time capsule of a movie makes your damn mind explode in gay joy. This 1968 documentary follows a drag pageant hosted by the one and only Flawless Sabrina, a.k.a. Jack Doroshow, in 1967. The movie details the rise of the young competitor Harlow as she competes for and wins the crown. It's packed with cameos by Andy Warhol, who was one of the judges for the night, as well as Mario Montez and the voice of Minette. A fascinating look at the gay and drag worlds before the Stonewall Riots, the film is finished off with the stunning and glorious rant of the one and only Crystal LaBeija, darling, of the famous House of LaBeija.

The Queen

Queer as Folk

A breakout hit for representation that showed gay lives as they were in the early 2000s, or at least as we wished they were, Showtime's *Queer as Folk* brought LGBTQ+ lives to televisions around the country in 2000. Set in Pittsburgh, the show tells of a group of friends who search for love and struggle with the external and internal influences around living an openly gay life in the new millennium. It took on a host of issues in its five-year run, from addiction and intergenerational relationships to HIV stigma and adoption. *Queer as Folk* was a show on the front lines of queer representation on mainstream television. Based on a British show of the same name created by Russell T. Davies, it starred Hal Sparks as the neurotic Michael, Gale Harold as sexy and sought-after loner Brian, and Randy Harrison as his younger partner Justin. Peter Paige played the ever-hopeful Emmett, and Scott Lowell played the humdrum Ted. Michelle Clunie and Thea Gill played the lesbian couple of Lindsay and Melanie, with Sharon Gless rounding out the cast as Michael's pro-LGBTQ+ mother and Jack Wetherall as Michael's gay uncle, Vic. The show was a hit with audiences and proved that LGBTQ+ stories were viable in a wider and diversifying television market.

Queer Eye for the Straight Guy

In this feel-good makeover show, a group of gay men, each with his own special power, shows up at someone's house and transforms them in a little under an hour. Sounds like magic, doesn't it? Well, it is. Gay magic. The show originally premiered in 2003 with the original, "Fab Five" of Ted Allen on food, Kyan Douglas on hair, Thom Filicia on design, Carson Kressley on wardrobe, and Jai Rodriguez on Lifestyle, and it was an immediate hit with audiences. The original show called it quits after five seasons, but in 2018 the idea was resurrected on Netflix with a new team of makeover-ers. The new series, now just *Queer Eye*, features Antoni Porowski on food, Jonathan Van Ness on hair, Bobby Berk on design, Tan France on fashion, and Karamo Brown on culture. The show has yet again proved a critical and cultural hit and has been renewed by Netflix for an additional three seasons.

Queer Music Heritage

A website and radio show hosted and curated by JD Doyle, it was a treasure trove of LGBTQ+ history and the music that has inspired and been created by the community. Beginning in 2000, the show ran for fifteen years and took deep dives into queer music and its history. Crossing genres and times, the show was a colossal achievement by Doyle, and definitely worth multiple visits for anyone interested in the history of queer music makers.

José Quintero (1924–1999)

One of the most respected directors in the history of Broadway, José Quintero was a master of making his work disappear and leaving the audience feeling as though the actors had just entered and begun talking. Anyone who worked with him knew that Quintero was deeply involved in making every gesture and movement look effortless and endlessly real. He was considered a master at the works of Eugene O'Neill, directing the world premiere of his greatest play, *Long Day's Journey into Night*. He was also a favorite of Tennessee Williams, directing many of his early works and returning to him in later years. He directed one film, *The Roman Spring of Mrs. Stone*, based on the novel by Tennessee Williams and starring Vivien Leigh and Warren Beatty.

Zachary Quinto (1977–)

A widely respected actor whose work on television and film has often existed in the realms of science fiction and horror, Quinto is perhaps most well known for his role as Spock in the recent additions to the *Star Trek* franchise. Prior to that, Quinto had been one of the breakout stars of the series *Heroes* in 2006. While Quinto has enjoyed his sci-fi roles on film and television, his roles on stage have been more varied. He played the role of Louis in the 2010 revival of *Angels in America*, Tom in the 2013 revival of *The Glass Menagerie*, and Harold in the star-studded revival of *The Boys in the Band* in 2018.

R is for . . .

Radical Faeries

Find five faeries and you'll find twenty-five opinions of what is a faerie is, so I'll try to take a crack. "A group of loving friends who meet in celebration of nature, shared queerness, and a comradery of affection, from the sexual to the kind" may be the least political and most kind way I can describe this radical anarchist movement that was started by Harry Hay, his partner John Burnside, and Don Kilhefner in the late '70s to reclaim queerness in the gay male community. It began as a response to the growing bar culture of the '70s, giving gay male adults a spiritual place with sex positivity and creativity. The Radical Faeries started as single event in Southern California and expanded to working communities of friends in queerness across the country. Though the "group" was started by gay men, the growing culture of queerness has been invited in for decades during and following the AIDS crisis, welcoming peoples of all genders and expression of queerness into the "fae-mily."

Randy Rainbow (1981–)

If the lies out of the White House ever get you down, look to Randy Rainbow for a laugh, and he will cure whatever ails you with a Broadway song parody. A satirist and comedian who has taken the world by storm with his stunning send-ups of the current political world, all set to the music of Broadway, he began as a pop-culture blogger. This led to a series of comedy videos featuring "staged interactions" with recorded voices of celebrities. But with the coming of the Trump administration, he began to shift his attention solely to the political. Writing new lyrics to popular songs from the Broadway cannon, Rainbow hilariously and astutely sends up the hypocrisies of the Trump administration. With parodies like "Unpopular" and "Fact-Checker, Fact-Checker," Rainbow has become a favorite around the country and a welcome laugh following the trying times of Trump.

Ma Rainey (1886–1939)

Often seen as the mother of the blues, Ma Rainey was one of the earliest and most beloved singers of this popular American artform. Known for her boisterous nature and her no-nonsense sensibility, Rainey was an expert singer, with phrasing that still rings true and clear even on the very scratchy recordings she left behind. She was a major blues star in her era, traveling the South in her own specially designed train car. A major influence and friend to Bessie Smith, she also toured with a young Louis Armstrong. Rainey sang frequently about her attraction to women in songs like "Prove It On Me." She retired from the music scene in 1935, moving to her hometown of Columbus, Georgia, and running three theaters there.

David Rakoff

David Rakoff (1964–2012)

One the funniest writers and performers of his generation, who we all lost too soon, Rakoff was a respected comedic writer and essayist whose work on NPR's *This American Life* first brought his wonderful voice to the masses. He became a regular contributor to the program, which spawned a series of books like *Fraud, Don't Get Too Comfortable,* and *Half Empty.* Through these collections of essays, Rakoff showed his power as a writer with a biting style that could at times be gentle and even self-deprecating. He established himself as a formidable master of the form, and his work was often lauded and awarded during his lifetime. *Half Empty* received the Thurber

Prize for American Humor in 2011. In 2010, Rakoff was diagnosed with cancer. He succumbed to the disease in 2012, right after finishing his novel in verse, *Love, Dishonor, Marry, Die, Cherish, Perish,* which was released in 2013.

Sara Ramírez (1975–)

An actress and activist who got her start on Broadway, Sara Ramírez won a Tony for the Monty Python musical, *Spamalot,* in which she played the Lady of the Lake. For this quite literally showstopping performance, Ramírez became the toast of Broadway. So when an ABC executive walked into her dressing room and asked her what she wanted to do next, Ramírez said she was a fan of *Grey's Anatomy* and joined the cast in 2006 as Dr. Callie Torres. It was just that easy. Her character, like Ramírez herself, was bisexual and had relationships with both male and female doctors during her ten-year run on the show. Since leaving *Grey's* in 2016, Ramírez continues to release music and act on a variety of television shows, including joining the cast of *Madam Secretary,* and will add an extra layer of queerness to the *Sex and the City* revival in 2022.

Andrew Rannells (1978–)

Rannells is the fresh-faced singer and actor who hit the Broadway stage in the 2011 mega-hit *The Book of Mormon,* for which he got a Tony nomination. Since his tenure as Elder Price, he has moved on to television projects, like the short-lived gay sitcom *The New Normal*. He found success playing Elijah, the vain and occasionally vapid gay friend of Hannah Horvath on HBO's *Girls*. Rannells returned to Broadway in the 2016 revival of *Falsettos*, for which he was nominated for his second Tony Award. Rannells's *Too Much Is Not Enough* is a memoir of his early days in show business.

Anthony Rapp (1971–)

A Broadway actor and singer who was the original Mark in *Rent*, Rapp played Charlie Brown in the celebrated 1999 Revival of *You're a Good Man, Charlie Brown* and Lucas in the musical *If/Then* in 2014 with *Rent* alumni Idina Menzel. He also has a long list of film credits, and has recently joined the cast of *Star Trek: Discovery* on CBS All Access. In 2017, Rapp accused actor Kevin Spacey of being sexually inappropriate with him in 1986, when he was just seventeen. Though Spacey apologized for the incident, it started a landslide of other accusers with similar stories.

Terence Rattigan (1911–1977)

Rattigan was a playwright of sophistication and wit who was often seen in company with Noël Coward for telling the stories of the wealthy and cosmopolitan. But further examination of his work since his death has demonstrated that Rattigan's work is unique, emotionally rich, and intensely gratifying. While much of his work varies from boulevard comedies to dark dramas, they all have the clipped sophistication that is his hallmark. He had major hits with plays like *The Winslow Boy* in 1946, *The Browning Version* in 1948, and *The Deep Blue Sea* in 1952. Rattigan fell out of fashion, however, with the advent of the "Angry Young Men," playwrights of the late 1950s like John Osborne and Harold Pinter. He loved the theatre and continued to write for the stage and film until his death in 1977.

Robert Rauschenberg (1925–2008)

One of the most prolific and varied visual artists of the twentieth century, Robert Rauschenberg was an ever-evolving artist who worked in a variety of mediums and materials, which made his work continually new and interesting. Rauschenberg was part of several art movements, sometimes called a "neo-Dadaist," along with his partner Jasper Johns. He often incorporated found objects into his paintings and sculpture, a move that would reach its zenith with his Combine period in the late 1950s. Rauschenberg also created sets and costumes for dance companies, many of which were headed by his dear friends, like Merce Cunningham and Paul Taylor. After his death, a memorial exhibition of his work was held at the Guggenheim Museum in 2008.

Johnnie Ray (1927–1990)

One of the earliest white singers who embraced rock-and-roll rhythms and sounds, Johnnie Ray was a teen idol and a powerhouse singer in the 1950s. With hits like "Cry" and "The Little White Cloud That Cried," both in 1951, Ray quickly became a sought-after singer. His high-intensity singing, as well as his strange and new inflections, made Ray a favorite among the ever-growing bobby-soxers set. Little did they know that Ray was partially deaf, which affected his phrasing. But there was much people didn't know about Johnnie Ray. While he continued to have hits throughout the 1950s, Ray had to continually hide his sexuality. Though Ray married, he was arrested several times in gay venues. As music changed in the 1960s, he couldn't keep up with trends. He suffered from alcoholism for years and eventually died from the illness in 1990.

Toshi Reagon (1964–)

An American musician, writer, producer, and a powerful singer for social change, Toshi Reagon began performing at a young age and quickly caught the attention of musicians and audiences alike. She released her first album, *Justice*, in 1990. While music is her passion, Reagon is often involved with and championing charitable and social-justice causes—something she may have learned from her godfather, the legendary Pete Seeger. She has worked with Sweet Honey in the Rock on the soundtrack for PBS's *Africans in America* and has produced several

other albums for the group. Reagon continues to tour and make music, and with a long-standing residency at Joe's Pub at the Public Theater in New York, Reagon has found a home to make music and make joy.

John Rechy and Toshi Reagon

John Rechy (1931–)

Not all professors can get out on the weekends for a little hustling, but John Rechy made it a priority. The bad boy of gay literature, Rechy wrote the classic *City of Night*. Published in 1963, the book was a huge best seller and established Rechy as a writer to watch. Anyone watching would see the good-looking young Rechy was a muscle queen's dream in the 1960s, who wanted to write with candor about the gay experience and the joys of sexual freedom. His second novel, *Numbers*, published in 1967, was all about these sexual adventures. While it received good reviews, it also directed Rechy to a more singular and devoted readership. Since *Numbers,* Rechy wrote several novels and a memoir, *The Sexual Outlaw,* which tells of his love to hustle.

Charles Nelson Reilly (1931–2007)

Paul Lynde's only rival for snarkiest gay of 1970's television, Reilly was the sarcastic master of *Match Game* and a comedian, writer, director, and teacher. His distinctive voice and dry-to-exasperated delivery made him a comedian's dream, and from 1973 to 1979 he was the mainstay of the comedic game show. He felt pigeonholed by appearing on game shows and often returned to his real love—the theater. He'd had his first big break in the musical *Hello, Dolly!* as the original Cornelius Hackl. In later years, he often directed and taught. He directed his friend Julie Harris in her one-woman show about Emily Dickinson, *The Belle of Amherst,* to critical acclaim. He often directed in television, as well, and was a very respected acting teacher at the HB Studio in New York.

Mary Renault (1905–1983)

Renault was a historian and novelist who wrote mostly about the ancient Greeks and in particular about the life of Alexander the Great. Unlike most writers of her period who chose to portray Alexander only as a willful he-man out to conquer the world, totally overlooking his homosexuality, Renault chose to put it front and center. She wrote one of her most famous books, *The Persian Boy,* totally from the perspective of Alexander's male concubine. Throughout her career, Renault wrote several novels about the ancient world, and was quite daring in her exploration of pre-Christian understandings of sexuality. Though a lesbian herself, most of Renault's novels are written with male protagonists, while her female characters are often not portrayed in the best light.

Reno (1956–)

A true trailblazer in LGBTQ+ comedy and storytelling, Reno brought her own unique take on politics and social commentary to the world in the late 1990s. Known for her charged and hilarious rants, Reno quickly caught the attention of icons like Lily Tomlin and used this attention to launch her first forays into television. In 2001, Reno launched her own reality show on Bravo, one of the first of its kind, which was produced by Tomlin and her partner Jane Wagner. In 2002, Reno starred in the wildly successful comedy special, *Reno: A Rebel without a Passion.* Since then, Reno has continued to be a voice for social injustice, bringing her unique perspective and particular rants to audiences around the world.

Rent

A rock musical by Jonathan Larson set in the gritty, or at least the imagined gritty, Lower East Side during the height of the AIDS crisis. It doesn't sound like it would be a hit, but a hit it was. A big one. The musical debuted off-Broadway in 1996, opening the night after Larson died tragically of a sudden heart attack. The show went on and proved very successful, moving to Broadway that same year. It also introduced some of Broadway's most beloved players, like Adam Pascal, Idina Menzel, Daphne Rubin-Vega, Taye Diggs, and Anthony Rapp. The musical was a mega-hit and won the Tony Award for Best Musical that year.

Adrienne Rich (1929–2012)

One of the most respected and lauded poets in American letters, Adrienne Rich was also an essayist and activist. She received praise and the Yale Younger Poets Award for her first collection of poems, *A Change of World*, in 1951. In the '50s, Rich settled into a life of writing and a heterosexual marriage that did not suit her. With the beginning of the '60s, she became very involved in the growing civil rights and anti-war movements, and it was during this period that she also had her sexual awakening and began to have relationships with women. She won the National Book Award in 1974 for *Diving into the Wreck*. Rich was a committed activist for change, and she would remain so until the end of her life. When offered the National Medal of Arts, Rich declined as a protest to the Republican-controlled house over their treatment of the NEA.

Robert W. Richards (1941–2019)

Illustrator and fashion plate, Robert W. Richards had a life that many people could have only dreamed of. He was on a close, personal basis with many of the greatest singers of the Great American Songbook, but it was his passion for drawing that led him in a thousand different directions, all with that particular Richards look: glossy, sexy, and sleek. Richards was a fashion and erotic illustrator whose work found its way into all sorts of magazines, from *Vogue* to *Inches*. With his black owl-like glasses and colorful cravats, his highly visual style set him apart, and as an older man Richards became a fashion model.

Miss Richfield 1981 and Arthur Rimbaud

Miss Richfield 1981

The iconic queen of Provincetown with her large black wig and trademark glasses, Miss Richfield 1981 is a legend. Many would recognize her from a series of commercials she did for the travel company Orbitz in the early 2000s. But for those of us who have been fortunate to see her perform live, that's just the tip of the iceberg. A talented comedian and storyteller, Miss Richfield 1981 mixes the perverted with the profound and keeps them laughing in her favorite P-town all season long.

Arthur Rimbaud (1854–1891)

The bad boy poet who peed in the middle of parties and told the world to fuck right off, Arthur Rimbaud defined the term *enfant terrible* for a century. He was loud, obnoxious, but also brilliant. A violent and insightful writer, his vision of what poetry could be was almost as powerful as a religious calling. The young Rimbaud moved to Paris at seventeen and took up with the older poet Paul Verlaine. Rimbaud and Verlaine became lovers, often arguing and fighting in public. Verlaine went so far as to famously shoot Rimbaud in the wrist during a typically bad argument. During his time with Verlaine, Rimbaud wrote some of the most shocking and provocative work that had ever been seen. His works *A Season in Hell* and *Illuminations* still stand as masterpieces. And then, at twenty-one, he left Verlaine, became a soldier and marine, and never wrote a word ever again. Perhaps the biggest fuck-off of all.

Herb Ritts (1952–2002)

A fashion photographer who reinvigorated black-and-white fashion photography for more than twenty years, Ritts took many famous portraits of celebrities, bringing an almost classical understanding to glamour and sensuality. He was also a favorite photographer of the emerging class of supermodels in the 1990s. His portraits of Cindy Crawford, Naomi Campbell, and Christy Turlington have become classics. His style also translated into music videos. He directed Madonna's video for "Cherish" and Chris Isaak's "Wicked Game."

The Ritz

Truly a "gay romp," *The Ritz* is a hilarious callback to a world that was. Originally a play by Terrence McNally, the film version was directed by Richard Lester in 1976. It starred Jack Weston, Jerry Stiller, F. Murray Abraham, and Rita Moreno, most of whom reprised their roles from the original Broadway production. The film and play are set in a bathhouse closely resembling the Continental Baths in New York. It's a farce in the classic sense of the word, with slamming doors and confused identities. The film was released to mixed reviews, but it stands as a loving testament to the lost world of the bathhouses in the 1970s.

Sylvia Rivera (1951–2002)

A trans pioneer whose years of activism made her into a patron saint of the movement for LGBTQ+ rights, Rivera was an outspoken activist for the rights of queer people while still in her teens, forming the legendary STAR, Street Transvestite Action Revolutionaries, with her friend Marsha P. Johnson. The two were trying to help their trans family, who felt they were often left out of the gay liberation movement. There are stunning clips of the young Rivera yelling at a group of gay men and women, who were shouting her down, but Sylvia demanded to be heard, as she did for the rest of her life. And while her own struggles with addiction and poverty led Rivera into personal difficulties over the years, her commitment to the rights of LGBTQ+ people never wavered. In 2002, the Sylvia Rivera Law Project was named in her honor to help trans people in legal matters. It still continues the work of Rivera to this day.

Jerome Robbins (1918–1998)

Jerome Robbins was one of the most successful and famous directors and choreographers of his day. His long and varied career includes everything from *On the Town* to his classical work with the New York City Ballet to directing the film version of *West Side Story*. Robbins was a true original, whose work with dancers and actors remains a hallmark of what is possible on the Broadway stage. He directed and choreographed the original *West Side Story* as well as the original *Fiddler on the Roof,* giving each a dance vocabulary that remains instantly recognizable and defines each work. He received numerous awards and accolades throughout his career, including five Tony Awards for his work in the theatre and an Oscar for *West Side Story*. Robbins was also awarded the Kennedy Center Honor for his contribution to the theatre and dance.

Robyn (1979–) `ICON`

A Swedish-born dance music diva who keeps her fans dancing on their own, Robyn got her start in the music industry at an early age, and she made a major breakthrough in 1997 with "Show Me Love" and "Do You Know." These two songs broke into the American charts, but it was with her later work, 2010's *Body Talk Pt. 1*, with hits like "Dancing On My Own" and "Call Your Girlfriend," that she hit pop and dance stardom in the United States. Her songs have been covered multiple times—a testament to her power as a writer—but her original versions are still the ones that get people up on their feet.

The Rocky Horror Picture Show

Are you just shaking with antica . . . pation? Well wait no longer, this cult classic has had a massive following in the LGBTQ+ community since it premiered in 1975. *The Rocky Horror Picture Show* was originally conceived as a stage musical by Richard O'Brein, but it's the camp-tastic film that has enraptured filmgoers and freaks for generations. The movie tells of a stranded couple, Brad played by Barry

The Rocky Horror
Picture Show

Bostwick and Janet played by Susan Sarandon, who get lost in a storm and head up to a haunted old mansion. The mansion belongs to the infamous Dr. Frank-N-Furter, played deliciously by Tim Curry, who's "just a sweet transvestite from Transylvania." The film has achieved cult status with lots of opportunities for audience participation and is often accompanied by a live reenactment when shown in theatres. This classic takes on everything, from pansexuality to the freedom of choice, with songs that make you want to let your freak flag fly. Because remember, there's a light . . .

Mj Rodriguez (1991–)

Rodriguez is an actress and activist taking Hollywood by storm with her leading role on FX's *Pose*. This newfound stardom hasn't taken her away from her first love, the musical theatre.

Rodriguez first started turning heads in the off-Broadway revival of the musical *RENT*. For her role as Angel, Rodriguez was awarded the Clive Barnes Award in 2011. It was after this experience that Rodriguez began her transition. She played many roles over the years until she was cast in the role of Blanca on *Pose* in 2018. With this newfound visibility, Rodriguez has broken down barriers for trans actors in Hollywood, becoming the first trans actress to win Best Actress at the Imagen Awards in 2019. She also made a huge splash in the role of Audrey in *Little Shop of Horrors* at the Pasadena Playhouse, and set the audience on its feet when singing, "Suddenly Seymour" on the *The Late Late Show with James Corden* in 2019. In 2021, Rodriguez became the first trans actress to be nominated for an Emmy for her work on *Pose*.

Sister Roma (1962–)

You can tell that porn is an important medium for the LGBTQ+ community, because when we want to talk about porn, we invite a nun. Sister Roma got her start as art director for the gay porn company Hot House Entertainment, but she soon found that her talents were best used in front of the camera. A longtime member of San Francisco's order of the Sisters of Perpetual Indulgence, Roma dons her habit and white face to talk about porn, politics, or whatever she really has on her mind. An emcee par excellence, Sister Roma has hosted everything from the Grabbys, an LGBTQ+ porn awards show, to movies at the Castro with Hollywood royalty. A proud supporter of the Folsom Street Fair, Sister Roma is a firm reminder of the importance of sex and sexuality in the LGBTQ+ community.

Ned Rorem (1923–)

Rorem is prolific classical music composer and diarist who was the golden-haired heartthrob of the post–Second World War classical world. With his art songs and song cycles, often setting the words of famous poets to music, Rorem became an international sensation and a respected composer. Though he wrote many forms of classical music, operas, orchestral, and chamber music, his songs remain some of his most famous works. He won the Pulitzer Prize for Music in 1976 for his *Air Music: Ten Etudes for Orchestra*. But Rorem had more up his sleeve. Throughout his life, he has been a committed diarist. He published his first diary in 1966, *The Paris Diary*, which caused a stir for its beautiful writing and its frank and at times hilarious renderings of gay sexuality. Rorem has published several more diaries since then, which have all shown him to be not only a scintillating truth teller, but also a writer of enormous skill and substance.

Diana Ross (1944–) ICON

A love supreme and living legend who has been making music and headlines for more than fifty years, Ross got her start as the lead singer of the Motown supergroup the Supremes. Ross and the Supremes ran neck and neck with the Beatles for the most hits of the 1960s. After leaving the group in 1970, Ross embarked on a stunning solo career that included hits like "Love Hangover," "Upside Down" and the ever-danceable "I'm Coming Out." She also broke into acting with films like *Mahogany* and *Lady Sings the Blues*, where she played legendary jazz singer Billie Holiday. Ross has always been a proud supporter of the LGBTQ+ community and has often lent her talent and her voice to the fight against AIDS.

Rubyfruit Jungle

What I love about *Rubyfruit Jungle* is that it was the first LGBTQ+ book to look at straight people like they were the strange ones. It's a classic 1973 novel on lesbian themes by Rita Mae Brown that is revered by young and old readers alike. One the first novels to deal with lesbianism in a positive light, Brown's novel tells the story of Molly Bolt as she comes to terms with her sexuality and embraces the larger lesbian world. The book has remained popular since its publication for its wit and insight, and while Brown has written many other novels on lesbian themes in her long and storied career, *Rubyfruit Jungle* remains her most endearing work.

Paul Rudnick (1957–)

One of the sharpest wits in the business, Paul Rudnick writes jokes so good, he makes the rest of us look like we're barely trying. Rudnick is famous for his plays like 1993's *Jeffrey*, which drew the first comparisons between Rudnick and Wilde. Indeed, when Rudnick is at his best, his lines swirl out like beautiful music. Rudnick later adapted *Jeffrey* for the film version, writing the screenplay. Rudnick's often written for film, most famously *Addams Family Values* in 1993, but he also wrote both the original *Sister Act* and its later sequel. Rudnick wrote a novel, 2013's *Gorgeous*, and he is writing the book for the musical version of *The Devil Wears Prada*.

RuPaul (1960–)

An icon. There's no two ways about it. Breaking the mold for what drag could be, entertaining the world with her insights, music, and that gorgeous laugh for over twenty years, RuPaul has done more for gay culture and visibility than can truly be calculated. It can be argued that there were drag queens before, but not with the same appeal, and never with the same reach. When RuPaul hit the big time with her 1993 hit, "Supermodel (You Better Work)," the world had never seen anything like her. Tall, undeniably gorgeous, and truly her own creation, RuPaul took the world by storm. She was featured in magazines and national ad campaigns, guest starred on television, and hosted on MTV. She had her own talk show, *The RuPaul Show*, from 1996 to 1998, and far from being some sort of oddity celebrity, RuPaul engaged in real and stunning conversations with a host of celebrity guests. At the turn of the millennium, RuPaul's output slowed down a bit, but soon she was back, releasing music and then unveiling her masterpiece, *RuPaul's Drag Race*. The show has been and continues to be a ratings juggernaut, and is now an Emmy darling.

RuPaul

RuPaul's Drag Race

RuPaul's Drag Race is one of the most popular shows in the country, and now the world. Among gay men and teenage girls, a new season is seen as something akin to March Madness. A mastery of marketing, everything on this show is a catchphrase and a callback, but far from feeling canned or insincere, it has allowed its viewership to feel a certain amount of ownership over the show. It's had a host of memorable moments and unforgettable lines—"This is not RuPaul's Best Friend Race"—and introduced a lot of gay terms and slang from ball and gay culture to the mainstream (it was quite a shock when my mom asked if I was a bottom or a top). The next time you hear an anchor on CNN comment that a senator was throwing shade, know you have *Drag Race* to thank. There is so much to say about *Drag Race*, and so many queens to talk about, but to do that would be its own book entirely. While some queens like Bianca Del Rio, Bob the Drag Queen, Trixie Mattel, Katya, Alaska, Valentina, Jinkx Monsoon, Shangela, Eureka, Willam, and Peppermint have broken out to other performing successes with television appearances and even Broadway shows, to talk about them all would be a huge undertaking. So I am creating a little cheat sheet for the *Drag Race* newcomers, with winners and notable queens from each season of American drag race. Now that the show has expanded to England, Thailand, Holland, Austrailia and New Zealand, and Spain, there's simply too many queens to keep up with!

SEASON ONE—2009

WINNER: BEBE ZAHARA BENET

STANDOUT QUEENS: NINA FLOWERS, SHANNEL, ONGINA, TAMMIE BROWN, and the legendary PORKCHOP

SEASON TWO—2010

WINNER: TYRA SANCHEZ

STANDOUT QUEENS: RAVEN, JUJUBEE, PANDORA BOXX, and SHANGELA

SEASON THREE—2011

WINNER: RAJA

STANDOUT QUEENS: MANILA LUZON, SHANGELA (again), CARMEN CARRERA, STACY LAYNE MATTHEWS, and ALEXIS MATEO

SEASON FOUR—2012

WINNER: SHARON NEEDLES

STANDOUT QUEENS: PHI PHI O'HARA, LATRICE ROYALE, WILLAM, and CHAD MICHAELS

SEASON FIVE—2013

WINNER: JINKX MONSOON

STANDOUT QUEENS: ALASKA THUNDERFUCK, ROXXXY ANDREWS, DETOX, ALYSSA EDWARDS, and COCO MONTRESE

SEASON SIX—2014

WINNER: BIANCA DEL RIO

STANDOUT QUEENS: ADORE DELANO, COURTNEY ACT, BENDELACREME, LAGANJA ESTRANJA, and MILK

SEASON SEVEN—2015

WINNER: VIOLET CHACHKI

STANDOUT QUEENS: GINGER MINJ, KENNEDY DAVENPORT, KATYA ZAMOLODCHIKOVA, TRIXIE MATTEL, and JASMINE MASTERS

SEASON EIGHT—2016

WINNER: BOB THE DRAG QUEEN

STANDOUT QUEENS: KIM CHI, NAOMI SMALLS, THORGY THOR, ACID BETTY, and CYNTHIA LEE FONTAINE

SEASON NINE—2017

WINNER: SASHA VELOUR

STANDOUT QUEENS: PEPPERMINT, SHEA COULEÉ, TRINITY TAYLOR, VALENTINA, EUREKA, and AJA

SEASON TEN—2018

WINNER: AQUARIA

STANDOUT QUEENS: EUREKA (AGAIN), ASIA O'HARA, MIZ CRACKER, MONÉT X CHANGE, THE VIXEN, and MAYHEM MILLER

SEASON ELEVEN—2019

WINNER: YVIE ODDLY

STANDOUT QUEENS: BROOKE LYNN HYTES, A'KERIA DAVENPORT, VANESSA VANJIE MATEO, NINA WEST, PLASTIQUE TIARA, and SCARLET ENVY

SEASON TWELVE—2020

WINNER: JAIDA ESSENCE HALL

STANDOUT QUEENS: WINDOW VON'DU, HEIDI N. CLOSET, GIGI GOODE, CRYSTAL METHYD, ROCK M. SAKURA, JAN, DAHLIA SIN, and BRITA FILTER

SEASON THIRTEEN—2021

WINNER: SYMONE

STANDOUT QUEENS: GOTTMIK (First Trans Man Queen), KANDY MUSE, ROSÉ, OLIVIA LUX, TAMISHA IMAN, UTICA QUEEN, DENALI, and TINA BURNER

For the Six Seasons of *All Stars*:

SEASON ONE WINNER: CHAD MICHAELS

SEASON TWO WINNER: ALASKA THUNDERFUCK

SEASON THREE WINNER: TRIXIE MATTEL

SEASON FOUR WINNER: TRINITY TAYLOR AND MONÉT X CHANGE

SEASON FIVE WINNER: SHEA COULEÉ

SEASON SIX WINNER: KYLIE SONIQUE LOVE

Craig Russell (1948–1990)

Russell was a Canadian actor and drag performer known for his ribald impressions of some of Hollywood's most dynamic leading ladies. From Mae West and Bette Davis to Joan Crawford and Judy Garland, Russell did them all. He had a huge success in 1977 with the film *Outrageous!* in which Russell starred as an actor and drag queen. He was nominated for a Canadian Film Award for his performance. He also starred in two sequels to the film and was a mainstay on the Canadian drag scene until his death of complications from AIDS in 1990.

Vito Russo (1946–1990)

Film historian, writer, and activist Vito Russo was an outspoken proponent of the contributions and portrayals of LGBTQ+ stories in the media, but he also hoped to change the narrative. His studies of classic film helped unlock a gay history that was hiding in the shadows of old Hollywood. Sharing movies with gay story lines or camp elements at the famous Firehouse in the West Village, Russo would regale his audiences with inside tidbits about the movies and their makers. These talks and lectures eventually became his book *The Celluloid Closet.* And it was this love of film that first brought him into activism. With the onset of AIDS, Russo became a fierce fighter on the front line of the crisis. Russo was also a co-founder of the organization GLAAD, a media watchdog group that cites and reviews LGBTQ+ content in the media. Since its founding, it has grown into one of the most respected media groups in the country.

Bayard Rustin (1912–1987)

A civil rights activist who organized the March on Washington in 1963, Bayard Rustin has often been cited as one of the key players behind the scenes of the civil rights movement, first working with A. Philip Randolph, then teaching Dr. Martin Luther King Jr. about nonviolence. King himself acknowledged Rustin as a key architect of the movement and friend. After an arrest for public indecency, Rustin, and indeed a lot of people around him, feared that his homosexuality would be used against him in an effort to discredit the movement. This kept him from assuming too much of the spotlight, so as not to draw attention away from the movement. After the March on Washington, Rustin continued his work in civil rights, assuming a key role in the A. Philip Randolph Institute. A lifelong activist, Rustin continued to work into the 1970s and '80s, adding the fight for LGBTQ+ rights to his long list of causes. Rustin died from a heart attack while on a humanitarian mission in Haiti at age seventy-five.

S

is for . . .

Yves Saint Laurent (1936–2008)

One of the world's most respected fashion designers, Yves Saint Laurent was known as a prodigy in the fashion world, when at the age of twenty-one, he took over the House of Dior. For the next twenty-five years, Saint Laurent was at the top of his game, designing for the chic and jet-set class and often seen as the most famous couturier of the 1960s and '70s. He was also part of the emerging global elite, dressing the fashionable and partying with them. He was one of the first couture designers to go into ready-to-wear, but remained true to the principles and vision of a true couturier. He struggled with addiction and mental health, but throughout his life enjoyed the success of being a true fashion visionary.

JD Samson (1978–)

JD Samson is a figure of infinite coolness. They joined the band Le Tigre in 2000, a punkish group of "underground electro-feminist performance artists." Le Tigre was the first taste the public got of Samson's enormous talents. After leaving the group after their final album in 2004, Sampson went on to form a new group, JD Samson and MEN. The band received a lot of critical acclaim, but since its founding in 2007, Samson has extended her talents to a multitude of projects, acting in John Cameron Mitchell's *Shortbus*, founding the performance art group Dykes Can Dance, and writing extensively for *HuffPost* about the struggles of modern queer artists in the twenty-first-century economy. Pretty cool, right? Very Cool.

Sapphire (1950–)

Most known for her novel *Push*, on which the 2009 movie *Precious* was

JD Samson and Sappho

---

based, Sapphire, a.k.a. Ramona Lofton, is an author and poet. She began her career as a slam poet, and it was from this scene that she was nicknamed Sapphire. She wrote *Push* in 1996 and had a tough time getting published. But once she found her way to Vintage Books, it became a hit. Since the novel, Sapphire has continued to write and perform her poetry, and in 2011 she wrote *The Kid*, a follow-up to *Push*.

Sappho (630–570 BC)

The original "lesbian" poet, in that she lived on the island of Lesbos and wrote poetry, Sappho also appears to have been a lesbian, which is where the term comes from. She is one of the few female writers to emerge from the ancient world, and most of her work survives only in fragments. She was greatly known and admired in her time and beyond, and her reputation and mystery have only grown in the modern day. For her stature as one of the first female poets in the Western canon, Sappho is often called the Tenth Muse.

José Sarria (1922–2013)

Some heroes need masks and capes; this one just needed a little black mourning dress and a veil. José Sarria was a pioneer for LGBTQ+ people in San Francisco. Also known as the Grand Mere, or the Absolute Empress I de San Francisco, or the Widow Norton, Sarria was a community builder in the early gay scene in San Francisco, and his love and support are still evident in the years since his passing. He served in the army in World War II, and afterward devoted himself to the rights of LGBTQ+ people. Long before Stonewall, Sarria was organizing groups to fight for the rights for the community. He formed the Imperial Court System that, to this day, is one of the largest LGBTQ+ organizations in the world. Sarria was also the first openly gay person to run for the San Francisco Board of Supervisors in 1961, and though he lost, he remained a constant in the community, performing in drag and singing for patrons at the legendary Black Cat. For his service to the people of San Francisco, a section of Sixteenth Street was named in his honor.

Dan Savage (1964–)

If you're looking for love advice and can take it dished out with no mercy, look to Dan Savage. His Savage Love advice column he offers shoot-from-the-hip advice about the sex you're having and the sex you want to have. In his no-nonsense, no-shame approach to sex has been hugely popular and made Savage a national figure. With this larger platform, Savage has continued to preach a message of acceptance and honesty that he has extended to a view of politics. Savage is never shy about taking a shot at politicians or pundits who defame the LGBTQ+ community. He renamed the fluid or fluids produced by gay sex "santorum" after anti-gay Senator Rick Santorum. He's also the founder of the It Gets Better Project with his husband, Terry Miller. This group focuses on preventing suicide in the young LGBTQ+ community.

Justin Elizabeth Sayre (1981–)

A writer, performer, and playwright whose friends said if they didn't include themself in their own book on gay culture, they would kill them. Sayre first came to prominence with their show *The Meeting of the International Order of Sodomites*—of which Sayre was the Chairman. Sayre oversaw *The Meeting* for eight years, making it the longest-running LGBTQ+ comedy variety show in New York. Sayre has written plays for La MaMa, Dixon Place, and the Celebration Theatre in Los Angeles. They've written for television on the shows *2 Broke Girls* and *The Cool Kids* as well as published three YA novels with Penguin Books. And they've written this book, so there.

Scott Turner Schofield

A groundbreaking actor, writer and director who has used his experience of his transition to create dialogues around justice, art and expression, Scott Turner Schofield began telling his own story in solo theatre performances like 2002's *Underground TRANSit*, to his most recent work, *Becoming a Man in 127 Easy Steps* which he is currently adapting to film. Besides his own work, Schofield has broken barriers in mainstream media, appearing on the soap opera *The Bold and the Beautiful* in 2015 as Nick. Most recently, Schofield appeared in 2018's *The Conductor*, for which he received incredible reviews.

Sarah Schulman (1958–)

Novelist, playwright, intellectual, and activist, Sarah Schulman is a writer of insight and depth, taking on the problems of the queer community and the world at large and turning them into beautiful and sensitive work. Some of Schulman's novels include *After Delores*, which was awarded the Stonewall Book Award from the American Library Association in 1989, and *The Cosmopolitans*, cited as one of the best books of 2016 by *Publishers Weekly*. She has written frequently for the stage as well, but it is her essays and nonfiction work that have perhaps been her most powerful. Her 2012 book *The Gentrification of the Mind* is a masterwork of free thought in an age of commodification, and her 2016 *Conflict Is Not Abuse* is a spellbinding read about conflict resolution and the healing needed in the LGBTQ+ community. As an activist, Schulman founded the Lesbian Avengers in 1992 and was a proud member of ACT UP. Schulman's latest work, *Let the Record Show*, a history of ACT UP in New York was released in 2021 to universal acclaim. The book has been optioned for television, and will be adapted by Andrew Haigh.

James Schuyler (1923–1991)

A poet of such painstaking and delicate beauty that to read him feels so intimate and raw that you may need to take a break and lie down, Schuyler was one of the famous New York poets of the 1950s and '60s, but even among them, he was often the most beloved. During his long and turbulent career, he wrote in many mediums, including plays, books, and diaries, but his poetry remains his greatest accomplishment. For his 1980 collection, *The Morning of the Poem*, Schuyler was awarded the Pulitzer Prize. He suffered from mental illness for most of his life and was often hospitalized.

Scissor Sisters

They put the camp in pop, and have given us all a reason to dance and laugh since their first self-titled album in 2004. Comprised of vocalists Jake Shears and Ana Matronic, multi-instrumentalist Babydaddy a.k.a. Scott Hoffman, and bassist/guitarist Del Marquis, the Scissor Sisters emerged on the scene in 2004 with their dance cover of Pink Floyd's "Comfortably Numb" and the irreverent and danceable "Take Your Mama." The band immediately became known for their wild costumes and openly gay aesthetic. They enjoyed a great success in the United States, but were even more beloved in the United Kingdom, where they often toured to sold-out crowds. More albums followed,

Ana Matronic and Jake Shears / Scissor Sisters

like 2006's *Ta-Dah*, and 2010's *Night Work*, to critical and commercial success. Their final album, 2012's *Magic Hour*, produced one of their biggest hits in the United States with "Let's Have a Kiki." Shortly after this release, the band announced that they would be going on an indefinite hiatus. Since the announcement, Matronic has had a very lucrative career as a broadcaster and DJ, and Shears has written the music for the musical version of *Tales of the City*, and his own solo album, titled *Jake Shears*, in 2018.

David Sedaris (1956–)

While you may know him for his stellar essays, David Sedaris will always be the man with the best Billie Holiday impression in the business, at least to me. The dry wit and humor of David Sedaris have made him one of the most popular comedic writers of his day. With books like *Naked*, *Me Talk Pretty One Day*, and even his earliest success, *The Santaland Diaries*, Sedaris has shown time and time again that he is a writer of both hilarity and pathos that leaves his readers with only one request: When can we get more? Long associated with the NPR show *This American Life*, on which he debuted many of his stories, Sedaris has also become famous for reading his stories. While he often uses his personal life for material, Sedaris has also shown his great skill in works of fiction, with the collection of animal short stories called *Squirrel Seeks Chipmunk* in 2013. He's recently published a collection from his diaries entitled *Theft by Finding* in 2017, and a new collection of essays, *Calypso*, in 2018. He's also written plays under the banner of the Talent Family with his sister, actress Amy Sedaris, in the 1990s.

Maurice Sendak (1928–2012)

Let the wild rumpus begin! Maurice Sendak was an author and illustrator most famous for his picture book *Where the Wild Things Are*, published in 1963. The book was an international success and put Sendak on a track to become one of the most respected authors and illustrators of children's literature in the world. In his long and storied career, he illustrated the first children's book written by Isaac Bashevis Singer, called *Zlateh the Goat and Other Stories*, for which he won the Newberry Honor; wrote and illustrated *Really Rosie*, which was turned into an animated special with songs by Carole King, and

worked with playwright Tony Kushner on the book *Brundibar*, a retelling of Czech composer Hans Krása's opera about the Holocaust. Sendak also illustrated the wildly popular *Little Bear* books with author Else Holmelund Minarik.

Julia Serano (1967–)

A writer, performer, and activist whose work *Whipping Girl* has become a rallying cry among trans people for its deep understanding of transphobia and its root causes, Serano openly identifies as a feminist and promotes ideas around inclusion, and her works have often been featured in workshops and classes teaching people how to understand and create dialogue with the trans community. Serano is also a spoken-word poet and musician who has appeared and performed at many queer festivals across the country, always carrying forward her message of equality and understanding for trans people.

John Sex (1956–1990)

This performance artist, actor, and musician could be said to be the visual prototype for the cartoon Johnny Bravo. They both had a long shock of blond hair standing straight up, but there's where the similarities end. Sex came to New York to paint in the 1970s, but soon found his way into go-go dancing and performance art. Linking up with friends like Joey Arias and Klaus Nomi, Sex came up with his own persona of a Las Vegas lounge lizard on hyperdrive. Sex performed songs and parodies, eventually releasing some of his own songs like "Hustle with My Muscle" and "Bump and Grind It." Sex was a staple of New York's downtown until his death of complications from AIDS in 1990.

Sex and the City

The question will inevitably come up at a brunch somewhere as to whether you are a "Carrie"? or maybe a "Samantha"? This HBO show starring Sarah Jessica Parker has made an indelible mark on modern culture with its frank talk about sexuality and relationship, and also its fabulous fashions. It was one of the first great hits for HBO, earning the show an unflappable audience that only continues to grow today. Audiences could see themselves in the freewheeling and at times a little irresponsible Carrie Bradshaw and her friend, uptight and judgmental Miranda Hobbes, played by Cynthia Nixon. Or perhaps they identified with the perky and perfect Charlotte York played by Kristin Davis, or the endlessly sassy sex maniac Samantha Jones played by Kim Cattrall. The show ran for six seasons, inspired two movies, and still touches the hearts and minds of an ever-growing fan base who wonder, like Carrie: Is love really possible? We'll all get a chance to find out with an announced revival in 2022.

Marc Shaiman (1959–)

One of the most lauded songwriters and musicians of the modern day, Marc Shaiman has done it all with many of the best that music has to offer. He's musical director for so many award shows and live events, and has a long-standing professional relationship with Bette Midler. Shaiman has written some of the most endearing scores to films in the last thirty years, like *Beaches*, *The Addams Family*, *A Few Good Men*, and *South Park: Bigger, Longer, & Uncut*. He's also written successful musicals with his partner Scott Wittman, like the smash-hit *Hairspray* in 2002, *Catch Me If You Can* in 2009, and *Charlie and the Chocolate Factory* in 2017. Shaiman and Wittman also wrote many of the songs for Disney's *Mary Poppins Returns* in 2018.

Omar Sharif Jr. (1983–)

This actor, model, and activist is the grandson of famed Egyptian actor Omar Sharif. He grew up in Canada and studied politics and performing arts in England. Sharif is an outspoken advocate for LGBTQ+ rights here in America and in the Middle East, hoping to use his celebrity and famous name to further the cause of LGBTQ+ equality across the region.

Shamir (1994–)

This nonbinary singer gives you the bops for life, and we can't wait for more. Shamir first came on the music scene with the EP *Northtown* in 2014, and started garnering quite a lot of attention for their great beats and beautiful countertenor voice. They were quickly signed to the XL label, where they released their single, "On the Regular." The song was a huge hit on the Internet and was used in an Android Wear commercial the following year. Since then Shamir has released a series of albums, each varying in style, but staying true to this groundbreaking nonbinary artist's vision of themself.

Jackie Shane (1940–2019)

Shane was a trans rhythm and blues singer whose outlandish stage presence made her a hit with Canadian audiences and a pioneer in the history of LGBTQ+ music. Shane started performing in clubs around her native Toronto and soon formed a reputation for stone-cold singing and her outrageous stage manner. With lots of makeup and sequins, Shane, who was then presenting male, used every moment on stage to let you know exactly who she was with hits like "In My Tenement" and "Any Other Way," in which Shane sings, "Tell her that I'm happy, tell her that I'm gay. Tell her that I wouldn't have it any other way." As Shane began her transition, she fell away from the music scene, but interest in her career and life only grew. Followed by candid interviews with the elusive star in national papers and the re-release of her records, Shane was rediscovered not long before her death in 2019.

Aiden Shaw (1966–)

Shaw is a devastatingly handsome man whose looks and talents have taken him down a myriad of fascinating roads. Shaw began his career as a porn star in the 1990s and was an instant favorite in the industry. He wrote about his experiences in two memoirs, *My Undoing* in 2006 and *Sordid Truths* in 2009. He is also the author of a series of novels, from 1996's *Brutal* to 2001's *Wasted*. Since retiring from porn, Shaw has a lucrative career as a runway and print model, and while he has at times used his birth name of Aiden Brady to distinguish himself from his far raunchier past, the unmistakable jawline and piercing eyes will let you know exactly who you're dealing with.

Peggy Shaw (1944–)

A writer, actor, and performance artist who's told stories from her own unique perspective as a butch woman for more than thirty years, Shaw became involved in theatre though a friendship with Bette Bourne, but quickly found the drag world not totally to her liking. She then co-founded the Split Britches company with friends Deb Margolin and Lois Weaver. Split Britches were doing both female and male drag and telling stories from a very queer, very female perspective. The group and Shaw won multiple Obies for their work and became a staple of the downtown theatre scene in

New York. A collection of Shaw's solo works was published by the University of Michigan under the title *A Menopausal Gentleman.*

Matthew Shepard (1976–1998)

The gruesome murder of Matthew Shepard in 1998 by Aaron McKinney and Russell Henderson made national news, and asked the nation to take a hard look at the treatment of LGBTQ+ people in this country. On October 6th, Shepard was beaten beyond recognition and left for dead, tied to a fencepost on the side of the road. When found, Shepard was still alive but he died six days later from his injuries. During his stay in the hospital, vigils were held around the country and the national conversation was focused on the horrific murder of this young man. After his death, the trial for McKinney and Henderson began, and while they never denied it, their lawyers tried to use the gay-panic defense, saying that Shepard had come on to them and they acted out of a fear of being perceived as gay. This tactic was used with the hope of avoiding a first-degree murder conviction that would lead to their execution. The trial started national conversation, not only about the gay-panic defense, but also about how much the motivation for a crime should be taken into consideration when charging. Both McKinney and Henderson were convicted of felony murder and received consecutive life sentences. Since the death of her son, Judy Shepard has become an outspoken advocate for the LGBTQ+ community and hate-crime legislation. In 2009, Congress passed the Matthew Shepard and James Byrd Jr. Hate Crimes Prevention Act, making hate crimes, or crimes motivated by social or racial prejudice, a federal crime.

Del Shores (1957–)

Southern charm never sounded so charming as it does from Del Shores. With his quirky and comical looks at southern lives, this writer and performer delivers Southern realness. Delighting audiences for almost thirty years, Shores first came to prominence with 1990's *Daddy's Dyin': Who's Got the Will?* The film was well received and pushed Shores into bringing his Southern twang to Hollywood. In 2000, Shores made the film *Sordid Lives*, a campy and hilarious take on his own family. The play would eventually become a film and then a short-lived but deeply loved series on Logo TV in 2008 starring Leslie Jordan and Rue McClanahan. Shores continues to make work for the theatre and television, performing his solo plays around the country and offering up a continuing chapter to *Sordid Lives* with the film *A Very Sordid Wedding* in 2017.

Shortbus

John Cameron Mitchell's 2006 movie about love, sex, and relationships was a breakout hit for its graphic yet totally realistic vision of sexuality. Set in New York, the film follows three story lines of people looking for connection and finally finding it in an all-out orgy hosted by the one and only Justin Vivian Bond. It was a success on the festival circuit and was a visionary look at how sex can be used as a storytelling device. It also featured an incredible soundtrack by singer-songwriter Scott Matthew.

Sia (1975–)

One of the most successful singer-songwriters of the modern era, Sia has written hits for performers like Beyoncé, Rihanna, and Kylie Minogue, and her own work stands on par with what she's written for others. With her powerful vocals and incredible video aesthetic, often working with choreographer Ryan Heffington, Sia has established herself as an artistic powerhouse in pop since her breakout

Sia

album, 2014's *1000 Forms of Fear*. She had huge hits with songs "Elastic Heart" and "Chandelier," but found the constant attention a bit unnerving. Sia famously didn't want to be seen while singing, thus employing Heffington's dance installations to take center stage and wearing huge stylized wigs to cover her face. Since 2013, Sia has released three more albums, all garnering commercial and critical success, and her long-banged wigs have become iconic of the emotional singer's desire to let her work speak for itself.

Michelangelo Signorile (1960–)

This radio host, journalist, and author has been an outspoken advocate for LGBTQ+ rights since the beginning of his career. His talk show on SiriusXM, *The Michelangelo Signorile Show*, debuted in 2003 and has been a great venue for him to talk about the issues of the day, always with his passion and wit at the ready. He's been an editor for *Out*, *The Advocate*, and the *Huffington Post* and has also authored several books, like *Queer in America*, *Outing Yourself*, and 2015's *It's Not Over*, a harrowing and prophetic book about the dangers of complacency in the modern age of seeming LGBTQ+ equality.

Sisters of Perpetual Indulgence

Every community needs a group of selfless individuals who give of their time for the betterment of the community. The LGBTQ+ community got a group of clowning nuns in white-face. Yup. They're great. Founded in 1979, this group, a.k.a. the Order of Perpetual Indulgence, is a charita-ble protesting body of drag nuns that show up for the community in lots of unlikely ways. Originally founded in San Francisco as a protest against outcry from the Catholic Church, the Sisters of Perpetual Indulgence have spread to most major cities in Amer-ica. Glee is still on the agenda with these nuns, and the Sisters have used their visibility as a touchstone for the community to collect for charity and speak out for causes like preventing the spread of HIV and the care of homeless LGBTQ+ youth. Even today, the Sis-ters are still a vibrant resource in the LGBTQ+ community and are open to all—so what about it? You wanna become a nun?

Sisters of Perpetual Indulgence

Troye Sivan (1995–)

If you look up the word *twink*, you might see a picture of Troye Sivan, but that's only one side of the pop star. Since his early days as a You-Tuber releasing personal videos and music, to his current success with the 2018's *Bloom*, Sivan seems to be on a trajectory that hasn't been seen for an openly gay pop star in a very long while. Sivan was hugely popu-lar on YouTube, and has used social media as an instrument to connect with his ever-growing audience. He has also turned his hand to acting, appearing in the 2018 film *Boy Erased*. His song for the film, "Revelation," was nominated for a Golden Globe for Best Song.

Small Town Gay Bar

This 2006 documentary about local gay bars tells the story of these little oases in towns all over the country. The film, made by Malcolm Ingram, followed the stories of gay bars in Mis-sissippi and Alabama, and looks at the history of each bar as they struggle to survive. It's a stunning and heartfelt look at these tiny gay spots that keep their communities alive in areas that often aren't thought to have gay com-munities at all.

Barbara Smith (1946–)

Smith is a stunning writer and driving force in the field of feminist theory, and a backbone to Black feminist thought in America. Throughout her long career, Smith has promoted and created opportunities for woman writers of color, founding the Kitchen Table: Women of Color Press in 1981 with the help of her sister Beverly, Demita Frazier, and her friend the poet Audre Lorde. The press published works by women of color and was widely successful until the death of Lorde and the press closed its doors in 1992. Smith has continued her own work as a writer, educator, and activist. She is a much-lauded resident of Albany, New York, and has been titled a Literary Legend there.

Bessie Smith (1894–1937)

The Empress of the Blues, Bessie Smith is a seminal figure in American music. Her loud and brassy tones, her stunning turns with lyrics, and the deep-rooted sorrow in her voice combine to make her recordings seem incredibly modern and touching almost a century later. Smith was a widely loved performer during her lifetime, primarily to Black audiences. Her recordings were cherished and were major influences on later singers like Billie Holiday, Dinah Washington, and LaVern Baker. Smith was also one of the first Black women to appear in talking pictures, with *St. Louis Blues* in 1929. Smith's recording of songs like "Downhearted Blues," "Empty Bed Blues," and "Nobody Knows You When You're Down and Out" have become classics.

Bob Smith (1958–2018)

A simple and soft-spoken gay comic who broke down a lot of doors for the LGBTQ+ community in the world of comedy, Smith was the all-American boy who, in 1994, was not only the first openly gay comedian to ever appear on the *Tonight Show*, but also the first openly gay comedian to have an HBO half-hour comedy special. Smith wanted to create space and opportunities for his gay contemporaries, forming the Funny Gay Males comedy troupe in 1988 with Jaffe Cohen and Danny McWilliams. Smith was also the author of several books, three collections of essays, and two autobiographical novels.

Jack Smith (1932–1989)

A pioneer of underground cinema and performance, Jack Smith is most remembered for his 1963 film *Flaming Creatures*. Sometimes called the father of American performance, Smith created performance work on stage about his life and sexuality. Always outrageous and thought-provoking, Smith's work is often seen as important to the progression of experimental filmmaking and theatre. Sadly, his work is largely out of circulation to this day. His photography work has been called masterful and important, though precious little of it is seen in galleries around the world and mostly held in private collections. Smith was an artist of mystery whose work influenced the artists who saw him live, but now it lives mostly in the imagination of younger generations.

Sam Smith (1992–)

The golden-voiced singer of such hits as "Stay with Me" and "Like I Can," which have skyrocketed their way into the music scene. Smith's debut album, 2014's *In the Lonely Hour,* immediately established Smith as a vocalist of power and subtlety, and certainly as someone to watch. Smith has proven themself to be the sensitive balladeer of the new millennium. While at times the rise to fame has been rough—Smith has struggled with body-image issues and faux pas with the press—Smith most often is cited for their expert musicianship and captivating way of communicating emotions in their songs. In 2017, Smith released *The Thrill of It All,* and a third album, *Love Goes,* in 2020, each achieving more and more commercial success. Smith came out as nonbinary in 2019.

Paul Soileau (1978–)

Some performers are freaky. Some performers are hilarious. But few combine the two. Paul Soileau does. This drag performer and musician is perhaps most famous for his drag persona, Christeene, the queen of "terrorist drag." Through Christeene, Soileau has taken on a host of social issues, all with a sense of play and anarchy through his performance and music. Christeene first hit the scene in a major way with the video for her song "African Mayonnaise" debuting in 2012. Soileau has since traveled the world with his weird and wonderful creation, as well as his other, more conservative persona, Rebecca Havemeyer. Both are hilarious, edgy, and ready to take you to places you've never been before.

Joey Soloway (1965–)

The writer and creator of Amazon's *Transparent* has won two Emmy Awards and a Golden Globe for Best Series. Soloway, who identifies as gender-nonconforming, uses *they* pronouns. With the huge hit of *Transparent,* Soloway has become an outspoken advocate for the LGBTQ+ community, and has done their best in hiring queer and trans writers and staff for the show. Soloway has also directed several episodes of the show, and their film *Afternoon Delight* was an official selection of the Sundance Film Festival. Soloway is also a writer, with a collection of novellas and two memoirs, *Tiny Ladies in Shiny Pants* in 2005, and 2018's *She Wants It.*

Some of My Best Friends Are…

Directed by Mervyn Nelson, this 1971 film about a single night in a gay bar follows its patrons through love and loss and all the complications that come with it. The film is an early example of gay cinema and remarkable for a few reasons, one being that there are many sympathetic characters and not everyone is a villain—a big step for the period. It also stars a young Rue McClanahan as a femme fatale fag hag, Fannie Flagg as a wisecracking hat-check girl, and a young Candy Darling. It's a hidden chestnut of gay cinema and definitely worth another viewing.

Stephen Sondheim (1930–)

If you've got angst and a song in your heart, Stephen Sondheim is the composer for you. Sondheim is considered the best composer and lyricist of musical theatre in the second part of the twentieth century. The list of his musicals is a reliving of some of the most brilliant moments in the American theatre. He was a protege of the famed lyricist Oscar Hammerstein II, and began his long and storied career writing lyrics for the musical *West Side Story*. He went on to write lyrics for the musical *Gypsy*, but Sondheim always wanted to write music all his own. From his earliest hit *A Funny Thing Happened on the Way to the Forum* in 1962 to the string of important works like *Company* in 1970, *Follies* in 1971, and *A Little Night Music* in 1973, Sondheim has time and time again proved his mastery of the lyric structure, producing words and music that delve into the depths of his character's feelings with wit and raw honesty. Though his 1979 musical *Sweeney Todd* is often considered his masterpiece, in the years since he has continued to write beautiful and

Stephen Sondheim and Jack Smith

challenging shows like *Merrily We Roll Along* in 1981, *Sunday in the Park with George* in 1984, and the international hit *Into the Woods* in 1987. Sondheim's contributions to musical theatre have made him an apocryphal figure, with some people breaking the art form into periods before Sondheim and after. Sondheim is the most awarded composer in Tony Award history. He has also won the Oscar, a Pulitzer Prize, the Presidential Medal of Freedom, and the Kennedy Center Honor. He has theatres bearing his name on Broadway and in London's West End.

Susan Sontag (1933–2004)

A deeply respected critic, writer, and pioneer in the realm of social criticism, Sontag is most remembered for her essay *Notes on Camp*, published in 1964. But that is just one essay in the long list of works by the prestigious writer. She wrote seriously about pop culture and, at times, was seen as elevating the criticism of her day by mixing high and low culture in interesting and thought-provoking ways. She wrote extensively about art and social change. A vehement and vocal advocate for social justice, Sontag wrote extensively about the plight of the underrepresented and oppressed. Sontag also wrote novels and plays, but her criticism and social thought have established her as one of the preeminent minds in American literature. Though Sontag never publicly came out in her lifetime, she had a long-term relationship with photographer Annie Leibovitz.

Southern Decadence

In this six-day festival in New Orleans, usually around Labor Day, the LGBTQ+ community descends on the city and takes partying in the Big Easy to the next level. The festival was started in 1972, and in the years since has grown into a major holiday weekend. There are parties and parades and lots of debauchery in a town known to celebrate just that. It's a fun time for all who come, and that's usually guaranteed.

Britney Spears (1981–) ICON

It's Britney, bitch. In the late 1990s and early 2000s, Britney Spears was the pop diva that the world was looking for. Starting out with an innocent look in her first video for " . . . Baby One More Time" to the more seductive "Toxic," Britney, much like Madonna, has given her gay audiences a lot to look at along with a lot of great songs to dance to.

She's also given us the story of modern stardom, with her short-lived marriage to dancer Kevin Federline and her very public breakdown in 2006. The pop princess has reinvented herself time and time again for an adoring audience that simply wants more.

Stephen Spender (1909–1995)

Spender was the third part of the small circle including W. H. Auden and Christopher Isherwood, who found enlightenment and sexual freedom in the Berlin of the late 1920s and early '30s. Spender was a poet, novelist, and critic who was a major influence on both of his friends. But while they chose to live their lives as openly gay men, Spender married Natasha Litvin in 1941. After the marriage, Spender began to tone down the homosexual content of his earlier work and publicly denied his homosexuality, though he continued to have homosexual affairs during his long marriage. Spender remains at one instance a writer of homosexual love and dignity and then a writer of the closet.

Jack Spicer (1925–1965)

A respected poet of the San Francisco Renaissance, Spicer was a gay writer who saw his work within a long lineage of gay poets. His conversational verse, with its touches of wit and stunning and revolutionary play with language, marked him as one of the most intriguing poets of his day. Though largely unrecognized during his lifetime, a collection of his work, *My Vocabulary Did This to Me*, released in 2009 won the American Book Award for poetry.

Dusty Springfield (1939–1999)

The black eyeliner. The beehive. The voice. I'm not talking about your failed Halloween costume; I'm talking about the legend Dusty Springfield. A stone-cold singer of "blue-eyed soul," she had a string of hits in her native England with songs like "I Only Want to Be With You," "Wishin' and Hopin'," and "You Don't Have to Say You Love Me." She was a favorite singer in the UK and a popular performer on television. Soon her hits began to cross over to America, where Dusty became a popular hitmaker in the 1960s. In 1968, she recorded the classic *Dusty in Memphis.* Recorded in Memphis with many soul musicians from the American music scene, the album became a huge hit and produced Springfield's signature song, "Son of a Preacher Man." Springfield fell somewhat out of favor in the late '70s, but made a stunning comeback, recording an album with the Pet Shop Boys in 1987.

Annie Sprinkle (1954–)

If there's one thing that Annie Sprinkle loves, it's sex. She talks about it, makes art about it, counsels people about it, and writes about it. Sprinkle is a certified sexologist, but that is merely the beginning of her work. She got started as a sex worker and actor in pornography, but wanted to make performance art to demystify sex and our drives to seek pleasure. Sprinkle has made works for the stage like *The Legend of the Ancient Sacred Prostitute* and her famous *Sluts and Goddesses* workshop. In her Public Cervix Announcement, Sprinkle famously used a speculum on stage and invited the audience to look at her cervix. She's been a longtime supporter of LGBTQ+ rights, and a champion for the rights and protections for sex workers around the world.

James St. James (1966–)

One of the famous Club Kids of New York who survived the period to tell the tale and pass his wisdom on to the children. James St. James was a staple of the scene in the late 1980s and '90s. With his outlandish and innovative costumes, St. James was front and center for a lot of the parties and the darker goings on. His 1999 memoir, *Disco Bloodbath*, was later retitled to *Party Monster.* It was made into both a documentary and a movie of the same name. St. James wrote another book, this time for teens, called *Freak Show*, which was made into a movie in 2017. He is a staple at WOW, World of Wonder Productions, interviewing queens and getting them to paint his face in their style. He's an enthusiastic supporter of drag and queer creativity, just as he's been since the beginning.

St. Vincent (1982–)

Electronic music never sounded so good or so inviting as it does when helmed by this visionary performer and songwriter. An accomplished musician and writer, St. Vincent continues to push the confines of modern pop with her fascinating music and her collaborations with fellow artists like David Byrne. St. Vincent first hit the scene with her album *Marry Me* in 2007, and she has since released four other solo albums, each achieving greater praise and notoriety. For her 2014 album, *St. Vincent*, she received her first Grammy Award for Best Alternative Album. In 2021, she released yet another hit with her '70s-inspired *Daddy's Home.*

Peter Staley (1961–)

This activist, writer, and educator is still at the forefront of the fight against AIDS and HIV. Staley was very involved in the early days of ACT UP in New York. He chronicled this fight in his memoir of the crisis, *How to Survive a Plague*, which was turned into a documentary in 2012. Staley has continued the work of ACT UP with other organizations, founding TAG, Treatment Action Group, to get patients the proper meds and work with drug companies to keep costs low. He's also worked with amfAR, the Foundation for AIDS Research, and founded the site POZ.com to provide people with clear information about their medications.

Starhawk (1951–)

A writer, teacher, and pagan goddess whose work on the reclaiming of Wicca and a closer relationship with the natural world has inspired millions around the world, Starhawk grew up in Minnesota, but soon found her way to the San Francisco area, where she first came into contact with Wicca. In 1979, she wrote *The Spiral Dance*, which focused on an earth-based religion with a goddess figure at the center. The book became a best seller and much-appreciated tome in the neo-pagan movement. Starhawk continues to write on the pagan religion and teach around the country.

Joey Stefano (1968–1994)

One of the early breakout stars of gay porn, whose bedroom eyes and all-American-boy looks were an instant hit with gay fans, Stefano paired up with friend and director Chi Chi LaRue early in his career and soon caught fire in the industry. He was so popular that Madonna used him as a model in her

Joey Stefano and Steven Universe

Sex book in 1992. He was a sex worker throughout his career, and was often connected to prominent gay figures. He struggled with addiction throughout his life and died from an overdose in 1994, at the age of twenty-six.

Gertrude Stein (1874–1946)

Gertrude Stein was Gertrude Stein was Gertrude Stein was a writer of novels, poetry, and plays. She was also a prominent art collector who collected a coterie of artists in her Paris apartment during the early decades of the twentieth century. She was a friend and mentor to Hemingway and Picasso, who painted the infamous portrait of her. She was an experimental writer, with repetitions of words as in her famous line, "a rose is a rose is a rose." Stein lived openly as a lesbian with her partner, Alice B. Toklas, whose name became synonymous with her famous brownie recipe that called for a healthy amount of marijuana in the mix.

Steven Universe

A cartoon about a young boy and his Crystal friends, created by Rebecca Sugar in 2013, the show grew a huge fan base among young viewers for its positive portrayal of LGBTQ+ characters and its hilarious adventures. As word spread about its serious themes of gender and its stress on the importance of healthy relationships, the show started to garner an adult fan base, as well. The show was awarded the first GLAAD Media Award for kids programming in 2019 for its portrayals of gender-nonconforming people and adult story lines. It was also awarded the prestigious Peabody Award for its writing in 2019.

Kristen Stewart (1990–)

You may know her as Bella from the *Twilight* series, or from her signature awkward-yet-strangely-too-cool way of speaking, but no matter how, you know who Kristen Stewart is. And that's just the beginning. Stewart got her start as a child acting in Hollywood roles like Jodie Foster's daughter in 2002's *Panic Room*, but it was playing opposite her on-again and off-again boyfriend Robert Pattinson in the wildly popular *Twilight* films that made Stewart a household name. Since then Stewart has continued to star in hits like *Snow White and the Huntsman* in 2012 and more indie fare like the *Clouds of Sils Maria* for which she won the Cesar Award for Best Supporting Actress in 2014. Stewart came out in 2017 on SNL with the phrase, "I'm like so gay, dude." And the LGBTQ+ community is so happy to have her.

Michael Stipe (1960–)

The melancholy in his voice made Michael Stipe stand out immediately as a dynamic and unusual singer at the head of the band R.E.M. From their forming in 1980 to their breaking up in 2011, Stipe's vocals gave the band a sound like no other. With their 1990s hits "Everybody Hurts," "Losing My Religion," and "Nightswimming"

R.E.M. has achieved a place in popular music seen by very few. Stipe has been a longtime activist and has often lent his talents as a singer and artist to many charitable causes. An outspoken social critic, social justice and equality have always been a part of Stipe's art. Since the dissolving of R.E.M., Stipe has continued to perform and create visual artwork. He and R.E.M. were inducted in the Rock and Roll Hall of Fame in 2007.

The Stonewall Riots

The famous riots that began a move-

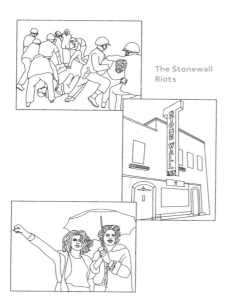

The Stonewall Riots

ment started in the early hours of June 28, 1969. Cops raided the mob-owned and operated Stonewall Inn on Christopher Street. Raids during this time on gay establishments were commonplace, but that summer their frequency and intensity had increased due in part to the efforts of Ed Koch, then head of the vice squad, who was told to clean up the city for the World's Fair. Judy Garland had died on June 22, and her body had been brought back to New York for an open viewing to throngs of fans. The mood in the murky city was hot and ready for something to happen. A few weeks prior, after another similar raid, a young man had been arrested and, while waiting to be booked, tried to sneak out and fell to his death. There was grumbling in the community about how much longer was this kind of harassment going to go on? Why were they allowing this to happen? What were they doing that was all that wrong? These people just wanted to dance. So when the cops came to bust up the Stonewall, tensions were high. When Stormé DeLarverie allegedly got physical with her arresting officer, the dam broke and the group of detainees turned on the police, forcing them back into the bar. The protest continued to grow as word spread that something vital was going on at the Stonewall. The protest grew and more police were called in. There was open taunting of the police with the famous chant and kick-line, "We are the Stonewall girls, we wear our hair in curls, we wear our dungarees, below our nelly knees." The riots stopped for the first night, but picked up again the next night, with larger crowds standing up against police brutality and fighting for the right to simply be. Though the original riots were very sparsely covered in the local press, legend of the event spread across the country and began to make people think that LGBTQ+ people had rights, and if they didn't, it was time to fight to get them.

Lytton Strachey (1880–1932)

A wit and writer of the famous Bloomsbury Group, Lytton Strachey was a friend of fellow writers Virginia Woolf and E. M. Forster, and emerged as their equal with his book of essays *Eminent Victorians* and his biographies of Queens Elizabeth and Victoria. Strachey was a conscience objector of the First World War, and had a long-term relationship with artist Dora Carrington. Though Strachey was gay and Carrington was bisexual, the two were devoted to each other. When Strachey died in 1932, Carrington, overcome with grief, killed herself just two months after. A film of their lives together, *Carrington*, was released in 1995 with Jonathan Pryce as Strachey and Emma Thompson as Carrington.

Straight to Hell

The original dirty zine, *Straight to Hell*, or *S.T.H.*, was subtitled with many names, from the *New York Review of Cocksucking* to the *Rimmer's Digest*. Started in 1971, this community-generated zine headed by Boyd McDonald was a chronicle of the sexual tales and desires of its readership. Readers would write to McDonald with details of their lurid sexual lives. The zine became very popular and continues to publish to this day, even after McDonald's death in 1993. *Straight to Hell* may come with a lot of different names, but it's a fascinating chronicle of desire and the men who sought it out in the later half of the twentieth century and beyond.

Strangers with Candy

The brainchild of Amy Sedaris, Stephen Colbert, Paul Dinello, and Mitch Rouse, this show told the tale of Jerri Blank, a forty-six-year-old high school student, who was a "boozer, a user, and a loser." Not often thought of as a "gay" show, the satire took the gay joke in a totally new direction. The joke was not homosexuality; it was homophobia itself. In a world where everything is backward, homophobia is just part of the absurdity. From the secret affair between Noblet and Jellyneck to Jerri's own bisexuality, the cult show was famously taking on queer love and the world that rejects it. The series ran for three seasons from 1999 to 2000, with a movie follow-up in 2005.

A Strange Loop

This autobiographical musical by Michael R. Jackson tells the story of a young Black queer man, Usher, as he searches for identity and wholeness through the world of musical theatre. The piece deals with everything from self-image to the sacrifces and trials that artists put into the making of their art. The show was a critical hit when it debuted at Playwrights Horizon in 2019, and won the Pulitzer Prize for Jackson as well as Lortel awards for leads, Larry Owens and John-Andrew Morrison.

Billy Strayhorn (1915–1967)

A jazz composer and lyricist who wrote one of the most beloved jazz songs, "Lush Life," when he was just nineteen years old, Billy Strayhorn became a long-term collaborator and co-composer with Duke Ellington. The two became so closely linked that to this day it is still confused as to which one of the pair wrote which songs. Strayhorn was known for his adventurous melodies and his searching and beautiful lyrics. With songs like "Take the 'A' Train," "Something to Live for," and "Satin Doll," Strayhorn certainly earned his stripes as a major composer of jazz. But as the years went on, Strayhorn felt continually overshadowed by his famous collaborator. He eventually left the Ellington band, but unfortunately died soon after.

Studio 54

The disco that in many ways defined the era, Studio 54 had it all and lost it all in quick succession. Opened in 1977 by Ian Schrager and Steve Rubell, Studio 54 soon became the hottest spot in New York to dance. It was often crowded with celebrities, from Liza Minnelli and Halston in one corner to Andy Warhol and Truman Capote in another with Grace Jones and Bianca Jagger in another. But it was also a hotbed for gay patrons who enjoyed not only the dancing on the floor but also the orgiastic goings-on in the balcony and the basement. Pictures from nights at Studio 54 became a national obsession, and lines around the block of eager people hoping to get picked to go in became a spectacle all their own. While the club was shut down in 1980 due to tax-evasion problems that sent both Rubell and Schrager to jail, the legend of Studio 54 remains palpable to this day. In 2018, a documentary about the legendary club, *Studio 54*, was released with first-hand accounts from patrons and Schrager himself. Steve Rubell died of complications from AIDS in 1989.

Lou Sullivan (1951–1991)

An author and activist who fought hard for trans visibility and rights, Sullivan was an early proponent for separating the concepts of sexual and gender identity. A trans male himself, Sullivan worked tirelessly for his community, connecting people to peer support and counseling as well as medical treatments and creating networks for the sharing of information among the community. Sullivan worked as the editor of *The Gateway* in San Francisco, a local newsletter for the trans community, and a founding member of the GLBT Historical Society. Sullivan died of complications from AIDS in 1991. His journals were published in 2019 under the title *We Both Laughed in Pleasure*.

Donna Summer (1948–2012) ICON
Summer was the queen of disco music

Lou Sullivan and Donna Summer

and hitmaker of the late 1970s. With hit songs like "Last Dance" and "Love to Love You Baby," she gave the world a reason to dance and remains a hallmark of the period. During her career, Summer had forty-two hits on the Billboard charts, and was one of the bestselling artists in the world. Her star was too big to be burned out with the demise of disco in the early '80s. Summer hit back with songs like "She Works Hard for the Money," and "No More Tears" with Barbra Streisand, showing the world she was here to stay. She was inducted into the Rock and Roll Hall of Fame in 2013, and a musical based on her life played Broadway in 2018.

Sunday Bloody Sunday
A 1971 film about a bisexual artist torn between his older male lover and his younger female girlfriend, it was in some ways revolutionary, simply for the fact that the older gay man, played by actor Peter Finch, was not a killer or a psychopath. He was just a well-adjusted man who loved other men. It may sound simple, but it was groundbreaking for its time. Besides Finch, the film stars Glenda Jackson, Murray Head, and Dame Peggy Ashcroft and was directed by John Schlesinger.

Wanda Sykes (1964–)
One of the most successful stand-up comedians of the modern era who continues to entertain audiences around the country, Sykes had been doing stand-up for years when she joined the writing team for *The Chris Rock Show* in 1997. She began to appear on the show, and parlayed this higher profile into more work in front of the camera. With appearances on *Curb Your Enthusiasm* and *The New Adventures of Old Christine*, Sykes soon became a favorite with audiences. In the years since, Sykes has been a major player in television and film, and still returns to stand-up specials with hilarious results. She is also an activist for the

LGBTQ+ community and the rights and representation of women of color in Hollywood.

Sylvester (1947–1988)

The queer disco diva of your dreams, Sylvester was out and outrageous before any of those things seemed possible. Born Sylvester James Jr. in Watts, Los Angeles, he began singing early in church. His enormous talent and unbelievable range set him apart, and so did his sense of the flamboyant. Sylvester left home at fifteen and started a group of trans musicians and drag artists called the Disquotays. He continued to sing, and through his friend Reggie Dunnigan, he was encouraged to move to San Francisco in the late 1960s and be a part of the counterculture. Through Reggie, Sylvester got involved with the Cockettes and quickly became a standout at their shows. After the Cockettes, Sylvester started his own band in 1972, Sylvester and the Hot Band. They toured the country, but Sylvester still didn't break through the way he thought he should. It was after the Hot Band broke up in 1974 that Sylvester met Martha Wash and asked her and her friend Izora Rhodes to join him as his Two Tons o' Fun (who eventually became the Weather Girls and released "It's Raining Men" in 1982). Record companies didn't know what to do with Sylvester. They tried to tame his androgynous looks, but it wasn't until they finally let him be his weird and wild self on his second solo album, 1978's *Step II*, that the true Sylvester started to shine. He scored his first mega hit, "You Make Me Feel (Mighty Real)," which remains a dance classic to this day. He was one of the first openly gay pop stars on television, continued to record until 1986, and throughout his career maintained his identification with the LGBTQ+ community. Sylvester died of complications from AIDS in 1988.

Sylvester

T is for ...

Tabboo! (1959–)

A drag queen of legendary status in New York, not just for her performances or her famous friends, but for her art, Tabboo! was a sickening queen for most of the 1980s and '90s, holding her own with the queens at the Pyramid Club. Tabboo! is also an accomplished painter and visual artist. Known by his civilian name of Stephen Tashjian, he has painted a number of murals on his beloved Lower East Side, showed with some of the most famous visual artists of his day, and was also a particular favorite of photographer of Nan Goldin.

George Takei (1937–)

George Takei has used his instantly recognizable voice and profile to be outspoken for the LGBTQ+ community and communities of color for decades. Most widely known for his role as Mr. Sulu on the original *Star Trek*, Takei has worked as an actor for years with large roles on *Heroes* and in Disney's *Mulan*. He returned to the stage in the 2015 Broadway show *Allegiance*, a musical about the

Japanese internment camps during the Second World War. Takei himself was interned in one of these camps, and he has been a fierce and vocal advocate for the rights of immigrants ever since.

Tales of the City

This series of nine books got turned into a television series, then another one, then most recently got a Netflix run, and has also been adapted as a musical. We simply can't get enough of the characters and the dreamy San Francisco in Armistead Maupin's novels detailing the goings-on at 28 Barbary Lane, owned and operated by the enigmatic Anna Madrigal. She welcomes the newcomer Mary Ann Singleton and the hopeless romantic Michael "Mouse" Tolliver and creates a little family at this idyllic San Francisco home. The books begin in the heady 1970s and continue to the modern day, becoming an international phenomenon along the way.

André Leon Talley (1949–)

The man of a thousand capes, and an eye for fashion that is undeniable, Andre Leon Talley is a respected voice in fashion and spent many years as an editor-at-large for *Vogue*, working closely with friend and editor Anna Wintour. He's worked with many luminaries, like Andy Warhol, Diana Vreeland, and Grace Coddington, and his writings on fashion have appeared in the *New York Times*, *Women's Wear*

Daily, and *Interview* magazine, but his longest tenure was at *Vogue*. A documentary on Talley's life and work in fashion, *The Gospel According to André*, was released in 2018 to rave reviews.

André Leon Talley

Tangerine

Proof you can make a beautiful movie on your iPhone, *Tangerine* is a masterwork. The sleeper hit of 2015, Sean Baker's film was shot mostly on his iPhone and stars Kitana Kiki Rodriguez and Mya Taylor as a pair of down-on-their-luck friends trying to navigate their way through Los Angeles. They share a lot, being both transsexual girls of color and knowing about the tough realities of the street. The movie is at times funny and at others tragic, and while some may scoff at the trope of transsexual hookers in a jam, the movie delves deeply into the humanity of two young women with little to hold on to in this world except each other.

Elizabeth Taylor (1932–2011) `ICON`

She's what you think of when you think of Cleopatra, or like me, when you were a kid who wanted to wear fur and toss diamond earrings on a table with the line, "These have always brought me luck." Elizabeth Taylor has often been called the most beautiful woman in the world, but that is only the beginning of understanding this mega-star to her fullest. Taylor started her career as a child actor at MGM, with hits like *National Velvet*. As she matured, she took on more serious roles, eventually winning two Oscars for her work in *Butterfield 8* and *Who's Afraid of Virginia Woolf?* Taylor was a star of the highest form—talented, beautiful, scandalous. Married eight times, Taylor did it all, and often looked like she was having a lot of fun doing it. And when trouble came, Taylor answered the call. When her dear friend and co-star Rock Hudson and many of her other gay friends were dying of complications from AIDS, Taylor jumped to their side. She became a public champion for AIDS research and the race to find a cure. Through her charitable organization, the Elizabeth Taylor AIDS Foundation, she put pressure on the FDA to release new drugs and raised millions in the fight against AIDS and HIV. It's a fight that continues now, even after her death. She was a brave and brilliant woman, who related deeply to the LGBTQ+ community. Even in her later years, she loved to be driven to the Abbey in West Hollywood, just to be around her people.

Paul Taylor (1930–2018)

One of the most prolific and provocative dancers and choreographers of the latter half of the twentieth century, Taylor began creating work in the 1960s at the Judson Dance Theater, and gained attention for his innovative choreography and his collaborations with visual artists. Over his long career, he created works with many of the biggest visual artists of his day, but his works like *Big Bertha* in 1970, *Last Look* in 1985, and *Brandenburgs* in 1985 set Taylor and his company apart for his unique vision and sense of dance. For his work, he was awarded the Kennedy Center Honor in 1992.

Rip Taylor (1935–2019)

Have you ever wanted to throw glitter right in people's faces? Too bad. Rip Taylor beat you to it. The boisterous and delightful glitter-throwing comedian made the scene of 1970s game shows, with his wild irreverence and sense of constant play. A character actor for many years, his unmistakable turned-up mustache and glitter made him a hallmark icon TV. His early routines were based on his ability to cry, and he was often called the crying comedian. His later outrageousness on shows like *Hollywood Squares, The $1.98 Beauty Show*, which he hosted, and *The Gong Show* made

Rip Taylor and Tchaikovsky

him a favorite. A friend and confidante to many of Hollywood's leading ladies, Taylor was a longtime resident of West Hollywood and was often seen out and about, always happy to give you a little sparkle wherever he went.

Pyotr Ilyich Tchaikovsky (1840–1893)

One of the greatest classical musical theatre composers in history, known for his beautiful melodies and his timeless scores to ballets like *Swan Lake* and *The Nutcracker,* Tchaikovsky was a very popular composer during his lifetime, and his work was thought to elevate the national artistic voice of Russia. He composed a number of orchestral works and ballets and also used the stories of Pushkin as the basis for operas, his most famous being *Eugene Onegin*, which is still in almost constant repertoire around the world.

Michelle Tea (1971–)

A prolific writer of deeply personal and often hilarious works, Tea has lived a life that is storied and varied, with work as a sex worker, a psychic, and a writer. Her work in books like *How to Grow Up* in 2015 and *Against Memoir* tells her story in honest and straightforward prose that makes no apologies for the queer and boundaries-free life she has led. Tea has also written a very successful series of YA novels about the lives of mermaids, including *Mermaid in Chelsea Creek*, and *Girl at the Bottom of the Sea.*

Tegan and Sara (1980–)

Twins. Lesbians. Rock stars. Are you intrigued yet? You should be. Tegan and Sara are a twin rock duo out of Canada whose great sense of indie pop has made them a huge success internationally. They released their first album, *Under Feet Like Ours*, in 1999, but their breakout success came in 2007 with their album, *The Con.* Their music had been categorized as mostly teen fare, but with *The Con* and 2009's *Sainthood*, Tegan and Sara broke out from that stigma for good. They have since released three more albums, including 2013's *Heartthrob.* They've also grown in mass appeal, with their music being featured in films like *Dallas Buyers Club* and *The Lego Movie*, for which they sang the theme song "Everything is Awesome."

Jewel Thais-Williams

People need places where they can just be themselves, and for LGBTQ+ people, it would be great if that place also had dancing. Jewel Thais-Williams created just such a place. A community organizer whose work and life are reflections of her continued commitment to the LGBTQ+ community, Williams opened the legendary Jewel's Catch One in Los Angeles in 1973, when there were still laws against same-sex couples dancing together in California. The Catch One became a mecca for the Black and Latino LGBTQ+ communities in Los Angeles, who felt unwelcome in the mostly white West Hollywood. When the AIDS crisis began, Thais-Williams used the club as a meeting place to organize and get information out to her community in peril. Catch One was one of the longest-running Black discos in the country. She sold the venue in 2015, though it still bears its original name. A documentary about Williams and the Catch One, *Jewel's Catch One*, was released in 2016.

Josh Thomas (1987–)

Words like *adorkable* were made for people like Josh Thomas. The actor, writer, and comedian has been making the world fall in love with his awkward and hilarious sensibility since the early 2000s. Born in Australia, Thomas first made a splash at the Melbourne

International Comedy Festival, winning the RAW comedy award in 2005. From there he wrote his solo show, *Please Like Me*, which he debuted at the Edinburgh Fringe in 2007. The show was eventually adapted into a television show of the same name, also starring Thomas in 2013. The show was a critical hit, and even nominated for an international Emmy in 2014. After four seasons of *Please Like Me*, Thomas moved on to America and created a new show for the Freeform network, *Everything's Going to Be Okay*, which debuted in 2020.

Michael Tilson Thomas (1944–)

A protégé of Leonard Bernstein, Michael Tilson Thomas is an American master conductor and composer who has been delighting audiences around the world for more than forty years. Much like Bernstein, Tilson Thomas sees the importance of musical education for young people and has made great efforts to keep music education in schools and make it accessible to children around the world. In 1987, Tilson Thomas founded the New World Symphony, bringing together talented young musicians from around the world to train for careers in classical music. He took this idea one step further in 2009, by working with YouTube to create the YouTube Symphony Orchestra, a group made up from young people who auditioned via the Internet platform. Tilson Thomas has been the musical director of the San Francisco Symphony since 1995, and in 2019 he was awarded the Kennedy Center Honor for his contributions to American Classical music.

Scott Thompson (1959–)

The brilliant mind behind the swishy and dishy character, Buddy Cole, Scott Thompson is an original member of the Canadian comedy troupe the Kids in the Hall. It was Thompson's addition of the openly gay character of Buddy Cole that made *The Kids in the Hall* series a comedy jackpot for young gay kids looking for representation in the 1990s. Though Cole was unapologetically a stereotype, Thompson reveled in putting on the lisp and dissecting social issues with a sharp eye and a sssinissster tongue. While Thompson has continued to work with the rest of his Kids in the Hall troupe, he's also broken out on his own with the recurring role on *The Larry Sanders Show* and the recurring role of Jimmy Price on *Hannibal*.

Tessa Thompson (1983–)

An actress and activist who is creating new visibility for bisexual representation in mainstream media, Thompson first hit the scene in 2005 in the cult series *Veronica Mars*. She made the leap to film in *Mississippi Damned* in 2009. The independent film thrust her into the limelight and she's been gaining momentum with every role, whether it's in *Creed* in 2015, its sequel in 2018, or a series of Marvel movies like *Thor: Ragnarok.* Thompson has most recently been announced to star in her own *Thor* spin-off, recreating her role of Valkyrie, who will be featured as a bisexual character.

Virgil Thomson (1896–1989)

This grand old man of American classical music was a composer and critic for most of the twentieth century. Thomson was prolific during his lifetime, composing operas, symphonies, and other orchestral works. But it was his role as a critic and a mentor that set him apart. Much like his friend and collaborator Gertrude Stein, Thomson collected a group of artists around him during his lifetime. He acted as friend and mentor to many composers, like Aaron Copland, Ned Rorem, and John Cage. Thomson is often remembered for hosting salons in his beautiful apartment in the Chelsea Hotel.

Tigger! (1965–)

In the world of burlesque, there are many legends. But when it comes to male burlesque, there's a real trailblazer, and that man is Tigger! An accomplished dancer and actor, Tigger! got his start dancing burlesque with friends like Dirty Martini in the 1990s and made strides for men to play along in this fun and fabulous world. His work is not only titillating, it's also political, as Tigger! has used his platform to speak out for the rights of the LGBTQ+ community. He is also

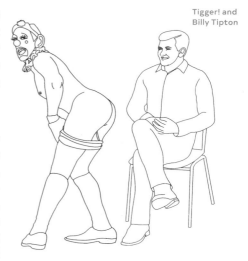

Tigger! and Billy Tipton

a longtime friend and collaborator of Taylor Mac, and has performed in many of Mac's plays and shows.

Tipping the Velvet

The 1998 novel by Sarah Waters tells the story of a young oyster girl named Nan who finds love and liberation on the Victorian music hall stage. She falls in love with a male impersonator named Kitty and eventually becomes one herself. Through trials and hardship, Nan uses her gender-bending skills to traverse a secret and hidden world of Victorian London, at one point even becoming a gay call boy. The novel was widely successful for talking about gay themes in a time of queer erasure, and eventually turned into a BBC miniseries starring Rachael Stirling as Nan.

Billy Tipton (1914–1989)

Jazz musician and talent agent Billy Tipton had a fascinating story. Living the majority of his life as a man, it was only revealed after his death that Tipton had been born a female. Tipton was a successful jazz musician playing in clubs across the Midwest throughout the 1930s and '40s. A talented pianist, Tipton was quickly brought to the West Coast to record and achieved a lot of success playing in Reno, Nevada. During his life, Tipton was married five times and adopted two sons. After his death, Tipton's biological gender was revealed and his story became tabloid gossip around the country.

To Wong Foo, Thanks for Everything! Julie Newmar

This 1995 drag cult hit, starring the most unlikely of queens, has become a hit with the drag community, and also a beloved favorite with the LGBTQ+ audience as a whole. It tells the story of Vida Boheme, played by Patrick Swayze, and Noxeema Jackson, played by Wesley Snipes. After winning a contest to go to Hollywood, the pair piles into a vintage car and heads across country with the drag newcomer, Chi-Chi Rodriguez, played by John Leguizamo. They run into car trouble and have to stop in the small town of Snydersville. They transform the town and its female inhabitants all before heading out to Hollywood and their dreams. The film did well at the box office, and has since become a classic for the LGBTQ+ community.

Jacob Tobia (1991–)

A writer and social commentator who has been on the forefront of the discussions on gender and identity for a number of years, Tobia has written for a variety of major print and Internet publications, and also become an on-camera personality discussing issues and news around gender and sexuality. Tobia created and starred in the NBC News series *Queer 2.0* in 2016. Tobia remains an outspoken and articulate writer on the subject of gender, and released a memoir, *Sissy*, in 2019 to rave reviews.

Colm Tóibín (1955–)

Tóibín is an Irish writer whose work has touched audiences and critics alike for more than twenty years. His prose has a beautiful, melodic quality that has often placed him in the canon of other poetic Irish writers. He is most known for his novels, *The Master*, based on the life of novelist Henry James, and *Brooklyn*, based on his mother's story of her immigration to America in the 1950s. *Brooklyn* was adapted for the screen in 2015 with Saoirse Ronan in the lead, and was nominated for Best Picture. Tóibín has written in a multitude of forms and has received three nominations for the Man Booker Prize, and won the Irish PEN Award for his contribution to Irish literature.

Tom of Finland, a.k.a. Touko Valio Laaksonen (1920–1991)

You know the images, absurdly buff men, hopping around on motorbikes or cops looking to write you a ticket, and they all scream Tom of Finland. Whether it's leather or sailors or businessmen taking a special meeting, Tom of Finland has become a staple of gay fare. You can even get them on sheets. Recently there was a fantastic movie about his life called, as he was, *Tom of Finland*, and it's about time. The drawings are always beautiful, and even though many of them are incredibly graphic, they all have a sense of fun and play that was new when talking about homosexual sex—especially between such masculine archetypes. I personally find them delightful, but that's because I imagine that if I ever heard these drawings talk, they would sound real, real gay. It's a fun party game; try it out for yourself.

Lily Tomlin (1939–)

Since the beginning of her career, doing characters in the 1960s, to her appearances on *Laugh-In*, introducing the nation to characters like her wisdom-doling toddler, Edith Ann, and her nosy and opinionated telephone operator, Ernestine, Lily Tomlin has created some of the most hilarious and powerful comedic moments in history. A true comedy legend and an intelligent and gifted actress, she has famously appeared in her partner Jane Wagner's work *The Search for Signs of Intelligent Life in the Universe*, for which she won the Tony Award in 1986. She has also been nominated for the Oscar for her role in Robert Altman's *Nashville*. Tomlin has been a mainstay in film with roles in the iconic *9 to 5* with Jane Fonda and Dolly Parton, *The Incredible Shrinking Woman*, *Big Business*, and recently *Grandma* in 2015. Tomlin has also had an illustrious career in television, recently capped off with the Netflix hit *Grace and Frankie*, again teaming up with longtime friend Jane Fonda. Even before she uttered her own coming out publicly, she was an advocate for the LGBTQ+ community. She and her partner Jane have contributed greatly to the LA LGBTQ+ Center, where the theatre is named in their honor. For her contributions to comedy, Tomlin received the Kennedy Center Honor in 2014.

Torch Song Trilogy

A triptych of plays written and performed by Harvey Fierstein tell the story of Arnold, a drag performer and wit who searches for love in the weird and wild world of late-1970s New York. The plays are all centered around Arnold, who meets a lover, loses his lover, and then gains a family to the horror of his mother. The first play, *International Stud*, debuted at La MaMa in 1978; the second, *Fugue in a Nursery*, in 1979; and *Widows and Children First!* debuted as part of the whole in 1981. The plays began an off-Broadway run, but eventually made their way to Broadway, winning Fierstein two Tony Awards for Best Play and Best Actor and introducing the world to Estelle Getty. Fierstein also made a film of the plays in 1988. A major revival of the plays was staged in 2017 with Michael Urie in the role of Arnold.

Torch Song Trilogy

Julio Torres (1987–)

Just when you think you think outside the box, you realize Julio Torres is questioning what makes a box a box at all. This writer and comedian's weird and wonderful queer takes on the world around him have set him apart, and on a quick trajectory to stardom. Torres began writing for television for *The Chris Gethard Show*, and soon found himself hired for *Saturday Night Live* in 2017. Torres quickly set himself apart from the pack with sketches like "Wells for Boys." Torres is also the writer and creator of HBO's *Los Espookys*, a Spanish-language horror comedy starring Torres and Fred Armisen. Torres's first HBO comedy special, *My Favorite Shapes*, debuted in 2019.

Nico Tortorella (1988–)

The genderqueer heartthrob of the TV series *Younger*, Tortorella is breaking gender stereotypes in front of a national audience. Tortorella immediately stood out as the young and sexy pursuer of Sutton Foster when the show debuted in 2015, but he had more up his sleeve. Since coming out as bisexual and genderqueer, Tortorella has made his case about his open, queer marriage to artist Bethany C. Meyers on national TV, released a successful book of poetry, and gone on to host MTV's *How Far Is Tattoo Far?* with *Jersey Shore* star Snooki.

Transparent

The groundbreaking brainchild of Joey Soloway, *Transparent* in some ways took Amazon to new heights as a serious platform for new programming but also broke boundaries for trans representation on television. This breakout hit centered on the Pfefferman family as they deal with the transition of their father into Maura, played by Jeffrey Tambor. With an all-star cast that included Judith Light, Amy Landecker, Gaby Hoffmann, and Jay Duplass, the show was a runaway hit when it debuted in 2014. It was a critical darling for most of its run, winning awards for Tambor and Solloway, but a sexual harassment scandal involving

Tambor rocked the show toward the end of its run. For the final musical episode, Tambor was killed off, and the whole cast got to sing themselves to resolution. If you haven't seen it, see it. It's jaw-dropping.

Tommy Tune (1939–)

Tune is a true Broadway legend who has been tap-dancing his way into our hearts for over forty years. As a director, actor, and choreographer, Tune has been behind some of Broadway's biggest hits, like *Nine* in 1982, *Grand Hotel* in 1989, and *The Will Rogers Follies* in 1991. He is the only person in Tony Award history to win consecutive awards in two separate categories (choreography and direction), and for his long and storied career, he has amassed ten Tonys. Tune has also had a great career on screen, playing young Ambrose in *Hello, Dolly!*, opposite Barbra Streisand, and most recently as Argyle Austero in *Arrested Development.*

Alan Turing (1912–1954)

See, you wouldn't have computers if it weren't for the gays. Often referred to as the father of modern computing, Alan Turing was a mathematician and scientist whose work during the Second World War led to technology that would later be used to make the computer a reality. He worked for the British government during the war, trying to decode intercepted messages from the Nazis, and in doing so pioneered theories on algorithm and computation that are still admired today. After the war, Turing was persecuted for being a homosexual, and was chemically castrated by the courts as an alternative to prison time. Turing took his own life in 1954. A film about Turing's life starring Benedict Cumberbatch, *The Imitation Game*, was released in 2014. In 2019, it was announced that Turing's image would be used on the Bank of England's £50 note.

Two Spirit

For many Native Cultures of the Americas, gender was rarely an either-or scenario. Some communities recognized as many as six genders, but many more saw that people existed outside the realm of merely male and female. Though this philosophy and culture existed in many tribes under many names, the term *two spirit* was first coined to represent a pan-Indian concept of gender nonconformity. Though the term has often been used and misused by people within and outside of the Native community, it is an attempt by Native communities to reclaim their own understanding of gender, prior to colonization, and to carry this tradition into a new era.

U

is for . . .

Karl Heinrich
Ulrichs

Karl Heinrich Ulrichs (1825–1895)

I'm a Uranian, are you? Karl Heinrich Ulrichs would say so. He was a writer and journalist who took up the cause of homosexual rights and came up with the term *Uranian* to define homosexual people before the use of the term *homosexual* in 1869. How did he come up with the term, you ask? Naturally, he derived it from the Greek goddess Aphrodite Urania, who was created out of the god Uranus's testicles. The German writer began writing articles about homosexual love under assumed names to protect himself from prosecution in the early 1860s. But by 1867, Ulrichs began using his own name and calling on governments and society as a whole to accept and embrace homosexuality as merely a variation in nature. Though his writings eventually caused him to leave his native country, Ulrichs continued to write and make the case for homosexuals until his death in 1895.

Michael Urie (1980–)

An actor perhaps best known for his role as Marc St. James on the ABC series *Ugly Betty*, Urie is a tremendous actor on the stage and has made his way between stage and screen with more than a hint of brilliance. He made his Broadway debut in 2012 in *How to Succeed in Business without Really Trying* opposite Daniel Radcliffe, and then continued to a stunning run in the solo play *Buyer & Cellar*. Most recently, Urie was seen in the lauded revival of *Torch Song Trilogy*, playing the role of Arnold, originally played by author Harvey Fierstein.

is for . . .

Alok Vaid-Menon (1991–)

A performance artist and activist making waves and sense around issues concerning the queer and trans community and for people of color, Vaid-Menon has created performance around their gender-nonconforming identity first with DarkMatter, a duo they created with Janani Balasubramanian, but in recent years has struck out on their own. With their outspoken style and stylish looks, they have become a favorite of the LGBTQ+ lecture and panel circuit, with appearances on *Logo30* and HBO's *Random Acts of Flyness.*

Valley of the Dolls

This movie has a special place in my heart since my ringtone is Neely O'Hara saying, "Start explaining, faggot." The very definition of camp, this 1967 film has it all. The rags-to-riches story tells of singer Neely O'Hara, played brilliantly and bizarrely by Patty Duke, the ditzy-yet-honest

Valley of the Dolls

Jennifer, played by Sharon Tate, and the icy-and-parochial Anne, played by Barbara Parkins. Rounding out the cast was the blousy queen of Broadway, Helen Lawson, played by Susan Hayward. It was based on the book by Jacqueline Susann, which was a sensation, combining Hollywood gossip based on stars like Ethel Merman and Judy Garland. Garland herself was originally cast in the role of Lawson, but was fired and replaced by Hayward. The movie tells of Neely's rise and fall in show business and it's filmed with ridiculousness and high fashion in equal measure. It's the perfect example of a great movie that's also so gorgeously bad it's good again. Instantly quotable, it's been a favorite example of high camp for generations.

Gus Van Sant (1952–)

A true American auteur, Van Sant is director and writer whose works in film have touched and inspired a generation of filmmakers. He's made his name with indie hits like 1989's *Drugstore Cowboy* and 1991's *My Own Private Idaho*, then tackled the box office with movies like *Good Will Hunting* in 1997 and the Oscar-winning *Milk* in 2008. Never one to shy away from controversy, Van Sant's 2003 film, *Elephant*, was loosely based on the Columbine high school shootings and won the Palme d'Or at the Cannes Film Festival.

Chavela Vargas (1919–2012)

One of Mexico's most beloved ranchera singers, Vargas was actually born in Costa Rica, but fell in love with the deeply felt ballads of ranchero, and made the mastery of these aching songs of love her life's work. Vargas was one of the most popular Rancheros singers in Mexico in the 1950s and '60s, but problems with alcohol led her to abandon performing and live in obscurity for a number of years. When Pedro Almodóvar used her early recordings in his films, a new interest in her began to emerge, and so did the long-reclusive Vargas. With the help of Almodóvar, Vargas toured the world as an older singer, still powerful and respected for the depth of her feeling and her raw delivery. A documentary about her life, *Chavela*, was released in 2017.

Chavela Vargas

Junior Vasquez (1949–)

One of the most popular and respected DJs in the world, Vasquez has remixed and produced tracks for the best and brightest in music, like Whitney Houston, Madonna, and Prince. Vasquez got started in the club scene in 1980s and quickly rose to the top of his profession. He has produced and mixed tracks for countless musicians and been associated with a multitude of hits. But don't cross him. Famously, after a falling-out with Madonna in 1996, Vasquez released a dance track under the name "If Madonna Calls." Only when hearing the track do you get the rest of the sentiment: "If Madonna calls, I'm not here."

Carl Van Vechten (1880–1964)

Van Vechten was a photographer and a writer who fell in love with Black culture and sought to promote its creations and creators. While he was acclaimed during his lifetime for his writings, it's his photography of notables like Billie Holiday, Eartha Kitt, and James Baldwin that have given Van Vechten a remaining allure in the modern culture.

Veneno

Cristina "La Veneno" Ortiz Rodríguez always made good television. From her earlier appearances in the 1990s on late-night talk shows, to her later controversial spots on tabloid panel shows, La Veneno was always captivating. Her rise from sex worker to superstar captured the heart of the Spanish audience, wanting to see what this outrageous woman would do next. It all sounds like great fodder for a television show, and in 2020, *Veneno* became a reality. Created by Javier Ambrossi and Javier Calvo, inspired by a memoir by Valeria Vegas, the HBO Max show followed Veneno through her rise and fall from fame, her time in prison, her problems with drugs and alcohol, and ultimately her tragic death. While the story may sound bleak from the onset, in the capable hands of Ambrossi and Calvo, you are left with more hope than regret. A story of compassion and truth, Veneno is a new standard in queer storytelling and introduced the world to Veneno's friend Paca La Piraña, who played herself in the television series.

Paul Verlaine (1844–1896)

A tremendous French poet, whose work has been somewhat eclipsed by his association with Arthur Rimbaud, Verlaine was already famous when he met the young Rimbaud. Their affair was the shock of the Belle Époque, and after Rimbaud ran off to join the army, Verlaine was left a ruined man. He taught, but was caught up in a love affair with a student. He drank to excess, but was still called by many of his contemporaries the King of the Poets. He also did a lot of work to promote the writings of Rimbaud, who, despite everything that passed between them, Verlaine still considered a genius.

Gianni Versace (1946–1997)

A genius designer whose work gave women power and sexuality in the 1980s and '90s, Versace was considered a maven and groundbreaker. Inventing his own fabrics and building an international fashion house out of a small storefront in Milan, there was little Versace couldn't do. His style sense combined the height of Roman art with the rococo at times, but brought it all together with a brimming sexuality that won him fans and famous clientele from around the world. Versace was murdered by the serial killer Andrew Cunanan in 1997. After his death, the Versace label was headed by Gianni's sister and partner Donatella, who maintains control to this day.

Vida

A stunning and heartfelt look into the queer Latinx community, this STARZ original series ran for three seasons from 2018 to 2020. Based on the short story "Pour Vida" by Richard Villegas Jr., the show centers on the relationship between two Mexican American sisters, Lyn and Emma Hernandez, as they deal with the death of their mother. The show was created by Tanya Saracho and starred Melissa Barrera and Mishel Prada as Lyn and Emma. *Vida* was almost universally acclaimed for its wit and stellar cast. It was awarded a 2019 GLAAD media award for Outstanding Comedy Series.

Gore Vidal (1925–2012)

The sneering wit of the post-war generation of American writers, Vidal was a novelist, essayist, playwright, and social commentator with a lot to say and a lot of class when he said it. He would also not want to be on this list. Vidal very famously said there was no such thing as a homosexual person, merely homosexual acts. He wrote many novels in a myriad of styles, from his early book *The City and the Pillar*, which talked about gay relationships, to his comic satire *Myra Breckinridge*, which trades on and defeats gender roles and sexual-identity myths left and right, to his successful historical novels like *Lincoln* and *Burr*. Vidal was a writer of varying style and substance that somehow made it all sound like Vidal. A staunch liberal, he wrote often about the corruption of power in Washington and was called upon to make the liberal case in debates

Sherry Vine and Bruce Vilanch

against conservative pundits. He was famously part of the Vidal-Buckley debates during the 1969 presidential election in which William F. Buckley, in a moment of rage, called Vidal a queer on national television.

Bruce Vilanch (1948–)

Chances are, if you heard a joke from someone on television in the last forty or so years, Bruce Vilanch probably wrote it. One of the most prolific and beloved writers of humor in the world, Vilanch has written for the likes of Bette Midler, Robin Williams, Whoopi Goldberg, and Billy Crystal, just to name a few. He also wrote the infamous *Star Wars Holiday Special* in 1978, so they can't all be winners. Vilanch has most often written for the Oscars, writing for the show from 1989 to 2014. With his Dutch-boy haircut and wacky T-shirts, Vilanch is known around the world as a storyteller with a hell of a story to tell.

Village People

Even today, when people think of gay people, the image of the Village People pops into their head. The cop, the cowboy, the biker, the Native American, and the construction worker didn't have names, which is understandable with the multitude of changes that happened to the lineup of the band. But the image of these dancing guys, singing hits like "YMCA" and "Macho Man," is etched into our minds as so very gay, even though a few of the original members were straight. With strong lead vocals by Victor Willis, and backup from the likes of Randy Jones, Glenn Hughes, Felipe Rose, and David Hodo, the group skyrocketed to fame in the late 1970s. Their hits were veiled hints at gay life that made America get up and dance. The band was so popular that they appeared in 1980's *Can't Stop the Music*, which is a delightful disaster of a film.

Sherry Vine

One of the hardest-working drag queens in the business, Sherry Vine's a bit of an institution. Vine began performing in New York in the 1980s, and came up through the ranks at places like Bar d'O in the 1990s with fellow performers like Jackie Beat, Raven O, and Justin Vivian Bond. Vine today is known for her hilarious and often scatological song parodies. Her version of Lady Gaga's "Bad Romance" is titled "Shit My Pants" and her take on Adele's "Hello" begins with Sherry on the toilet. Vine performs around the country, often with friend and long-time collaborator Jackie Beat. In 2021, Vine debuted her show, *The Sherry Vine Variety Show* on Apple TV.

Luchino Visconti (1906–1976)

A master of Italian cinema, Visconti was a theatre and opera director in his native Italy, but it was his work in the cinema that brought his genius to people around the world. He started his career in film assisting the famous French auteur Jean Renoir, and quickly began learning the tools of the trade. He released his first film, *Obsession*, in 1943. He followed it with classics like *Rocco and his Brothers* in 1960, *The Leopard* in 1963, and *Death in Venice* in 1971. His theatre work was also respected, and his efforts with Maria Callas on the operatic stage was a huge success for Visconti and the diva herself.

Paula Vogel (1951–)

One of the most thought-provoking and interesting playwrights of the late twentieth century and beyond, Paula Vogel has written plays that defy time and space to make stories come to life in new and exciting ways. She won the Pulitzer Prize for her 1998 play *How I Learned to Drive*. Besides writing a myriad of plays, Vogel has been an influential and passionate teacher of dramatic writing, first with a long tenure at Brown, and then as a Eugene O'Neill professor and playwriting department chair at the Yale School of Drama. Her recent work *Indecent* was Vogel's long-overdue Broadway debut and was nominated for Best Play by the Tony Awards.

Ocean Vuong (1988–)

A poet and novelist who has hit the contemporary literature scene with gusto and won the prestigious T. S. Eliot Prize in 2017 for his collection *Night Sky with Exit Wounds*, Vuong immediately became a poet to watch and read. He immigrated to the United States from Vietnam at just two years old, and his experiences as an immigrant figure largely into his subtle and beautiful poetic work. Recently, Vuong released a novel, *On Earth We're Briefly Gorgeous*, to wide critical acclaim and audience raves.

W

is for . . .

Lana Wachowski (1965–) and Lilly Wachowski (1967–)

The dynamic directing team behind *The Matrix* and its sequels, Lana and Lilly Wachowski are visionary storytellers who had us all wondering about the reality we see before us every day. Since its premiere in 1999, *The Matrix* has spawned a million conspiracy theories and legions of fans, but it was only the beginning for the Wachowskis. Since completing those films, they have crafted many more eye-opening works, including *V for Vendetta* and the cult hit *Sense8* for Netflix.

Rufus Wainwright (1973–)

His sonorous voice and honest songwriting have led Wainwright into the spotlight of pop music, though his talents also extend into the classical world with his poperas *Hadrian* and *Prima Donna*. Wainwright stepped into the public spotlight with his self-titled debut in 1998. Since then, his albums have included his beautiful melodies and a series of experiments with just how far pop music can go. While his breakout hit came from a cover version of Leonard Cohen's "Hallelujah" for the first *Shrek* film, Wainwright's own music continues to push boundaries. With 2003's *Want* double album, two operas, and a Judy Garland tribute album where Wainwright recreated her legendary Carnegie Hall concert, he remains a thrilling and experimental artist with much more to say.

Lena Waithe

Lena Waithe (1984–)

Waithe is a writer and actor who first came to prominence after writing and starring in the Netflix series *Master of None* with Aziz Ansari. The "very-special" episode of the show addresses her character's coming out and was a hit with audiences and critics alike. It also won Waithe an Emmy for her writing of the show, making her the first-ever African American woman to do so. Since *Master of None*, Waithe has used her platform to promote LGBTQ+ rights and been an outspoken champion for communities of color. She is also the creator of Showtime's *The Chi* and BET's *Twenties*. Waithe also has the honor of portraying the first LGBTQ+ character in the Pixar Universe by playing Officer Spector in *Onward* in 2020.

Alice Walker (1944–)

Walker is most widely known for her novel *The Color Purple*, which won the National Book Award and the Pulitzer Prize. A poet, novelist, essayist, and educator, Walker has continually used her work as a healing balm to the world's trouble. An outspoken critic and social-justice advocate, Walker has been a firm supporter of the Free Palestine Movement, as well as many other worthy causes around the globe.

Alexander Wang (1983–)

A designer whose use of color in high fashion and streetwear have set him apart in a crowd of competing visions, Wang launched his first women's collection in 2007 and quickly caught the eye of the fashion industry. Since that first collection, Wang has continued a rise through the industry, doing huge collections for his own self-titled label while also taking on the creative directorship of the legendary Balenciaga fashion house in 2012. While Wang stepped down from Balenciaga in 2014,

his own line has continued to grow in prominence.

Andy Warhol

Andy Warhol (1928–1987)

Andy Warhol created the world we're living in, where everyone is interested in their fifteen minutes of fame, and the images we see are repeated and manipulated over and over again. Perhaps the most influential artist of the twentieth century, Andy Warhol is an icon. With his 1962 show of his famous take on Campbell's Soup cans, Warhol set the art world on fire and began a trajectory to take him and many of those around him to art superstardom. Besides his paintings, like the famous screenprints of Marilyn Monroe and the mourning Jackie Kennedy, Warhol experimented in film. Following early works like *Empire* and *Blow Job*, Warhol moved to more narrative works like *Chelsea Girls* and *The Nude Restaurant*. After Warhol was shot by Valerie Solanas in 1968, his work began to change. He started collaborating with Paul Morrissey on films (these later films, primarily directed by Morrissey, featured Holly Woodlawn, Candy Darling, Jackie Curtis, and Joe Dallesandro), turned to working in still photography with Polaroids, and began to work with younger artists like Jean-Michael Basquiat and Keith Haring.

John Waters

John Waters (1946–)

The dirty old man of the late-night movie, John Waters is a master of filth. A director, writer, and artist whose weird and profane view of the world has made him an outsider icon for the film world, Waters starting making movies with his friends in the suburbs of Baltimore. Waters was infamous for his early midnight movies, like *Multiple Maniacs* and *Mondo Trasho*, which could be shown late at night for a weirder and more adult audience. His breakout hit was 1971's *Pink Flamingos*, which ended with his muse and superstar Divine eating dog shit. After *Pink Flamingos*, a string of Waters's movies began to gain popular traction, with *Female Trouble, Desperate Living, Polyester,* and *Cry-Baby*, all leading up to his breakout studio hit, 1988's *Hairspray*. Waters has continued to bring his subversive comedy with works like *Serial Mom* and *Pecker*. Waters has also become a regular performer and lecturer, and has written several successful books, like *Role Models* and *Mr. Know-It-All*.

Lois Weaver (1949–)

A writer, activist, and performer who is a legend in the world of performance art and experimental theatre, Weaver met friend and collaborators Peggy Shaw and Deb Margolin in the late 1970s and the three founded Split Britches, a company seeking to create work around female and queer identity. She wrote many works for the company, focusing much of it on the premise of a conversation with the audience. Weaver also started the Women's One World Cafe company in 1980, and has continued to make thought-provoking and creative theatre in both New York and London.

Weekend

Have you ever wished that a hookup would lead to love? Then *Weekend* is the wish-fulfillment movie for you. A film by Andrew Haigh, it was heralded by the press and fans alike as a breakthrough in gay cinema. Released in 2011, the film starred Tom Cullen and Chris New and was a major hit at the SXSW festival. After the UK and US release, the film was a success and paved the way for Haigh to direct the series *Looking* for HBO. For its honesty and intimacy, *Weekend* deserves a second and even a third glance.

David Weissman (1950–)

Weissman is a documentarian and activist who has been telling gay stories for decades in films that chronicle our creativity and our care for one another. His first major hit was 2002's *The Cockettes*, which detailed the rise and fall of the famous drag troupe in San Francisco. Weissman has since taken on darker subjects. His *We Were Here*, released in 2010, talks in harrowing detail about the AIDS crisis and the community response in San Francisco. He's recently toured with an ongoing project titled *Conversations with Gay Elders*, which fosters intergenerational conversations about the changing world of the LGBTQ+ community.

We'wha (1849–1896)

A member of the Zuni tribe of Native peoples living in New Mexico, We'wha was one of the first recorded *lhamana* people in Western literature. In Zuni culture, some male-bodied people live and work as women, performing all rights and rituals associated with female-bodied people. We'wha was first "discovered" after the Zuni sent a delegation to Washington, DC, to discuss Zuni relations and Native culture with the impeding American government. The talks drew the attention of anthropologist Matilda Coxe Stevenson, who wrote extensively about We'wha and the Zuni culture. We'wha was also a notable artist and textile worker, and in this role as *lhamana* was able to defy the laws of Western gender norms with great authority and personal expression. We'wha is often seen as an early example of the Native American two spirit philosophy.

James Whale (1889–1957)

A film director most famous for horror classics like *Frankenstein, The Invisible Man*, and *Bride of Frankenstein*. While Whale is known for his stunning use of light and giving his scary monsters humanity, he was also a great purveyor of humor and camp in all his films. *Bride of Frankenstein*, in particular, is an excellent example of Whale's love of the weird and wondrous. Whale continued to make a host of movies until his retirement in 1941. A film of Whale's final years, *Gods and Monsters*, was released in 1998, starring Ian McKellen.

Ben Whishaw (1980–)

An actor of enormous talent who first came to attention with a star turn as Hamlet when he was just twenty-three, Whishaw was instantly hailed as a fantastic classical actor and continued to perform on stage in Shakespeare. He also began making films. Independent films like *Perfume* and *I'm Not There* led

Whishaw to more commercial movies, like taking on the role of Q in recent Bond movies, and the Disney hit *Mary Poppins Returns*. Whishaw continues to be a tremendous classical actor, garnering praise for his role of Richard II in the BBC series *The Hollow Crown*.

Edmund White (1940–)

You may never find a more beautifull description of "corn-holing" as you will in Edmund White's *A Boy's Own Story*. White's writing has been groundbreaking for LGBTQ+ literature. Known most widely for his trilogy of semi-autobiographical novels, *A Boy's Own Story* in 1982, *The Beautiful Room Is Empty* in 1988, and *The Farewell Symphony* in 1997, White uses simplicity and depth to tell gay stories with the gravity and humor they truly deserve. As a founding member of the legendary Violet Quill group, White has always been a proponent of LGBTQ+ writers. His work encompasses a number of genres, with a series of successful memoirs, a host of novels, biographies of writers Jean Genet and Marcel Proust, and the manual *The Joy of Gay Sex*. White is a legend in the realm of LGBTQ+ literature and a much-admired writer in the larger Western canon.

White Party

Gay men love a theme. And when the theme is something as simple as "white," most people can rally and get themselves together. The White Party has become a staple of the gay dance calendar. It's a weekend filled with techno, drugs, sex, and white clothes that don't usually stay on that long. The Miami White Party is an annual fundraiser for HIV/AIDS research, and other White Parties have popped up around the globe.

Walt Whitman (1819–1892)

Still screaming that barbaric yawp, the great gray poet was also a great gay poet. Walt Whitman is often seen as the first great American poet. He is most famous for his mammoth work *Leaves of Grass*. First published in 1855, he would go on to edit and re-edit, adding poems and deleting others, for the rest of his life. From the beginning, *Leaves of Grass* was controversial; Whitman's rhapsodic writings of sex and his open appreciation of the male form made the faint of heart turn away and for many years. A reevaluation in the 1940s and '50s made Whitman a titan in the annals of American verse. Most remembered today for poems like "O Captain! My Captain!" and "I Sing the Body Electric," Whitman's "Calamus" section of *Leaves of Grass* holds some of the most beautiful same-sex love poems in history. Though Whitman's sexuality has been debated by scholars, they find in Whitman no help. The poet continually edited out the gay content of his work in subsequent editions. Whether or not Whitman himself was indeed gay, his poetry certainly made it seem Walt enjoyed the company of his male comrades.

Randy Wicker (1938–)

An activist, archivist, and writer who has been a major part of gay history since before the days of Stonewall, Wicker came out in the 1950s, and wanted to create political action and awareness around homosexuals and their lives. In the 1960s, he was a vocal proponent for homosexual rights and was a witness to the Stonewall Riots. After the riots, Wicker joined the Gay Activists Alliance and became a friend and roommate to Marsha P. Johnson. He continues to fight for visibility for the LGBTQ+ community and is a hero who has been part of the movement for more than sixty years.

John Wieners (1934–2002)

An American poet whose romantic sensibility and cheeky modernism made him a favorite among poets and readers alike, Wieners was originally a poet of the San Francisco Renaissance, with strong ties to the Beat community. He suffered with mental illness, and while holding firm to the ideals of poetry, at times lived in poverty. He was an advocate for politically liberal views and a supporter of LGBTQ+ rights, contributing a large amount of work to LGBTQ+ publications like *Gay Sunshine* and *Fag Rag* within his lifetime. Wieners became known as a Boston poet, living in his beloved city for more than thirty years

and creating a scene there with other writers.

Wigstock

A festival celebrating all the weird and wonderful art that gets made under the umbrella of drag, Wigstock, created by Lady Bunny, was one of the first festivals of its kind and ran every summer for many years. Bunny got the idea for Wigstock in the 1980s, paying homage to the legendary Woodstock Festival of 1969 with her own feel-good festival in Tompkins Square Park in New York City. Throughout the years, it played host to many of drag's biggest and brightest, with performances by Leigh Bowery, Flotilla DeBarge, Lypsinka, the Dueling Bankheads, performance artist John Kelly, and even RuPaul herself. A documentary about the festival, also called *Wigstock*, was released 1995. Though in recent years, Wigstock had lost its home in Tompkins Square Park and was less regular, a revival took place in the summer of 2018 on Pier 17 of the South Street Seaport, which was also documented in the film *Wig*, released by HBO in 2019.

Oscar Wilde (1854–1900)

Every gay man may think himself funny, but chances are he's no Oscar Wilde. With his wit and love for aphorism, Wilde is an instantly quotable humorist with phrases like, "I have nothing to declare but genius," and "we are all in the gutter, but some of us are looking up at the stars." While

Wilde is often remembered for his quips, he is also a literary genius that wrote a host of works from his deeply gothic novel, *The Picture of Dorian Gray*, to plays like *The Importance of Being Earnest* and *An Ideal Husband*. As widely known as his work, his life also plays a seminal role in the Wilde legend. A flamboyant figure even in his own time, Wilde was constantly in the headlines. Though Wilde was gay, he married Constance Lloyd in 1884, had two children by her, and continued to have affairs with male lovers. Though Wilde had other homosexual relationships, none were as outlandish as his open affair with Lord Alfred Douglas, or Bosie, as he was called. When Douglas's father, The Marquess of Queensberry, accused Wilde of being a "sodomite" in public, Wilde decided to sue for libel. The plan backfired, and after losing his case, Wilde was put on trial for gross indecency and sentenced to two years hard labor. While in prison, Wilde wrote two of his most famous works, *De Profundis*, a long love letter to Bosie, and *The Ballad of Reading Gaol*. After his release, Wilde lived in Europe, but financial and health trouble eventually led to his early death at age forty-six.

Thornton Wilder (1897–1975)

Perhaps most famously known for his play *Our Town*, Thornton Wilder was the winner of three Pulitzer Prizes during his lifetime. His play *The Matchmaker* was later adapted into the Broadway musical *Hello, Dolly!* His novel *The Bridge of San Luis Rey* is often seen as a masterwork of storytelling. Wilder wrote many works that are perhaps less well known, but in each he shows himself as a writer of deep insight and playful experimentation. Widely respected among dramatists, his deceptively simple plays belie a depth and insight into the human psyche that few have matched.

Kehinde Wiley (1977–)

Contemporary portraiture in the style of the grand rococo, Kehinde Wiley is reexamining who gets portrayed in art, and who gets to make it. His striking works give voice and height to faces often underrepresented in art. Using the works of old masters, Wiley takes

Oscar Wilde

on the modern Black world with stunning and insightful portraiture. Never afraid of controversy, his play on Caravaggio's *Judith Beheading Holofernes*, in which he painted two majestic portraits of Black women brandishing the decapitated heads of a white women, caused a huge stir in 2012. In 2017, Wiley was commissioned by the White House to paint the official portrait of President Obama. His stunning portrait was revealed in 2018 to universal praise.

Will & Grace

The show that President Joe Biden says made gay marriage happen in America, and the source of endless gay puns that still make me giggle, *Will & Grace*, the brainchild of Max Mutchnick and David Kohan, debuted in 1998 and brought the world the long-standing friendship between gay men and the women who love them. The show centers around best friends Will Truman, played by Eric McCormack, and Grace Adler, played by Debra Messing, as they journey through life and love together in the ever-changing world of sexual politics in New York. It also brought us two of the funniest comedic inventions on screen—the dynamic sidekicks of Karen Walker, played by Megan Mullally, and Jack McFarland, played by Sean Hayes. The show originally ran for eight seasons, garnering many awards for both the writers and the

actors. In 2017, the series was revived and ran for three additional seasons finally ending in 2020.

Tennessee Williams

Tennessee Williams (1911–1983)

If you're a Southern Belle looking for the kindness of strangers, or wondering how to get off this hot tin roof, look no further than the works of Tennessee Williams. One of the most respected writers of the twentieth century, Williams has at times been called the American Shakespeare. For his heightened sense of poetry and his brutal characterizations, Williams set himself apart from his fellow dramatists in the 1940s with his plays *The Glass Menagerie* in 1944 and *A Streetcar Named Desire* in 1947. Following these two hits, he wrote a series of successful plays like *Cat on a Hot Tin Roof* in 1955, for which he won the

Pulitzer Prize, *Sweet Bird of Youth* in 1959, and *The Night of the Iguana* in 1961. Many of these plays were turned into successful films, starring the likes of Marlon Brando in his break-out performance as Stanley Kowalski in *Streetcar*, Elizabeth Taylor in *Cat on a Hot Tin Roof*, and Geraldine Page in *Sweet Bird of Youth*. Williams's work often dealt with homosexuality, which was plenty taboo in the 1950s and '60s, but his poetry and sensuality made even the most taboo subject sound better than anyone could have imagined.

Doric Wilson (1939–2011)

A playwright and director whose plays were directed by and for the gay community, Doric Wilson got his start at the Caffe Cino in the 1960s. Writing almost exclusively about gay themes when the subject was still somewhat taboo, Wilson became a trendsetter in the fight for gay voices on stage. In 1974, Wilson with others founded TOSOS, The Other Side of Silence, a theatre company that hoped to offer a home for emerging gay voices. The company was wildly successful for a number of years, but eventually fell apart. A second TOSOS company emerged in 2001, with Wilson still lending a hand. He was an outspoken artist and activist for gay stories and the lives of the people who live them.

Lanford Wilson (1937–2011)

A great American playwright, whose work told of people in crisis with a beautiful simplicity that made him a giant in the field, Wilson started writing short works at the Caffe Cino in New York in the 1960s, but with plays like *The Hot L Baltimore* and *Balm in Gilead*, he soon moved to bigger and more prominent venues. In 1969, he co-founded the Circle Repertory Company with Marshall W. Mason and there put on some of his most import-ant works. His trilogy of plays, *The Fifth of July*, *Talley's Folly*, and *Talley & Son*, were widely acclaimed, and *Talley's Folly* won Wilson the Pulit-zer Prize. His most successful play, *Burn This*, was recently revived on Broadway with Adam Driver and Keri Russell in 2019.

Edie Windsor (1929–2017)

The little old lady who loved to talk 'bout gay sex and won the right for everyone to get married, Edie Windsor was an unlikely LGBTQ+ advocate, but when she took her case all the way to the Supreme Court and won, making gay marriage the law of the land, Edie was ready for the spotlight. Windsor had lived with her partner, Thea Spyer, for decades, but after Spyer's death, Windsor was required to pay hundreds of thousands of dollars in inheritance taxes. She sued the federal government for the wrongful taxation and took the case all the way to the

Supreme Court and won. During the trial it was rumored that her lawyers didn't want Windsor to talk about how hot her relationship with Thea had been, but it was her favorite subject. On top of Windsor's determination for justice, she was also a warm and funny activist, whose sense of fun and fairness endeared her to the heart of her community and the country as whole. Her memoir, *A Wild and Precious Life*, was released two years after her death.

David
Wojnarowicz

David Wojnarowicz (1954–1992)

The most poetically rageful voice to emerge from the AIDS crisis, David Wojnarowicz was a multidisciplinary artist and writer whose work took the AIDS crisis and America's stagnant response to the disease on headfirst. Wojnarowicz worked in a multitude of forms, including painting, collage, and a stunning amount of photographic work. Most famously his Rimbaud in New York series, where he wore a flat paper mask of the famous French poet around New York, has become a classic. He also explored film with his controversial work *A Fire in My Belly*, which is often cited by conservatives as a blasphemous work for its depiction of ants crawling over a crucifix. His written works and diaries have also made Wojnarowicz stand out as a chronicler of the AIDS crisis and a powerful writer on LGBTQ+ themes and sexuality. A retrospective of his work, *History Keeps Me Awake at Night*, was presented at the Whitney Museum in 2018, exposing the huge vision of Wojnarowicz's work to rapt viewers as well as huge critical praise.

George C. Wolfe (1954–)

Wolfe is a playwright, director, and filmmaker whose works have illuminated the Black experience and created new vistas of exploration in the American theatre. George C. Wolfe's writing first came into the public eye in the 1980s with plays like *The Colored Museum* in 1986 and *Spunk* in 1989. Wolfe went on to direct and create stunning musicals, first with *Jelly's Last Jam* in 1991, and then *Bring in 'da Noise, Bring in 'da Funk* in 1995. Wolfe served as the artistic director of New York's Public Theater from 1993 to 2004, fostering new works and continuing a line of enormous successes. He directed the original production of Tony Kushner's *Angels in America* on Broadway in 1991, for which he won the Tony Award. Since leaving the Public, Wolfe has continued to make thought-provoking and brilliant work in the theatre, most recently directing Denzel Washington in *The Iceman Cometh*.

BD Wong (1960–)

An actor of enormous skill and understanding, Wong had his first flush of stardom in 1988 with David Henry Hwang's play, *M. Butterfly*. For his role as the gender-bending opera star and spy Song Liling, Wong won praise and a host of awards, including the Tony Award for Best Actor. Wong has since been a constant on stage, television, and film, with roles in *Law & Order: SVU*, *Mr. Robot*, and the *Jurassic Park* franchise. Wong has been a longtime advocate for the rights of LGBTQ+ people and the representation of Asian artists in the media.

Holly Woodlawn (1946–2015)

"Holly came from Miami, F-L-A." Immortalized in Lou Reed's "Walk on the Wild Side," before Woodlawn was known around the world as a Warhol, she was an actress, singer, performer, and writer whose lust for life and outrageous laugh made her a beloved figure for the LGBTQ+ community. With Candy Darling and Jackie Curtis, Woodlawn was part of the holy trio of Warhol superstars. She starred in Paul Morrissey's *Trash* in 1970, and her performance in this film was so good, famed director George Cukor openly campaigned for her to be nominated for an Oscar. After *Trash*, Woodlawn continued to act in independent films and theatre productions with Jackie Curtis, Charles Ludlam, and Hibiscus and the Angels of Light. She also had a wildly successful solo career as a cabaret artist. Woodlawn wrote a memoir of her heady days at the Warhol Factory and the downtown New York art scene of the 1970s titled *A Low Life in High Heels*.

Work in Progress

Life is tough when you're counting almonds until you kill yourself, or so Showtime's *Work in Progress* would like you to believe. This hilarious and heartfelt take on queer lives and mental illness is the brainchild of comedian Abby McEnany and Tim Mason and stars McEnany in the central role. The show debuted in 2019 to rave reviews and follows the life of Abby as she navigates the world of her mental health as well as a new relationship with a transman named Chris played by trans actor Theo Germaine.

World Famous *BOB*

The Voom in the Va-Va-Voom. World Famous *BOB* is the curvatious queen of queer burlesque. Bob hit the scene in the 1990s, bringing the scintillating art of the striptease to queer audiences around the country. Known for her bubbling personality and her ample bosom, *BOB* infiltrated the old world of the hoochie coochie with a new energy and vitality that was more open and willing to see not only women empowered in their sexuality, but people of all genders. Bob brought the world of burlesque into a queer setting and has continued to push the art form ever since. She has worked with countless photographers and artists over her career, always looking to foster the idea of inclusion and acceptance around body positivity and sexuality into the art she creates.

Hector
Xtravaganza

a consultant on the FX television show *Pose*, yet again bringing the world of ballroom to the public.

Hector Xtravaganza (1965–2018)

One of the greatest exponents and promoters of the ballroom scene, Hector Xtravaganza was legendary in the truest sense of the word. A dancer, fashion stylist, and activist, he shot to prominence when he was featured in *Paris Is Burning*. Using this film as a launching pad, Xtravaganza used this opportunity to expose the broader entertainment world to the style of ballroom. He was a stylist for many artists including Lil' Kim and Foxy Brown, and used his platform to speak out against AIDS and fight for the lives and the rights of his community. Xtravaganza was also

Bowen Yang (1990–)

Who knew we could all fall in love with an Iceberg? Bowen Yang is bringing the gayness to *Saturday Night Live* in ways that have never been seen before, and we're LIVING! Yang originally went to NYU to study microbiology but, inspired by his hero, Sandra Oh, decided to pursue a career in comedy. He started releasing videos online and garnering attention, which eventually led him to his podcast, *Las Culturistas*, which he co-hosts with comedian Matt Rogers. The podcast was a major hit, and he soon found himself writing for *SNL* in 2018. In 2019 he joined the cast, becoming the first Asian American cast member and only the third openly gay cast member. Since then Yang has been a breakout hit, bringing a gay sensibility that is much needed on the *SNL* stage.

Jaboukie Young-White (1994–)

A comedian and actor who is making a huge splash with his regular contributions on *The Daily Show with Trevor Noah* as the resident gay correspondent, Young-White debuted on the *Tonight Show Starring Jimmy Fallon* in 2017 and since then he's been on *Big Mouth* and *Crashing*, with an appearance in Disney's *Ralph Breaks the Internet* in 2018.

Marguerite Yourcenar (1903–1987)

A Belgian novelist and essayist who was the first woman elected to the Académie Française, Yourcenar published her first novel at just twenty-six and continued to write and translate literary works throughout her life. Her most famous work, *Memoirs of Hadrian*, published in 1951, she became an international sensation. The novel is told from the point of view of the famous Roman emperor Hadrian as he deals with the sorrows and realizations at the end of his life, including his long affair with his male companion Antinous.

YouTube

It's more than just cat videos and people breaking their aboveground pools. Since its beginning, YouTube has offered a platform for LGBTQ+ people to reach audiences of kids and adults who feel different, just like them. In a great way, it has provided an online community for young and old alike to see and hear from people they can relate to, and the platform has offered solace in the face of bullying. It has become a major venue where LGBTQ+ entertainers and personalities can thrive. With stars like Shane Dawson, Hannah Hart, and Natalie Wynn all reaching huge audiences and becoming major cultural figures in their own right, YouTube continues to be a major platform for the community.

Pedro Zamora (1972–1994)

Going on MTV was part of his activism, for it gave Pedro Zamora a voice and a platform in the fight against AIDS. Zamora was cast on the third season of MTV's groundbreaking series *The Real World*, and immediately became a focal point of the show. Wise, yet fun, Zamora was very popular to fans of the show and even his new roommates, except for the controversial roommate Puck. Even when the two sparred, Zamora maintained his cool and was able to bring the story of his life living with HIV to viewers around the world. Zamora also married his partner, Sean Sasser, on the show. He saw being on the show as a chance to humanize people with HIV, and for millions of viewers, Pedro did just that.

Franco Zeffirelli (1923–2019)

Leave it to a gay man to create some of the grandest opera productions in the twentieth century. Franco Zeffirelli was a film and opera director with a lavish eye for detail and spectacle. He scored huge successes on screen with his 1968 version of *Romeo and Juliet* and his 1967 adaptation of *The Taming of the Shrew* with Elizabeth Taylor and Richard Burton. But it was on the opera stage that Zeffirelli may have created some of his greatest work. His productions of *Aida*, *La Bohème*, and *Turandot* became mega-hits for the Metropolitan Opera for decades. He was also a favorite of the diva, directing a legendary production for opera stars like Maria Callas, who was also a close friend, and for Dame Joan Sutherland's legendary performance in *Lucia di Lammermoor*.

This book is dedicated to my gay family;
my gay godparents,
Jim Fouratt, Robert Croonquist, and Jackie Rudin;
my gay sisters
MxC, Dusty, Shane-Shane, Howl,
Tyler, Madeleine, and Rudy;
and all my gay babies yet to come.

Index

Bushwig, 44, 55
Butcher, Rhea, 44–45
butch lesbians, 44
But I'm a Cheerleader, 44
Butler, Judith, 45
BUTT, 45, 94

C

Cadmus, Paul, 46
Caffe Cino, 46, 92, 214, 288
Cage, John, 46–47, 68, 268
La Cage aux Folles, 99, 127, 157
Cahun, Claude, 47
Caldwell, Sandra, 82
Callas, Maria, 47–48, 150, 165,
    173, 184, 217, 278, 294
Callen, Michael, 48, 85
Call Me by Your Name, 47, 138
Calvo, Javier, 276
camp, 48
Campbell, Bobbi, 48–49, 51
Campbell, Naomi, 191, 233
Canals, Steven, 220
Capote, Truman, 38, 49, 260
Caprotti, Gian Giacomo, 70
Carangi, Gia Marie, 49–50
Cardi B, 18
Carey, Mariah, 50
Carlile, Brandi, 50
Carlos, Wendy, 50
Carmichael, Elizabeth, 85
Carpenter, Edward, 50
Carpenter, Kelli, 206
Carr, Alan, 51
Carrington, Dora, 259
Carroll, Diahann, 86
Casa Susanna, 51
Casita del Campo, 47, 51
The Castro, 51, 144, 187, 198
The Catch One, 266
Cather, Willa, 51–52

Catillano, Jordan, 195
Cattrall, Kim, 246
Cavafy, Constantine, 52
Cavern Club, 51, 90
Cayne, Candis, 52
Cazuza, 52–53
Cazwell, 53
The Celluloid Closet, 53, 240
Cernuda, Luis, 53
Chalamet, Timothée, 47
Channing, Carol, 53–54, 127, 187
Chapman, Tracy, 54
Charlene, 54
Chauncey, George, 109
Chee, Alexander, 54
Chekhov, Anton, 163, 197
Cher, 6, 9, 34, 54–55, 177
Cheren, Mel, 55
Cherry, Merrie, 55
Chin, Justin, 55–56
Cho, Margaret, 25, 56
A Chorus Line, 26
Christine and the Queens, 56
Christopher Street, 56–57
Cino, Joe, 46
The City and the Pillar, 57, 277
City of Night, 57, 230
Clarke, Shirley, 220
Clarke, Vince, 91
Clary, Julian, 57
Clift, Montgomery, 57–58
Clinton, Hillary, 94, 183
Clinton, Kate, 58, 135
clones, 58
Clooney, Rosemary, 97, 187
Club Kids, 58–59
Club My-O-My, 59
Cobra Woman, 59
The Cockettes, 59–60, 82, 159,
    190, 262, 283
Cocteau, Jean, 22, 60, 110
Cohen, Andy, 60, 62, 100

S